DK EYEWITNESS

T0019099

TOP 10
BERLIN

Top 10 Berlin Highlights

The Top 10 of Everything

CONTENTS

Berlin
Area by Area

Streetsmart

Within each Top 10 list in this book, no hierarchy of quality or popularity is implied. All 10 are, in the editor's opinion, of roughly equal merit.

Title page, front cover and spine *Berliner Dom and boats on the Spree River at sunset*
Back cover, clockwise from top left
Gingerbread cookies, Gendarmenmarkt; Oberbaumbrücke, Kreuzberg; Reichstag's dome; Berliner Dom and Spree River; interior of Potsdamer Platz

The rapid rate at which the world is changing is constantly keeping the DK Eyewitness team on our toes. While we've worked hard to ensure that this edition of Berlin is accurate and up-to-date, we know that opening hours alter, standards shift, prices fluctuate, places close and new ones pop up in their stead. So, if you notice we've got something wrong or left something out, we want to hear about it. Please get in touch at **travelguides@dk.com**

Welcome to
Berlin

Few European cities have witnessed as much upheaval and renewal as Berlin. From Prussian powerhouse and Nazi bastion to Cold War zombie and revitalized capital of a reunited Germany – Berlin has seen it all, and then some. This fascinating city is perpetually in a state of becoming, and with DK Eyewitness Top 10 Berlin, it's yours to explore.

Even today, the layers of history are evident. A stroll along **Unter den Linden** leads you from the classical columns of **Brandenburger Tor** past former Third Reich ministries to the world-class treasures of **Museumsinsel**. Just beyond lies the Socialist architecture of **Alexanderplatz**, compelling in an entirely different way. This kaleidoscope of eras lends richness to Berlin's eclectic charm.

For many visitors, the city's star attractions are its exciting arts scene and variety of bars, cafés and restaurants. The spirit of the Golden Twenties lives on here, and Berlin keeps going around the clock. How late you stay out depends on your stamina – as any bleary-eyed reveller will tell you, this isn't a city of morning people (the after-parties don't count). For a buzzing metropolis, Berlin is surprisingly green, with vast parks such as the **Tiergarten** or **Volkspark Friedrichshain** teeming with sunbathers, families having a barbecue, joggers and cyclists – in a country known for its *autobahns*, Berliners are proud bike riders.

Whether you're visiting for a weekend or a week, our Top 10 guide brings together the best of everything that Berlin has to offer, from the hip cafés of **Prenzlauer Berg** to the gritty nightlife of **Kreuzberg** and the royal stamping grounds of **Charlottenburg**. The guide has useful tips throughout, from seeking out what's free to places off the beaten track, plus 14 easy-to-follow itineraries, designed to tie together a clutch of sights in a short space of time. Add inspiring photography and detailed maps, and you've got the essential pocket-sized travel companion. **Enjoy the book, and enjoy Berlin.**

Clockwise from top: Berliner Dom, Sony Center at Potsdamer Platz, Hackescher Markt near Hackesche Höfe, Schloss Charlottenburg, Marx-Engels-Forum, the Philharmonie concert hall

Exploring Berlin

For a sprawling, historic metropolis whose charms are widely scattered, Berlin is a surprisingly easy place to navigate. There's something for every interest and budget, and excellent public transport takes you from sight to sight with clockwork efficiency. Here are a few ideas to maximize your fun and minimize your planning.

The Kaiser-Wilhelm-Gedächtnis-Kirche stands as a reminder of the horrors of war.

Key
— Two-day itinerary
— Four-day itinerary

Two Days in Berlin

Day ❶

MORNING

Begin at **Alexanderplatz** (see pp102–9) and ascend the **Fernsehturm** (see p104) for an unequalled panorama of Berlin. View Babylonian treasures at the **Pergamonmuseum** (see pp24–6).

AFTERNOON

Stroll along historic **Unter den Linden** (see pp16–19). Admire the iconic **Brandenburger Tor** (see pp12–13) and take a guided tour of the **Reichstag** (see pp14–15) before enjoying a classical concert at the **Philharmonie** (see p38).

Day ❷

MORNING

Begin with the ruins of the **Kaiser-Wilhelm-Gedächtnis-Kirche** (see pp32–3) before exploring stores along **Kurfürstendamm** (see pp30–31) and in **Kaufhaus des Westens** (see p76).

AFTERNOON

After lunch, wander through **Schloss Charlottenburg** (see pp34–7) and linger in its Baroque-style gardens. Seek out **Savignyplatz** (see pp120–21) for cocktails and an evening bite.

Four Days in Berlin

Day ❶

MORNING

Explore the **Reichstag** (see pp14–15) and government district, then take a boat tour through Berlin's waterways (see p167). There are piers in the **Großer Tiergarten** (see p113) next to the Haus der Kulturen der Welt.

AFTERNOON

Have lunch at **Hugo & Notte** (see p93), and visit **Gendarmenmarkt** (see p86). Promenade on **Unter den Linden** (see pp16–17) before admiring the **Brandenburger Tor** (see pp12–13). Catch an evening show at the **Friedrichstadt-Palast** (see p67).

The Reichstag, one of Berlin's most symbolic buildings, is a popular sight.

The Neues Museum contains spectacular treasures, including the bust of Nefertiti.

Friedrichstadt-Palast Pergamon-museum Neues Museum Alexander-platz

Reichstag Fernsehturm

Klosterstrasse station

Unter den Linden Hugo & Notte Gendarmenmarkt

Brandenburger Tor MITTE

Potsdamer Platz U-BAHN

U-BAHN KREUZBERG

Gneisenaustr. station

SCHÖNEBERG

0 kilometres 1
0 miles 1

Potsdamer Platz, untouched for nearly 50 years in rubble, has now been regenerated into a vibrant city hub.

Day ❷

MORNING

Take the lift up to the **Fernsehturm** observation deck (see p104). Peruse the collections of **Museumsinsel** (see pp24–7), particularly the Neues Museum, home to the Nefertiti bust, and the Pergamonmuseum.

AFTERNOON

Head to **Potsdamer Platz** (see pp20–23) for striking modern architecture and the Marlene Dietrich exhibit at the Deutsche Kinamathek. Stroll in the **Tiergarten** (see p113).

Day ❸

MORNING

Start at the **Kaiser-Wilhelm-Gedächtnis-Kirche** (see pp32–3), then choose between the **Zoologischer Garten** (see p119) or shopping on **Kurfürstendamm** (see pp30–31).

AFTERNOON

Marvel at Prussian riches at **Schloss Charlottenburg** (see pp34–7) and

wander its beautifully landscaped park. Stop by the **Gipsformerei Staatliche Museen** (see p77) for gift sculptures, or visit the fascinating **Käthe Kollwitz Museum** (see p35). For dinner, head to Kantstraße and choose from the numerous Asian restaurants.

Day ❹

MORNING

Start the day at the **Kulturforum** (see pp38–41). There are several cultural institutions to be explored in this complex, but a wise use of time is to view the Renaissance masters at the Gemäldegalerie. Have lunch at Potsdamer Platz.

AFTERNOON

The splendid town of **Potsdam** and the stunning gardens in the palace complex of **Sanssouci** (see pp156–61) are a short trip away from the city by commuter train. Stay for dinner at one of the many Italian restaurants.

Top 10 Berlin Highlights

The grand auditorium of the Berlin
Staatsoper Unter den Linden

TOP 10 Berlin Highlights

Berlin is Germany's liveliest city and one of the most fascinating capitals in the world. Here, art and culture, museums and theatres, entertainment and nightlife are more diverse and exciting than perhaps in any other place. Once reunited, Berlin quickly developed into a cosmopolitan city, and today there is an air of great energy and vibrancy about it.

Brandenburger Tor and Pariser Platz ①

The Brandenburger Tor is in Pariser Platz, where the embassies and the Hotel Adlon Kempinski exude stylish elegance *(see pp12–13).*

② Reichstag

No other building is a more potent symbol of Germany's history than the Reichstag. Its vast egg-shaped dome affords fantastic views across the city *(see pp14–15).*

③ Unter den Linden

This magnificent, leafy boulevard has always been a central axis along Berlin's most important historic buildings *(see pp16–19).*

Potsdamer Platz ④

The new heart of the old city is Potsdamer Platz, where exciting modern structures have been erected *(see pp20–23).*

7 Museumsinsel

Among the museums in this complex are the Pergamonmuseum, which houses the Pergamon Altar, the Altes and the Neues museums (see pp24–7).

8 Kaiser-Wilhelm-Gedächtnis-Kirche

The tower ruins of the memorial church, built to commemorate Kaiser Wilhelm I, still stand today as a silent reminder of the horrors of war (see pp32–3).

5 Kurfürstendamm

Berlin's much visited strolling and shopping avenue is the main thoroughfare in the western part of the city (see pp30–31).

9 Schloss Charlottenburg

The former Hohenzollern summer residence and its beautiful Baroque gardens offer visitors a slice of Prussian history (see pp34–7).

10 Kulturforum

This complex includes the Gemäldegalerie, the Berliner Philharmonie, the Kunstgewerbemuseum and the Neue Nationalgalerie (see pp38–41).

6 Jüdisches Museum Berlin

Exhibits at Berlin's Jewish Museum trace the turbulent German-Jewish relationship over the centuries (see pp42–3).

⭐ Brandenburger Tor and Pariser Platz

One of Berlin's best-known symbols, the Brandenburg Gate stands proudly in the middle of Pariser Platz, asserting itself against the modern embassy buildings that now surround it. Crowned by its triumphant Quadriga sculpture, the famous gate has long been a focal point in Berlin's history: rulers and statesmen, military parades and demonstrations – all have felt compelled to march through the Brandenburger Tor.

Brandenburger Tor ①
Built by Carl G Langhans in 1789–91 and modelled on the temple porticoes of ancient Athens, the Brandenburg Gate **(right)** is the undisputed symbol of Berlin. Since the 19th century, this iconic land-mark has been the backdrop for many events in the city's turbulent history.

② Quadriga
The 6-m-(20-ft-) high sculpture **(below)** was created in 1793 as a sym-bol of peace by Johann Gottfried Schadow. The sculpture, which depicts the goddess of victory driving her four-horsed chariot, is the gate's centrepiece.

③ Hotel Adlon Kempinski Berlin
Destroyed in World War II, the city's most elegant hotel **(below)** is a recon-struction of the original, which hosted celebrities such as Greta Garbo, Thomas Mann and Charlie Chaplin.

④ DZ Bank
This modern building, designed by the American architect Frank Owen Gehry, combines the clean lines of Prussian architecture with some daring elements inside *(see p53)*.

⑤ Akademie der Künste
Built in 2000–2005 and designed by Günter Behnisch and Manfred Sabatke, the Academy of Arts incorpo-rates, behind a vast expanse of win-dows, the ruins of the old art academy, which was destroyed in World War II.

⑥ French Embassy
Christian de Portzamparc built this elegant building in 2001 on the site of the old embassy, which was ruined in World War II. Its colonnades and windows are a homage to the original.

8 Palais am Pariser Platz

This complex **(left)** by Bernhard Winking is a successful modern interpretation of Neo-Classical architecture. Inside you will find a café, a restaurant and a souvenir shop around a pleasantly shaded courtyard.

NEED TO KNOW

MAP K3 ■ Pariser Platz

Visitor information:
Brandenburger Tor southern gatehouse; (030) 25 00 25; open Apr–Oct: 9:30am–7pm daily (Nov–Mar: until 6pm daily); www.visitberlin.de

DZ Bank: Pariser Platz 3; open 10am–6pm Mon–Fri

■ For a quick pit stop between sights, visit the Starbucks on Pariser Platz 4A.

■ You can trace the Wall along the former border patrol road, following the green-and-white Berliner Mauerweg signs. Sites of historic interest and natural beauty alternate along the trail.

---

10 Haus Liebermann

Josef P Kleihues built this in 1996–8, faithfully recreating the original that stood on the same site. The house is named after the artist Max Liebermann, who lived here. In 1933, watching Nazi SA troops march through the gate, he famously said: "I cannot possibly eat as much, as I would like to puke."

7 American Embassy

The last gap around Pariser Platz **(above)** was finally closed in 2008. A dispute had delayed building for years: the US wanted a whole street moved for reasons of security, but had to concede the point in the end.

9 Eugen-Gutmann-Haus

With its clean lines, the Dresdner Bank **(right)**, built in 1997 by gmp, recalls the style of the New Sobriety movement of the 1920s. In front of it is Pariser Platz's famous original street sign.

TOP 10 ★ Reichstag

Of all the buildings in Berlin, the Reichstag, seat of the Bundestag (parliament), is probably one of the most symbolic. The mighty structure, erected in 1884–94 by Paul Wallot as the proud manifestation of the power of the German Reich, was destroyed by arson in 1933 and bombed during World War II. In 1995, the artist Christo wrapped up the Reichstag and, in 1999, the British architect Lord Norman Foster transformed it into one of the most modern parliamentary buildings in the world.

The Dome 1
The Reichstag dome **(right)** by Lord Norman Foster affords breathtaking views of Berlin. It is open at the top to air the building and – a symbolic touch – to allow for the free and open dissemination of debates throughout the country. A ramp winds its way up to the top.

2 Plenary Hall
The plenary hall **(above)** is the seat of the Deutscher Bundestag – the German parliament – which has convened here again since 20 April 1999. Technologically, the hall is one of the most advanced parliament buildings in the world. The federal eagle caused a row: considered too "fat", it had to be slimmed down.

3 Portico "Dem deutschen Volke"
The dedication "To the German People" was designed in 1916, against the will of Wilhelm II.

4 Restored Façade
Despite extensive renovations, small World War II bullet holes are still visible in the building's façade.

THE REICHSTAG FIRE

When the Reichstag went up in flames on 27 February 1933, the Dutch Communist van der Lubbe was arrested for arson. It is, however, likely that the Nazis started the fire themselves. Hitler used it as an excuse to get the "Enabling Act" passed, which let him dispose off his opponents and marked the start of a 12-year reign of terror.

5 Käfer im Reichstag
This popular luxury restaurant (see p117) on the Reichstag's roof **(right)** offers an excellent view of the historical centre of Unter den Linden.

8 The German Flag
The giant German flag **(left)** was first raised on the occasion of the official national celebrations of German reunification on 3 October 1990.

9 Weiße Kreuze Memorial
Opposite the southern side of the Reichstag, a memorial recalls the Wall, which stood only a few steps away. The white crosses commemorate the people who died at the Wall while trying to escape to West Berlin.

10 Memorial by Dieter Appelt
Unveiled in 1992, the memorial **(below)** in front of the Reichstag commemorates 97 Social Democratic and Communist delegates who were murdered under the Third Reich.

6 Platz der Republik
Celebrations often take place on the lawn **(below)** in front of the Reichstag, as in 2006, when Germany hosted the Football World Cup.

7 Installation "Der Bevölkerung"
Hans Haacke's work of art "To the People" is a counterpoint to the portico inscription opposite and uses the same style of lettering.

NEED TO KNOW

MAP K2 ▪ Platz der Republik 1 ▪ Dome: (030) 22 73 21 52; Käfer: (030) 22 62 99 33 ▪ www.bundestag.de

Open Dome: 8am–midnight (last entry 10pm); Käfer im Reichstag: 9am–1pm & 7–11pm Thu–Sat, 9am–1pm Sun

▪ To visit the Reichstag dome register online two to three days in advance. Try for same-day admission at the Visitors' Service Centre *(open Apr–Oct: 8am–8pm daily; Nov–Mar: until 6pm daily)* next to the Berlin Pavilion on Scheidemannstraße. You will need your passport/identity card.

▪ If a meal at Käfer im Reichstag exceeds your budget, many stalls nearby sell *Bratwurst* (sausages).

TOP 10 ⭐ Unter den Linden

"As long as the lime trees still blossom in Unter den Linden, Berlin will always be Berlin," sang Marlene Dietrich about this magnificent avenue. The lime trees blossom more beautifully than ever and the street's old buildings have been extensively restored. The Linden, once a royal bridle path linking the king's town residence (the Stadtschloss) and Tiergarten, became Berlin's most fashionable street in the 18th century. Today, the street remains one of the city's most important arteries.

Deutsches Historisches Museum ❶

Germany's largest history museum (right) offers an overview of more than 1,000 years of German history. Housed in the Zeughaus, it is the oldest and architecturally the most interesting building [see p18] on Unter den Linden.

❷ Staatsoper Unter den Linden

The richly ornamented State Opera House (above) is one of Germany's most attractive. Neo-Classical in style, it was built by architect Georg Wenzeslaus von Knobelsdorff between 1741–3 as Europe's first free-standing opera house, to plans devised by Frederick the Great [see p85] himself.

❸ St.-Hedwigs-Kathedrale

Designed by von Knobelsdorff in 1740–2 and modelled on the Pantheon in Rome, this (below) is the seat of Berlin's Catholic archdiocese. It was commissioned [see p48] by Frederick the Great to appease Berlin Catholics after the conquest of Silesia.

❹ Humboldt-Universität

Berlin's oldest and most highly regarded university (above) was founded in 1890, on the initiative of Wilhelm von Humboldt. Twenty-nine Nobel Prize winners were educated here, including Albert Einstein.

Neue Wache
The central German memorial **(above)** for all victims of war was created in 1816–8 by Karl Friedrich Schinkel. A reproduction of Käthe Kollwitz's moving *Pietà* stands here.

Kronprinzenpalais
Originally created in 1669 as a private residence by Johann Arnold Nering, the building was remodelled in 1732–3 into a Neo-Classical palace by Philip Gerlach and was a residence for several Hohenzollern heirs. After World War I it became an art museum, before the East German government housed state visitors there. The German reunification agreement was signed here in August 1990. It now holds cultural events and exhibitions.

Bebelplatz
Originally named Opernplatz, this wide open space was designed by Georg W von Knobelsdorff as the focal point of his Forum Fridericianum. The elegant square was meant to introduce some of the splendour and glory of ancient Rome to the Prussian capital. In May 1933, it became the scene of the infamous Nazi book burning.

Opernpalais
The building next to the Staatsoper, built in 1733–7, once served as a palace for Friedrich Wilhelm III's daughters. Today it houses a centre for contemporary arts and culture, PalaisPopulaire.

Russische Botschaft
The gigantic Russian Embassy, built in Stalinist "wedding-cake style", was the first building to be erected on Unter den Linden after World War II.

Frederick the Great's Statue
One of Christian Daniel Rauch's grandest *(see p85)*, this equestrian statue **(above)** shows "Old Fritz" (13.5 m/44 ft high) in his tricorn and coronation mantle.

NEED TO KNOW

Deutsches Historisches Museum: **MAP K5**; Zeughaus, Unter den Linden 2; (030) 20 30 40; closed for renovation until 2025; Pei Bau: open 10am–6pm daily, adm €10; www.dhm.de

Staatsoper Unter den Linden: **MAP K4**; Unter den Linden 7; (030) 20 35 45 55; www.staatsoper-berlin.de

St.-Hedwigs-Kathedrale & Bebelplatz: **MAP K4**; Bebelplatz; closed for renovation until 2023; www.hedwigs-kathedrale.de

■ Take a break at the Café LePolulaire in the Deutsche Bank's Palais-Populaire at Opernpalais, Unter den Linden 5.

Deutsches Historisches Museum

 The Dying Warriors
The 22 reliefs by Andreas Schlüter, displayed on the walls of the courtyard rather than in one of the museum's exhibitions, portray the horrors of war in an unusually immediate way.

 Europe and Asia
This group of 18th-century Meissen porcelain figures reflects the fascinating relationship between the two continents.

 Steam Engine
A full-sized steam engine from the year 1847 marks the entrance to the exhibition on the Industrial Revolution.

 Martin Luther
Luther's portrait, by Lucas Cranach the Elder, is the focal point of exhibition rooms devoted to the Reformation and Martin Luther himself.

A Nazi Germany V2 rocket engine

5 Clothes from the Camps
Among the many exhibits here that illustrate the years under Nazi rule is the jacket of a concentration camp inmate – a chilling reminder of the Third Reich.

6 V2 Rocket
Exhibited in the section on Nazi Germany is a V2 rocket engine, displayed next to an 88-mm flak gun. The V2 missile was one of the *Wunderwaffen* ("wonder weapons") used by German troops at the end of World War II.

7 Soldiers Plundering a House
This painting by Flemish-Baroque painter Sebastian Vrancx, dating from around 1600, depicts a scene from the wars of religion that tore the Netherlands apart during the 16th century.

8 Saddle
A valuable saddle, dating from the middle of the 15th century, is decorated with elaborately carved plaques made of ivory.

9 The Berlin Wall
An original section of the Berlin Wall, together with banners of a peaceful pro-unification demonstration in 1989, commemorates the fall of the Wall.

10 Gloria Victis
The moving allegorical figure of Gloria Victis, created by the famed French sculptor Marius Jean Antonin Mercié, bears witness to the death of his friend during the conclusive days of the Franco-Prussian War of 1870–71.

Martin Luther by Lucas Cranach

ZEUGHAUS UNTER DEN LINDEN

Originally the royal arsenal, the Zeughaus was built in 1706 in Baroque style according to plans by Johann Arnold Nering. It is an impressive structure, with the building surrounding a historical central courtyard that is protected by a modern glass cupola roof. Especially memorable are Baroque sculptor Andreas Schlüter's figures of 22 dying warriors, lined up along the arcades in the courtyard. They portray vividly the horrors of war. Behind the main building stands a cone-shaped glass annex designed by the Chinese-born architect Ieoh Ming Pei in 2001 for special exhibitions and temporary shows. The permanent exhibition in the main historical building includes a collection entitled "Images and Testimonials of German History". Highlighting the most significant periods and events in the history of the country, the displays include a surprising variety of exhibits dating from the days of the early Medieval German Empire up to 1994. Featured are the period of the Reformation, the Thirty Years' War, the wars of Liberation and the failed Revolution of 1848, and, of course, the two World Wars.

TOP 10 UNTER DEN LINDEN EVENTS

1 1573 Elector Johann Georg has a bridle path built, linking the royal Stadtschloss and the Tiergarten

2 1647 During the reign of the Great Elector, the road is planted with *Linden* (lime trees)

3 From 1740 Frederick the Great has grand buildings erected

4 1806 Napoleon and his troops march along Unter den Linden

5 1820 The road turns into a grand boulevard

6 1928 Unter den Linden and Friedrichstraße epitomize the world city

7 1933 Troops celebrate Hitler's victory

8 1945 The avenue is razed to the ground

9 1948–53 Revival of the boulevard

10 October 1989 Demonstrations lead to the fall of the East German regime

Entry of Napoleon into Berlin, 27 October 1806 (1810) by Charles Meynier shows the victorious French at the Brandenburg Gate, Unter den Linden.

TOP 10 ⭐ Potsdamer Platz

The heart of the new metropolis of Berlin beats on Potsdamer Platz. This square, where Berliners and tourists alike now flock to cinemas, restaurants and shops, was a hub of urban life in the 1920s. After World War II, it became a desolate wasteland, but since the fall of the Wall, Potsdamer Platz – for a while Europe's largest building site – has become a city within the city, surrounded by imposing edifices that began to appear in the 1990s, and are still being added to today.

Sony Center ①
The Sony Center **(right)** is the most ambitious, successful and architecturally interesting building in the new Berlin. The cupola structure, designed by Helmut Jahn, is the German headquarters of the Sony company, and with its cinemas and restaurants it is also a social magnet.

② Deutsche Kinemathek
This museum **(below)** takes visitors backstage at Babelsberg and Hollywood with Marlene Dietrich's costumes *(see p22)* and other exhibits.

Weinhaus Huth ④
The only building on Potsdamer Platz to have survived World War II, the restored Weinhaus **(right)** today accommodates restaurants and the excellent Daimler Contemporary, which showcases modern art.

③ Frederick's
This glamorous hybrid restaurant-bar is housed in the Sony Center. With a restaurant, two bars, lounge and deli set in plush, extravagant interiors, Frederick's brings the spirit of the 1920s back to life.

⑤ Boulevard der Stars
Berlin's walk of fame features stars such as Marlene Dietrich, Werner Herzog, Fritz Lang, Hans Zimmer, Christoph Waltz, Diane Kruger and Romy Schneider **(left)**. The coloured asphalt evokes the red carpet.

6 LEGOLAND® Discovery Centre

This LEGO® wonderland features brick models, a miniature Berlin, a train ride to a land of dragons and a DUPLO® Village with bigger blocks for the tots *(see p65)*.

7 Theater am Potsdamer Platz

The theatre at Marlene Dietrich Platz seats 1,800 and hosts theatrical performances, musicals and shows. Every year in February, it transforms into a venue for the Berlinale film festival, the "Berlinale Palast".

Map of Potsdamer Platz

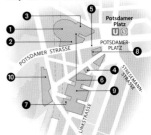

10 Spielbank Berlin

Berlin's casino invites visitors to *faites vos jeux*. Roulette and Black Jack are played, and gambling machines cover one floor.

8 Kollhoff Tower

Designed by Hans Kollhoff, this postmodern high-rise building was completed in 1999. It features Europe's fastest elevator that takes passengers to the 25th floor viewing platform **(below)** in just 20 seconds.

9 The Playce

Opened in 2022 and previously known as Potsdamer Platz Arkaden, this shopping mall is now a food and entertainment venue. Inside, a food market, Manifesto, offers sustainable products and street food.

NEED TO KNOW

MAP L2

Sony Center: Potsdamer Platz; www.sonycenter.de/en

Deutsche Kinemathek: Potsdamer Str. 2; open 10am–6pm Wed–Mon; adm €9, free for under-18s; www.deutsche-kinemathek.de

Frederick's: Bellevuestraße 1; (030) 31 19 67 36; hours vary, check website; www.fredericksberlin.com

Kollhoff Tower: Potsdamer Platz 1; (030) 25 93 70 80; open 11am–7pm daily (winter: until 6pm); adm €7.50, family €17.50, VIP €11.50

LEGOLAND® Discovery Centre: Potsdamer Str. 4; open 10am–7pm daily (last entry 5pm); adm €19 (€15 online); www.legolanddiscoverycentre.de

Spielbank Berlin: **MAP F4**; Marlene-Dietrich-Platz 1; open 11am–3am daily; adm €2; (ID required); www.spielbank-berlin.de

Deutsche Kinemathek Exhibitions

Marlene Dietrich's famous costume collection

industry's victims: some stars allowed themselves to be used for the Nazis' benefit, others refused to cooperate. The life and work of Jewish actor Kurt Gerron, who was persecuted and murdered, is documented as an exemplary case.

 Marlene Dietrich
This exhibition of the film star's estate includes her film costumes, her touring luggage, film clips, posters, photographs, letters and notes.

Metropolis
This iconic 1927 film, directed by Fritz Lang, has an alarming vision of a futuristic urban dystopian world as its subject. Models and props from the film are on display.

Caligari
The best known German film of the 1920s, *The Cabinet of Dr Caligari* (1920), was an influential masterpiece of Expressionist filmmaking by Robert Wiene.

Weimar Republic
The exhibits here are dedicated to the works of the legendary directors of German cinema's golden age from 1918 to 1933.

Olympia
This exhibition reveals the technical tricks used in the Nazi propaganda film *Olympia*, a staged documentary by Leni Riefenstahl made in 1936–8 after the Olympics.

 National Socialism
This exhibition has documents relating to the use of film as propaganda, everyday cinema and the

 Post-War Cinema
The story of films and filmmaking in East and West Germany is shown here with props and costumes of popular stars of post-war German cinema such as Hanna Schygulla, Romy Schneider, Heinz Rühmann and Mario Adorf.

Transatlantic
This exhibition of letters, documents, keepsakes and souvenirs retraces the careers of German film stars in Hollywood, both of the silent era and the "talkies" that followed after 1928.

Exhibits in the Transatlantic section

 Pioneers and Divas
The early days of cinema are featured here, as well as stars of the silent era such as Henny Porten and the Dutch actress Asta Nielsen.

 Exile
Documents in this exhibition relate the difficulties encountered by German filmmakers when making a new start in the USA in 1933–45.

THE NEW CENTRE OF BERLIN

In the 1920s, Potsdamer Platz was Europe's busiest square, featuring the first automatic traffic lights in Berlin. During World War II this social hub was razed to the ground. Ignored for almost 50 years, the empty square shifted back into the centre of Berlin when the Wall came down. During the 1990s, it was Europe's largest building site. New skyscrapers were built, old structures were restored – some preserved rooms of the ruined historic Grand Hotel Esplanade were even physically moved into the Sony Center. Millions of people came to follow progress from the famous Red Info Box, which was removed in 2001. Altogether, around €17 billion was invested to create the present square.

TOP 10 POTSDAMER PLATZ ARCHITECTS

1 Helmut Jahn
Sony Center

2 Renzo Piano and Christian Kohlbecker
Atrium Tower, Spielbank Berlin, Musical-Theater, Spielbank, Weinhaus Huth

3 José Rafael Moneo
Hotel Grand Hyatt, Mercedes-Benz Headquarters

4 Hans Kollhoff
DaimlerChrysler Highrise Building, Kollhoff Tower

5 Giorgio Grassi
Park Colonnades

6 Ulrike Lauber and Wolfram Wöhr
Grimm-Haus, CinemaxX

7 Sir Richard Rogers
Office Block Linkstraße

8 Steffen Lehmann and Arata Isozaki
Office and Retail House Linkstraße

9 Heidenreich & Michel
Weinhaus Huth

10 Bruno Doedens and Maike van Stiphout
Tilla-Durieux-Park

Grand Hotel Esplanade remnants, Sony Center

Brightly lit skyscrapers at dusk on Potsdamer Platz

🔟 ⭐ Museumsinsel

Formed by the two arms of the Spree River, the Museumsinsel is home to the world's most diverse museum complex. Built between 1830 and 1930, the museums, which hold the Prussian royal collections of art and archaeology, were turned into a public foundation in 1918. Heavily damaged in World War II, the complex was restored and declared a UNESCO World Heritage Site in 1999. Renovations will go on until 2027 during which an underground path, linking the four museums, will be constructed.

Bode-Museum **1**

Located at the northern tip of Museumsinsel, the Bode-Museum is a stately structure dominated by a cupola **(right)**. The building holds the Sculpture Collection, the Museum of Byzantine Art and the Numismatic Collection, made up of a diverse collection of over 500,000 objects.

2 Pergamonmuseum

Built in 1909–30, this is one of the world's most important museums (see p26) of ancient art and architecture, with a vast collection of antiquities. The huge Ishtar gate **(above)** dates from the 6th century BCE.

5 Neues Museum

Spectacularly revamped by British architect David Chipperfield, the building itself is as fascinating as its exhibits. As well as the Museum of Pre- and Early History, the Ägyptisches Museum is also housed here.

3 Ägyptisches Museum

Housed within the Neues Museum, this museum (see p54) features portraits of Egyptian royals and monumental architecture.

4 Alte Nationalgalerie

First opened in 1876, the Old National Gallery was beautifully restored in the 1990s **(right)** and now holds 19th-century sculptures and paintings (see p56), including works by Schadow and Max Liebermann.

MISSING TREASURES

During World War II, many of the island's exhibits were hidden in underground bunkers. Some pieces of "Priam's Gold", excavated from the site of ancient Troy, were taken by the Red Army as war booty and remain in Moscow. The Neues Museum points out where there are gaps in the collection.

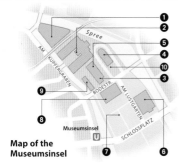

Map of the Museumsinsel

8 Altes Museum
The first building to be completed on Museumsinsel in 1830, the Altes Museum *(see p51)* resembles a Greek temple. Originally meant to hold paintings, it now houses the collection of Classical antiquities **(right)**.

9 James-Simon-Galerie
Named in honour of James Simon (1851–1932), a patron of the Berlin State Museums, this building, was designed by David Chipperfield. The museum was completed and opened in 2019.

10 Colonnade Courtyard
This columned courtyard between the Neues Museum and the Alte Nationalgalerie connects the museums and is an atmospheric venue for open-air concerts.

7 Lustgarten
This "pleasure park", with a fountain in its centre, is located in front of the Altes Museum *(see p51)*. The lawns are popular with tired visitors.

6 Berliner Dom
Easily the island's most overwhelming structure *(see p48)*, this Baroque-style cathedral **(above)** is unusually ornate for a protestant church. Organ concerts and services can be enjoyed in this exquisitely restored church.

NEED TO KNOW

MAP J5 ■ (030) 266 424 242 ■ www.smb.museum

Open 10am–6pm daily, until 8pm Thu (most museums); Pergamonmuseum: closed for renovation until 2027

Adm €12 per museum; Museumsinsel day pass €19; 3-day Berlin Museum Pass €29; extra fee for exhibitions; free for under-18s

■ Altes Museum, Neues Museum, Bode-Museum and James-Simon-Galerie, all have cafés, the latter with a nice terrace.

■ It's best to set aside a whole day for the Museumsinsel. There are several parks nearby where you can take breaks. Sundays can be very busy with long queues and large groups.

Pergamonmuseum

Detail, frieze from Darius's palace

5 Pergamon Altar

The Pergamon Altar from the eponymous Greek city (in modern Turkey) dates from 160 BCE. The altar will remain closed for renovation until 2027.

6 Giant Sculpture of a Bird of Prey

The nearly 2-m- (7-ft-) high Riesensonnenvogel (huge sun bird) was discovered during excavations in Tell Halaf, Syria, the centre of the ancient Aramaic city-state of Guzana.

7 Aleppo Room

Taken from a Christian merchant's house in Syria and dating from the early 17th century, this small room features magnificent wooden cladding and is a beautiful example of Ottoman architecture.

1 Frieze from the Palace of Darius

A frieze dating to around 510 BCE from the palace of Darius in Susa (Iran) is made of exquisitely coloured glazed brick and depicts a row of Persian warriors holding lances and carrying bows and quivers.

2 Ishtar Gate

The Ishtar Gate, built under the reign of Nebuchadnezar II in the 6th century BCE in Babylon, and the Processional Way are fully preserved. Original faïence tiles depict the sacred lions.

3 Market Gate of Miletus

This vast gate (100 CE) is over 16 m (52 ft) high. To the right of the entrance, a hairdresser has carved an advertisement for his shop into the stone.

4 Assyrian Palace Room

The reconstructed room of the Assyrian kings' palace (9th century BCE) features impressive door figures and 13th-century BCE wall paintings.

8 Mosaic of Orpheus

This delightful mosaic floor, depicting Orpheus playing his lyre amid animals enchanted by his skill, comes from the dining room of a private home in Asia Minor (200 CE).

9 The Mshatta Façade

A gift from Ottoman Sultan Abdul Hamid II to Kaiser Wilhelm II, this stone façade elaborately carved with arabesque and animal forms was the south face of a desert fort built in 744 CE in Mshatta, Jordan.

Market Gate of Miletus

10 Victory Stele of Esarhaddon

This monumental stele, excavated in 1888 in Zincirli, commemorates Esarhaddon's victory over Pharoah Taharqa (671 BCE).

SAVING THE MUSEUMSINSEL

Visitors at the spectacular Neues Museum

The island of museums is a treasury of antique architecture, but until recently it had been slowly decaying. Since 1992, however, €1.8 billion has been spent on the renovation and modernization of Museumsinsel. A master plan created by renowned architects that include David Chipperfield and O M Ungers will transform the complex into a unique museum landscape – just as it was first conceived in the 19th century by Friedrich Wilhelm IV, when he established the "free institution for art and the sciences". Once completed, an "architectural promenade" will serve as a conceptual and structural link between various individual museums, except the old National Gallery. This promenade will consist of a variety of rooms, courtyards and vaults, as well as exhibition halls. The core of the complex will be the James-Simon-Galerie, a central building opened in 2019. The Pergamonmuseum, which is undergoing extensive restoration, is scheduled to reopen in 2027.

TOP 10 MUSEUMSINSEL EVENTS

1 1810 Plan for a public art collection created

2 1830 The Altes Museum, Prussia's first public museum, opens

3 1859 Completion of the Neues Museum

4 1876 Opening of the Alte Nationalgalerie

5 1904 Completion of the Kaiser-Friedrich-Museum (Bode-Museum)

6 1930 Opening of the Pergamonmuseum

7 1958 Most museums reopen after renovation after they were bombed in 1943

8 1999 Museumsinsel declared a UNESCO World Heritage Site

9 2009 The Neues Museum reopens

10 2019 The new central entrance building, the James-Simon-Galerie, is completed

The eye-catching entrance to James-Simon-Galerie

TOP 10 ★ Kurfürstendamm

After years of decline, the Kurfürstendamm, or Ku'damm for short, has once again become a fashionable hot spot. Breathtaking architecture, elegant boutiques and a lively street artist scene around Breitscheidplatz have made this shopping boulevard one of Berlin's most attractive and – at 3.8 km (2.5 miles) – also its longest avenue for strolling.

1 Breitscheidplatz
Here, in the heart of the western city, artists, Berliners and visitors swarm around J Schmettan's globe fountain, known by locals as "Wasserklops" (water meatball).

2 Kaiser-Wilhelm-Gedächtnis-Kirche
While the church itself was destroyed during World War II, the church tower (see pp32–3) stands in the centre of the square (**left**), serving as both memorial and stark reminder of the terrors of war.

3 Europa-Center
The oldest shopping centre (**below**) in West Berlin, opened in 1962, is still worth a visit. Here you will find fashion boutiques, a comedy theatre and an official Berlin Tourist Info centre.

5 Bikini Berlin
The Bikini-Haus building (**above**), built in 1956, was renovated to house the splendid Bikini Berlin, an ultra-hip boutique mall that also offers great views of the nearby zoo.

4 Neues Kranzler Eck
This glass and steel skyscraper was built in 2000 by architect Helmut Jahn. The legendary Café Kranzler was retained as a bar in front of the office block. There is an official Berlin Tourist Info centre here.

WHEN KU'DAMM WAS NO MORE THAN A LOG ROAD

In 1542, Ku'damm was just a humble "Knüppeldamm", or log road. It served the Electors as a bridle path, linking their town residence (Stadtschloss) and their hunting lodge (Jagdschloss). It was not until 1871 that the area around the boulevard developed into a fashionable "new west end". Chancellor Otto von Bismarck had the boulevard modelled on the Champs Elysées in Paris, lined with houses, shops, hotels and restaurants.

Previous pages The Reichstag and the Paul Löbe legislative building reflected in the Spree

7 Lehniner Platz

The square is home to the Schaubühne theatre **(left)**, built as Universum cinema in 1928 by Erich Mendelsohn and converted in 1978.

8 Fasanenstraße

A small street *(see pp120–21)* off Ku'damm, Fasanenstraße **(below)**, with its galleries, expensive shops and restaurants, is one of Charlottenburg's most elegant areas.

9 Traffic Turret

On the corner of Joachimstaler Straße stands an old-fashioned traffic turret or *Verkehrskanzel*, the last one in the city and now a heritage monument. A police officer sat in the raised glass cabin to control traffic lights manually from 1955 to 1962, when the signals went automatic.

6 Iduna-Haus

The turreted building at No. 59 at the Leibnitzstraße corner is one of the few surviving bourgeois houses from the late 19th century. The ornamented Jugendstil (Art Nouveau) façade **(below)** has been lavishly restored. The building is home to a number of banks.

10 RT&W Galerie

The Neo-Classical building housing this art gallery gives visitors a glimpse of Ku'damm's erstwhile splendour.

NEED TO KNOW

Europa-Center:
MAP P5; Tauentzienstr. 9; (030) 348 00 80; open 24 hours (shops and Berlin Tourist Info: 10am–8pm Mon–Sat); www.europa-center-berlin.de

Bikini Berlin: **MAP N4**; Budapester Str. 38–50; open 10am–8pm Mon–Sat, noon–6pm Sun; www.bikiniberlin.de

■ Few original cafés in the Kurfürstendamm area have survived. The most charming of these is the Café Wintergarten, located in the Literaturhaus on Fasanenstraße *(see p126)*.

■ On Saturdays, Ku'damm is usually busy with locals and tourists shopping and meeting for brunch.

TOP 10 ⭐ Kaiser-Wilhelm-Gedächtnis-Kirche

This ruined Neo-Romanesque church is one of Berlin's most haunting symbols. It was consecrated in 1895 and named Kaiser Wilhelm Memorial Church in honour of Wilhelm I. Following severe damage by bombing raids during World War II, the ruins of the tower were left standing as a memorial. Egon Eiermann built a new church next to it in 1957–63.

Tower Ruins ①

Only the church tower **(right)** survived the Allied bombing raids that razed much of the city to the ground in 1943. Today only 71 m (233 ft) high, the tower once rose to 113 m (370 ft). The rough hole in its roof has given rise to its nickname "the Hollow Tooth".

New Bell Tower ②

The hexagonal bell tower **(right)** rises 53 m (174 ft) high next to the tower ruins on the site of the old church's main nave.

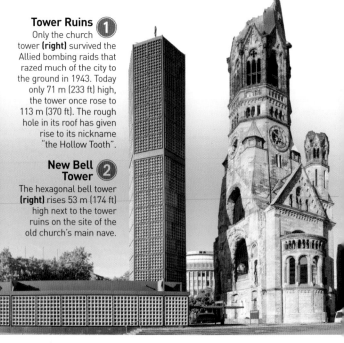

Tower Clock ③

The tower clock **(left)** is based on a Classical design, with Roman numerals. At night, it is lit blue by modern light-emitting diodes to match the lighting inside.

Russian Orthodox Cross ④

This gift from the bishops of Volokolomsk and Yuruyev was given in memory of the victims of Nazism.

Kaiser's Mosaic ⑤

One of the preserved mosaics shows Heinrich I on his throne, with imperial orb and sceptre **(right)**. Originally decorated with scenes from German imperial history, the interior was meant to place the Hohenzollerns within that tradition.

6 Main Altar

The golden figure of Christ **(above)** created by Karl Hemmeter is suspended above the main altar in the modern church. In the evening light, the windows behind the altar glow an overwhelming dark blue.

7 Mosaic of the Hohenzollerns

The vividly coloured mosaic **(above)** of the Hohenzollerns adorns the vestibule of the church ruins. It depicts Emperor Wilhelm I together with Queen Luise of Prussia and her entourage.

Original Mosaics 8

Glittering mosaics **(right)** in Jugendstil style showing Prussian dukes and princes are preserved on the walls and ceilings along the stairways.

9 Figure of Christ

Miraculously, the vast, plain sculpture of Christ, which is suspended from the ceiling, survived the bombing of the church.

A CHURCH WITH TWO LIVES

The Kaiser-Wilhelm-Gedächtnis-Kirche has the Berliners to thank for its preservation: in 1947, the Senate had planned to demolish the tower ruins for safety reasons. In a referendum only about 10 years later, however, one in two Berliners voted for its preservation. And so the idea came about to build a new church next to the ruin and to preserve the vestibule of the old church as a striking memorial hall to the horrors of war.

NEED TO KNOW

MAP N4 ■ Breitscheidplatz ■ (030) 218 50 23 ■ www.gedaechtniskirche-berlin.de

Open Church: noon–6pm daily; Memorial hall: noon–5pm daily; Services: 10am & 6pm Sun

Free guided tours at 12:15pm, 1:15pm, 2:15pm & 3:15pm daily; 11:15am & 4:15pm Fri & Sat (donations welcome); group tours in English available for a small fee

■ Visit the new church on a sunny day around lunchtime, when the blue glass window is at its most impressive.

■ Special music services take place at 6pm every Saturday.

10 Coventry Crucifix

This small crucifix was forged from old nails that were found in the ruins of Coventry Cathedral in England. It honours the bombing of Coventry by the German Luftwaffe in 1940.

🔟 ⭐ Schloss Charlottenburg

The construction of Schloss Charlottenburg, designed as a summer residence for Sophie Charlotte, wife of the Elector Friedrich III, began in 1695. The Orangerie was extended and a cupola was added by Johann Friedrich Eosander between 1701 and 1713. Subsequent extensions were undertaken by Frederick the Great, who added the Neuer Flügel in the mid-1700s.

1 Altes Schloss
The Baroque tower (above) of the oldest part of the palace (dating to 1695) by Johann Arnold Nering is crowned by Richard Scheibe's golden statue of Fortuna.

2 Porzellankabinett
This small, exquisite mirrored gallery (below) has been faithfully restored to its original glory. Among the exhibits on display are valuable porcelain items from China and Japan.

3 Schlosskapelle
The luxurious splendour of the palace chapel recalls the once magnificent interior design of the palace, before it was destroyed in World War II. However, apart from the original altar, the entire chapel – including the king's box – is a costly reconstruction.

4 Monument to the Great Elector

The equestrian statue of the Great Elector Friedrich Wilhelm (right) is thought to be one of his most dignified portraits. Made by Schlüter in 1696–1703, it originally stood on the Rathausbrücke, near the destroyed Stadtschloss.

5 Neuer Flügel
Built between 1740 and 1747 by Georg W von Knobelsdorff, the new wing contains Frederick the Great's private quarters, as well as a large collection of 18th-century French paintings.

8 Schlosspark
The palace has a lovely Baroque garden, beyond which lies a vast park, redesigned by Peter Joseph Lenné in 1818–1828 in the English style with rivers, artificial lakes and small follies.

Map of Schloss Charlottenburg

7 Belvedere
Friedrich Wilhelm II liked to escape to the romantic Belvedere **(below)**, a summer residence built in 1788 by Carl Gotthard Langhans, which served as a tea pavilion. Today it houses a collection of precious porcelain objects from Berlin.

9 Neuer Pavillon
This Italianate villa, designed by Schinkel for Friedrich Wilhelm III in 1825, was inspired by the Villa Reale del Chiatamone in Naples and clearly shows the Hohenzollerns' love of the Italian style.

10 Mausoleum
Slightly hidden, this Neo-Classical building **(below)** by Schinkel is the final resting place of many of the Hohenzollerns.

6 Käthe Kollwitz Museum
This museum showcases the work of sculptress and graphic artist Käthe Kollwitz (1867–1945). She was the first woman to be elected to the Prussian Academy of Arts and was later ostracized by the Nazis. Works on show include 200 drawings and prints, sculptures, a woodcut series about the war and self portraits spanning 50 years.

NEED TO KNOW

MAP A/B3 ■ Spandauer Damm ■ (030) 32 09 10 ■ Adm ■ www.spsg.de

Altes Schloss: open Apr–Oct: 10am–5:30pm Tue–Sun (Nov–Mar: until 5pm)

Neuer Flügel: open Apr–Oct: 10am–5:30pm Tue–Sun (Nov–Mar: until 5pm)

Käthe Kollwitz Museum: Spandauer Damm 10, Theaterbau building; open 11am–6pm daily; www.kaethe-kollwitz.berlin

Belvedere: open Apr–Oct: 10am–6pm Tue–Sun

Neuer Pavillon: open Jan–Mar: noon–4pm Tue–Sun, Apr–Oct:

10am–5:30pm; Nov–Dec: noon–4pm Tue–Sun

Mausoleum: open Apr–Oct: 10am–6pm Tue–Sun

■ The Orangery Café has an attractive garden.

■ Try a romantic midweek evening stroll to avoid the crowds (*park: 6am–dusk*).

Schloss Charlottenburg Rooms

Goldene Galerie in the Neuer Flügel

 Goldene Galerie
The festival salon in the Neuer Flügel, 42 m (138 ft) long, was designed in Rococo style by Frederick the Great's favourite architect von Knobelsdorff. The richly ornamented room has a cheerful appearance.

 Eichengalerie
The wooden panelling of the Oak Gallery is carved with expensively gilded portraits of Hohenzollern ancestors.

3 Gris-de-Lin-Kammer
This small chamber in Friedrich's second palace apartment is decorated with paintings, including some by his favourite artist, Antoine Watteau. The room was named after its wall coverings in violet-coloured damask (*gris-de-lin* in French).

4 Schlafzimmer der Königin Luise
Queen Luise's bedchamber, designed in 1810 by Karl Friedrich Schinkel, features the clear lines typical of the Neo-Classical style. The walls are clad in silk fabrics and wallpaper.

5 Winterkammern
Friedrich Wilhelm II's early Neo-Classical rooms contain fine paintings, tapestries and furniture.

 Bibliothek
Frederick the Great's small library has outstanding elegant bookcases and a vibrant, light green colour scheme.

 Konzertkammer
Furniture and gilded panelling in the concert hall have been faithfully recreated as during Frederick the Great's time. Antoine Watteau's *Gersaint's Shop Sign*, considered to be one of his most significant works, hangs here; the king bought the work directly from the artist.

 Grünes Zimmer
The green room in Queen Elisabeth's quarters is an excellent example of royal chambers furnished in 19th-century Biedermeier style.

Queen Elisabeth's Grünes Zimmer

9 Rote Kammer
The elegant chamber, decorated entirely in red and gold, is adorned by portraits of King Friedrich I and Sophie Charlotte.

10 Friedrich I's Audienzkammer
The ceiling paintings and Belgian tapestries depict allegorical figures symbolizing the fine arts and the sciences. There are also magnificent lacquered cabinets, modelled on Asian originals.

THE HOHENZOLLERNS AND BERLIN

Friedrich Wilhelm, the Great Elector

In 1412, Burggraf Friedrich of the Hohenzollern dynasty of Nuremberg was asked by Sigismund of Luxemburg to support him in the princely feuding before the imperial election for the throne. When Sigismund became king, he gave Friedrich, in 1415, the titles of Margrave and Prince-Elector of Brandenburg as a reward for his services – this is where the histories of the Hohenzollerns and Berlin first became entwined, a relationship that was to last for 500 years. From the start, the family tried to limit the powers of the town and of the Brandenburg nobility. Culture, however, flourished under the new rulers, especially the Great Elector 200 years later, who invited 20,000 Huguenot crafters to Berlin and founded an art gallery and several schools. His grandson Friedrich Wilhelm I, father of Frederick the Great, transformed the city into a military camp, with garrisons and parade grounds, and scoured the town for tall men to join his bodyguard. In the 19th century, however, relations between Berlin and the Hohenzollerns became decidedly less cordial.

TOP 10 HOHENZOLLERN RULERS

1 **Friedrich Wilhelm** the Great Elector (1620–88)

2 **Friedrich I** (1657–1713)

3 **Friedrich Wilhelm I** (1688–1740)

4 **Friedrich II** the Great (1712–86)

5 **Friedrich Wilhelm II** (1744–97)

6 **Friedrich Wilhelm III** (1770–1840)

7 **Friedrich Wilhelm IV** (1795–1861)

8 **Wilhelm I** (1797–1888)

9 **Friedrich III** (1831–88)

10 **Wilhelm II** (1859–1941)

The Great Elector Receiving Huguenot Refugees, 18th-century etching by Daniel Chodowiecki

🔟⭐ Kulturforum

The Kulturforum is a unique complex of museums, concert halls and libraries west of Potsdamer Platz. Here, some of the most outstanding European art museums, as well as the famous concert hall of the Berlin Philharmonic Orchestra, attract millions of visitors interested in culture and music. The complex, based in the former West Berlin, has been growing steadily since 1956 as a counterpoint to the Museumsinsel in the former East Berlin. The Kulturforum also contains some of Berlin's best examples of modern architecture.

Gemäldegalerie ①

Berlin's largest art museum **(right)** holds masterpieces of European art. They are displayed in the modern Neubau, built in 1998 by Heinz Hilmer and Christoph Sattler. The collection includes Bosch, Holbein, Dürer, Gossaert, Vermeer, Brueghel the Elder, Titian, Caravaggio and Rembrandt.

② Neue Nationalgalerie

Located in a striking steel and glass building **(above)** designed by Mies van der Rohe, this gallery *(see p52)* displays 20th-century art, with an emphasis on German Expressionism.

③ Philharmonie

This tent-like building **(right)** was the first new structure *(see p66)* to be built in the Kulturforum in 1960–3. Considered one of the best concert halls in the world, it is the home of the Berlin Philharmonic Orchestra. Kirill Petrenko is conducting the orchestra from 2019 onwards.

④ Kunstgewerbe-museum

Craft objects **(left)** from across Europe from the Middle Ages to the present day are on show at this museum *(see p55)*, including valuable items like the Guelphs' treasure, Lüneburg's silver and Renaissance faïence.

⑤ Musikinstrumenten-Museum

Concealed behind the Philharmonie is this fascinating little museum *(see p55)* of musical instruments. More than 800 exhibits are on show here, particularly early instruments such as harpsichords **(right)** and a 1929 Wurlitzer.

NEED TO KNOW

MAP L1–L2 ▪ West of Potsdamer Platz ▪ (030) 266 424 242 ▪ www. smb.museum

Adm €16 (day pass for all museums)

Gemäldegalerie: Matthäikirchplatz 4/6; open 10am–6pm Tue–Sun (until 8pm Thu)

Neue Nationalgalerie: **MAP E4**; open 10am–6pm Tue–Sat; www.smb.museum

Philharmonie: Herbert-von-Karajan-Str. 1; (030) 25 48 80; Box Office: open 3–6pm Mon–Fri, 11am–2pm Sat & Sun; www.berliner-philharmoniker.de

Kupferstichkabinett: Matthäikirchplatz 8; open 10am–6pm Tue–Sun

St Matthäuskirche: Matthäikirchplatz 1; (030) 262 12 02; open 11am–6pm Tue–Sun; organ concert 12:30pm; adm for concerts; www.stiftung-stmatthaeus.de

Kunstbibliothek: Matthäikirchplatz 6; open 10am–6pm Tue–Sun

▪ The Kulturforum restaurant and café is a convenient spot for coffee.

⑥ Kammermusiksaal

The smaller relative of the larger Philharmonie, this concert hall *(see p53)* is one of Germany's most highly regarded chamber music venues.

⑦ Kupferstichkabinett

The Gallery of Prints and Drawings holds more than 550,000 prints and 110,000 drawings from all periods and countries, including a portrait of Dürer's mother.

⑧ St Matthäuskirche

This church **(right)** is the only historical building pre-served in the Kulturforum. Built in 1844–6 by Stüler, it is also a venue for art installations and classical music concerts.

Map of the Kulturforum

⑨ Staatsbibliothek

Built in 1978 by Hans Scharoun, the National Library is one of the world's largest German-language libraries, with five million books, manuscripts and journals.

⑩ Kunstbibliothek

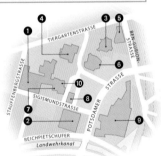

The Art Library has a collection of advertising and art posters, among other items, and also hosts art and architecture exhibi-tions and design shows.

Gemäldegalerie

1 Portrait of Hieronymus Holzschuher

Albrecht Dürer painted this portrait of the mayor of Nuremburg in 1529.

Key to Floorplan
■ Exhibition area

Floorplan of the Gemäldegalerie

Holbein's *Portrait of Georg Gisze*

2 Portrait of the Merchant Georg Gisze

This 1532 painting by Hans Holbein, showing the Hanseatic League merchant Georg Gisze counting his money, reflects the rise of the rich citizen during the Renaissance.

3 Madonna with Child and Singing Angels

A 1477 painting by Sandro Botticelli, this depicts the Madonna and Child, surrounded by angels carrying lilies.

4 The Birth of Christ

Martin Schongauer's altar painting (c.1480) is one of only a few religious paintings by the Alsatian artist that have been preserved.

5 Victorious Eros

Caravaggio's 1602 painting, follows Virgil's model and shows

Eros, the god of love, trampling underfoot the symbols of culture, glory, science and power.

6 Portrait of Hendrickje Stoffels

In a 1656–7 portrait of his lover Hendrickje Stoffels, Rembrandt's focus is entirely on the subject.

7 The French Comedy

This painting by Antoine Watteau belonged to the collection of Frederick the Great.

8 The Glass of Wine

A skilfully composed scene, Vermeer's *The Glass of Wine* (1658–61) shows a couple drinking wine.

Detail, Botticelli's *Madonna with Child*

9 Venus and the Organ Player

Painted by Titian (1550–52), this piece reflects the playful sensuality typical of the Italian Renaissance.

10 Dutch Proverbs

Pieter Brueghel beautifully incorporated and literalized more than 100 proverbs into this 1559 painting.

ARCHITECTURE IN THE KULTURFORUM

The tent-like roof of the Berlin Philharmonie

The Kulturforum was planned to fill the area between Potsdamer Straße and Leipziger Platz that had been destroyed during the war. The idea for a varied townscape of museums and parks is credited to Berlin architect Hans Scharoun, who had designed plans for this between 1946 and 1957. It was also Scharoun who, with the building of the Philharmonie in 1963, set the character of the Kulturforum: the tent-like, golden roofs of the music hall, the Kammermusiksaal and the national library, designed by him and – after his death – realized by his pupil Edgar Wisniewski, are today among Berlin's top landmarks. All the buildings are characterized by the generous proportions of their rooms and, although controversial when they were built, are today considered classics of modern architecture.

**The auditorium of the
Berlin Philharmonie**

TOP 10 ★ Jüdisches Museum Berlin

The Jewish Museum is one of the most important memorials to the history and culture of Germany's Jewish community. Reopened in 2020 after extensive modernization, the permanent exhibition is housed in the landmark Libeskind Building. It comprises three areas symbolizing Jewish life in Germany – the Axis of Exile, the Axis of the Holocaust and the Axis of Continuity. The building's symbolic design, along with the museum's important exhibits, leave a long-lasting impression.

1 Libeskind Building

Designed by Daniel Libeskind, this building echoes the complex German-Jewish history – its zig-zagging floor plan, concrete "voids", angled walls and windows, sliced into the façade, are all symbolic of the Jewish experience.

2 Old Building

This Baroque building **(below)**, built in 1735 as the Prussian Court of Justice, serves as the entrance to the Libeskind Building. The two buildings are connected via an underground passage. The Old Building houses the ticket counter, visitor information desk, a shop and the Eßkultur café.

3 Permanent Exhibition

The new core exhibition, "Jewish Life in Germany: Past and Present" **(above)**, covers, curates and explicitly presents the culture, traditions, religion and, of course, the history of the Jewish community in Germany, from the Middle Ages to present day.

4 The Voids

A straight line of five concrete spaces, or the "voids", cut through the entire vertical axis of the Libeskind Building. These voids are intended to represent the permanent physical emptiness left behind after the Holocaust.

6 Shalekhet Installation

One of the most poignant exhibits at the museum is the *Shalekhet* (Fallen Leaves) installation **(left)** by Israeli sculptor Menashe Kadishman. It features over 10,000 iron plates, with open-mouthed faces, which visitors must walk over to cross the "Memory Void" on the ground floor of the Libeskind Building.

9 Holocaust Tower

At the end of the Axis of the Holocaust lies the Holocaust Tower. Designed with only one narrow slit for sunlight, the concrete tower imparts a sense of oppression and anxiety to visitors.

10 The Garden of Exile

Set on a slope, The Garden of Exile **(above)** represents the disorientation and instability of life in exile. The garden is a perfect square made of 49 concrete columns, with the central column filled with earth from Jerusalem.

7 Objects

A highlight of the museum's permanent exhibition are the objects and personal effects **(left)** that narrate the history of German Jews. The collection includes art, photographs, applied art and religious artifacts.

5 Music Room

This room celebrates Jewish music and its prominent role in religious and everyday Jewish life. Immerse yourself in mellifluous chantings and compositions.

8 Courtyard

The stunning glass-enclosed courtyard, part of Libeskind's design in the Old Building, and the adjoining garden provide a calm place for reflection.

NEED TO KNOW

MAP G5 ▪ Lindenstr. 9–14 ▪ (030) 25 99 33 00 ▪ www.jmberlin.de

Open 10am–7pm daily (last entry 6pm)

Adm €8; free for under-18s

▪ Eßkultur café, located in the Old Building, serves lunch specials that change daily, often featuring traditional Jewish and Israeli dishes as well as cakes and coffee.

▪ The entire permanent exhibition is accessible to visitors with specific requirements.

The Top 10
of Everything

Gendarmenmarkt's imposing Deutscher Dom, with the Konzerthaus entrance in the foreground

Moments in History

The Neues Palais in Potsdam, the town where the 1685 edict was signed

1 1685: Edict of Potsdam
Berlin's history as a cultural capital began in 1685, when the Edict of Potsdam proclaimed that around 20,000 Huguenots would be taken in by Berlin. Many craftsmen and scientists, who had fled Catholic France, brought a new age of cultural ascendancy to the town.

2 1744: Frederick the Great
Although Frederick the Great preferred the isolation of Sanssouci to the bustle of Berlin, in 1740 he began to transform the city into a metropolis. The "Forum Fridericianum" in Unter den Linden brought new splendours to the town. Masterpieces such as the national opera house made Berlin an important European city.

3 Golden Twenties
Between 1919 and 1933, Berlin became an influential metropolis. Film, theatre, cabaret shows, restaurants and bars transformed the town into an international entertainment centre. Berlin also set new standards in the realms of science, industry, architecture and fine art, particularly the Bauhaus movement.

4 1945: Surrender
Signed in Berlin-Karlshorst on 8 May 1945, Germany's unconditional surrender marked more than the end of World War II. The previous Jewish population of 161,000 had virtually disappeared and Berliners called their city "the empire's fields of rubble".

5 1953: Workers' Uprising in East Germany
East Berlin construction workers in Frankfurter Allee protested against an increase in the average rate of production and work quotas on 17 June 1953. Soviet tanks suppressed the rebellion while, in West Berlin, the uprising was interpreted as a demonstration for German unification.

6 1961: Building of the Berlin Wall
The building of the Berlin Wall, which commenced during the night of 12 August 1961, was a traumatic event for many. Families were torn apart by the concrete wall and more than 100 people were to be killed over the following 30 years at the border dividing East and West.

Soviet tanks during the 1953 uprising

7 1963: "I am a Berliner"

 No other politician was as enthusiastically received in Berlin as the US President John F Kennedy. On 17 July 1963 he declared to the cheering crowd: "Ich bin ein Berliner". Kennedy confirmed that the Western Allies would stand by Berlin and support the town, just as they had done during the blockade of 1948–9, when the US and Britain airlifted food to the "island" of West Berlin.

8 1968: The late Sixties

During the late 1960s, West Berlin students transformed Germany. Rudi Dutschke and others proposed political change and a reappraisal of Germany's Nazi past. The movement came to an untimely end when Dutschke was injured in an assassination attempt by Josef Bachmann in April 1968.

People celebrating the fall of the Wall

9 1989: Fall of the Wall

The fall of the Berlin Wall on 9 November 1989 marked a new dawn for the city and the country. For the first time in 30 years, Berliners from both sides of the Wall were able to visit each other. The town celebrated all along Ku'damm and in front of the Brandenburg Gate.

10 1991: Berlin becomes the capital of Germany

In June 1991, Berlin was officially declared the capital of the reunified Federal Republic of Germany. Allied Forces left the city during 1994, but Berlin became the capital only when the Bundestag, the German parliament, moved here on 19 April 1999.

TOP 10 NOTABLE EVENTS

1 World's first electric locomotive
Presented by Werner von Siemens at the Berlin Trade Fair in 1879.

2 Berliner Secession
In 1898, a group of 65 artists, headed by Max Liebermann, broke away from the conservative Royal Academy.

3 Hauptmann von Köpenick
Regarded as a folk hero, Friedrich Wilhelm Voigt masqueraded as a Prussian military officer in 1906 and "confiscated" 4,000 Deutsche marks.

4 Bauhaus
Founded in 1919 by Walter Gropius, this "School of Building" gave rise to an influential Modernist movement.

5 Traffic lights
In 1924, a five-sided traffic light tower (with the first traffic lights in Berlin) was installed in Potsdamer Platz *(see p23)*.

6 Nazi book burning
On 10 May 1933, members of the SS, the SA and Nazi youth groups set fire to books by "un-German" authors.

7 Assassination attempt on Hitler
A group of army officers planned to assassinate Hitler *(see p115)*. The attempt failed on 20 July 1944.

8 Berlin Airlift
When the Soviet Union cut off surface traffic to West Berlin in June 1948, allied forces began flying in supplies by air.

9 Bridge of Spies
The first exchange of spies during the Cold War took place on Glienicker Brücke on 10 February 1962.

10 Construction of Berlin Marzahn
The first topping ceremony in Berlin Marzahn was held in September 1977.

Sketch of an electric locomotive

⭐10 Churches and Synagogues

Baroque-style exterior, Berliner Dom

1 Berliner Dom

MAP K5 ▪ Am Lustgarten
▪ (030) 20 26 91 19 ▪ Open Apr–Sep:
9am–8pm daily; Oct–Mar: 9am–
7pm daily (opening hours subject
to concert schedule, check website)
▪ Adm ▪ www.berlinerdom.de

Berlin Cathedral, the largest and
most lavish church in the city, was
reopened in 1993, after almost 40
years of restoration work. Designed
by Julius Raschdorf between 1894
and 1905, the building (see p25)
reflects the empire's aspirations
to power. In particular, the black
marble imperial stairs are a sign
of the proximity of the Hohenzollern
residence opposite the cathedral.
Members of this powerful ruling
dynasty are buried in the crypt.
The main nave, topped by an 85-m
(279-ft) high dome, is remarkable.
The church is dominated by a splendid 20th-century Neo-Baroque
pulpit and the giant Sauer organ.

2 St.-Hedwigs-Kathedrale

Berlin's largest Catholic church
(see p16) was built by Frederick the
Great in 1747–73. The cathedral is
closed for renovation until 2024.

3 Marienkirche

Work started in 1270 on
the Church of St Mary (see p104),
which nestles at the foot of the
Fernsehturm. Gothic and Baroque
in style, it has an impressive Neo-
Gothic tower, added in 1790 by
Carl Gotthard Langhans. The font
(1437) and the fresco Dance of the
Dead (1485) are among the oldest
treasures of the church. The richly
ornamented Baroque pulpit was
made by Andreas Schlüter in 1703.

4 Nikolaikirche

MAP K6
▪ Nikolaikirchplatz
▪ Open 10am–6pm
daily ▪ Adm ▪ www.
en.stadtmuseum.de

Berlin's oldest sacred
building, this church
was built in 1230 in the
Nikolaiviertel quarter.
The present structure
dates to around 1300.
It is particularly famous
for the portal on the west
wall of the main nave,
created by Andreas
Schlüter. It is adorned
with a gilded relief depicting a goldsmith and his
wife. The church was
rebuilt in 1987 and com-
pletely restored in 2009.
It is now a museum

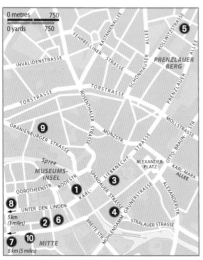

exploring the history of the church and the surrounding area. Events and concerts are held here regularly.

5 Synagoge Rykestraße
The largest synagogue (see p139) in Berlin, Rykestraße is one of the few Jewish places of worship in Germany to have survived Kristallnacht. It looks the same today as when it was originally built over 100 years ago.

6 Christi-Auferstehungs-Kathedrale
MAP B6 ▪ Hohenzollerndamm 166 ▪ Open only during service 10am & 6pm Sat, 10am Sun
Berlin's largest Russian-Orthodox church, the Church of Christ's Ascension is known for its green onion domes. Services are held in Russian, following Orthodox rituals.

7 Friedrichswerdersche Kirche
Werderscher Markt
This Neo-Gothic church, built in 1824–30 by Karl Friedrich Schinkel, was originally meant to serve the German and French communities of the Friedrichswerder district. Today, the rededicated church holds the sculpture collections of the Alte Nationalgalerie (see p24).

8 Neue Synagoge
Once Berlin's largest synagogue, this (see p95) was built originally in 1859–66. It was

demolished in World War II and partially reconstructed in 1988–95. Its ornate dome is visible from afar.

Kaiser-Wilhelm-Gedächtnis-Kirche

9 Kaiser-Wilhelm-Gedächtnis-Kirche
A West Berlin landmark, this Church (see pp32–3) successfully combines modern architecture with the ruins of the church tower.

10 Französischer Dom
MAP L4 ▪ Gendarmenmarkt 5 ▪ Open summer: 10am–7pm daily; winter: 10:30am–6:30pm daily ▪ www.franzoesischer-dom.de
At 66 m (216 ft) high, this domed Baroque tower (see p86), which dates back to between 1780 and 1789, is a magnificent ornamental addition to the Friedrichstadtkirche serving Berlin's Huguenot community.

Beautiful dome of the Neue Synagoge

TOP 10 Historic Buildings

 Brandenburger Tor
More than a mere symbol, the Brandenburg Gate (see pp12–13) is synonymous with Berlin.

 Schloss Charlottenburg
This palace (see pp34–7) features Baroque and Rococo splendours and a beautiful park, making it one of the most attractive in Germany.

Façade of Schloss Charlottenburg

 Schloss Bellevue
MAP E4 ■ Spreeweg 1 ■ Not open to the public ■ www.bundespraesident.de/EN

Built by Philipp Daniel Boumann in 1785–90, this was the residence of the Hohenzollerns until 1861. Since 1994 the stately building with its Neo-Classical façade has been the official residence of the President of the Federal Republic. The modern, egg-shaped Presidential Offices stand next to the old palace.

 Reichstag
The seat of the Deutscher Bundestag, the German parliament (see pp14–15), with its spectacular dome, is a magnet for visitors.

 Rotes Rathaus
Berlin's Town Hall (see p103), also known as "Red Town Hall" because of the red bricks from Brandenburg province with which it was built, harks back to the proud days when Berlin became the capital of the new Empire. Built in 1861–9 according to designs by Hermann Friedrich Waesemann, the town hall was one of Germany's largest and most magnificent buildings, built to promote the splendour of Berlin. The structure was modelled on Italian Renaissance palaces, and the tower is reminiscent of Laon cathedral in France. The exterior was decorated with *Die Steinerne Chronik* (the stone chronicle) in 1879, depicting scenes from the city's history.

Konzerthaus
The Concert Hall is one of Karl Friedrich Schinkel's masterpieces. Built in 1818–21, it was once known as the *Schauspielhaus* (theatre), and was used as such until 1945. It was damaged during World War II, and then reopened in it's new avatar as the Konzerthaus (see p86) in 1984. The building has a portico with Ionic columns

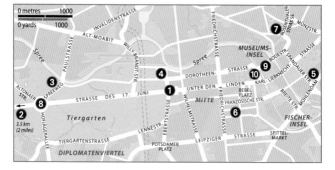

The Neo-Classical exterior of the Konzerthaus

and statues of allegorical and historical personages, some riding lions and panthers, as well as deities, muses and bacchants.

7 Hackesche Höfe

This complex (see p95) of 19th-century buildings has eight interlinked courtyards, some of which are decorated in Jugendstil style, originally by August Endell. In the early 1990s the complex was completely renovated. The first courtyard is particularly attractive: coloured glazed tiles with geometric patterns decorate the house from the foundations up to the guttering. In the last courtyard, trees are grouped around an idyllic well. The Hackesche Höfe is one of Berlin's most popular spots, especially on weekends, with restaurants, cafés, a cinema and the Chamäleon Theatre.

8 Siegessäule

The Victory Column (see p113) in Tiergarten is topped by the statue of Victoria. Designed by Heinrich Strack after Prussia's victory in the Danish-Prussian War of 1864, it was refurbished in 2010.

9 Altes Museum and Lustgarten

The façade of the Old Museum, possibly one of the most attractive Neo-Classical museum buildings in Europe, is remarkable for the 18 Ionic columns supporting a portico. Built in 1830 to Karl Friedrich Schinkel's design, it was at the time one of the first buildings to be created specifically as a museum. Originally it was to house the royal collection of paintings; today it is home to a collection of antiquities (see p25). In front of the museum is a garden designed by Peter Joseph Lenné. Conceived as the king's herb garden, it is now decorated with a 70-ton granite bowl by Gottlieb Christian Cantian and a fountain.

10 Zeughaus

Designed by J A Nering as the first Berlin Baroque building, the former Royal Prussian Arsenal is now the Deutsches Historisches Museum (see pp16–19), with a modern addition by I M Pei.

Siegessäule

🔟 Modern Buildings

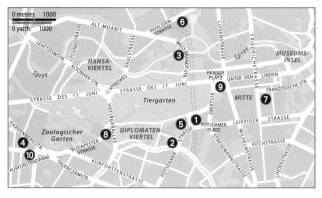

1 Sony Center
The spectacular Sony Center (see p20), with its unique roof, is one of Berlin's largest structures.

Glass membrane roof, Sony Center

2 Neue Nationalgalerie
This impressive structure (see p38) was constructed in 1965–8 by Mies van der Rohe. It was the first building by the pioneering Bauhaus architect after his emigration to the USA. He made use of his earlier designs for the Havana headquarters of the Bacardi company, which had been abandoned after the Cuban Revolution. The collection here brings together the best of 20th-century art from Europe and North America.

3 Bundeskanzleramt
MAP K2 ■ Willy-Brandt-Str. 1
■ **Closed to the public**

Berliners are not too fond of the Chancellor's modern offices, although this is the only government building to have been designed by a Berlin architect. Axel Schultes developed a vast, elongated office complex, which extends north of the Reichstag, in a bend of the Spree, even stretching across the river. In the centre of the modern building stands a gleaming white cube with round windows, which Berliners quickly nicknamed the "Washing Machine". Critics describe the design as pompous, while civil servants dislike their small offices. The interior of the building is decorated with valuable modern paintings. The Chancellor's office on the 7th floor has a view of the Reichstag building.

Exterior of the Bundeskanzleramt

Ludwig-Erhard-Haus

4 Ludwig-Erhard-Haus

MAP N4 ■ Fasanenstr. 85
■ Open 8am–5pm Mon–Thu
(until 4pm Fri)

The seat of the Berlin Stock
Exchange, Ludwig-Erhard-Haus was
designed by British architect Nicholas
Grimshaw in 1994–8. Locals refer to
it as the "armadillo", because the 15
giant metal arches of the domed
building recall the animal's armour.

5 Philharmonie and Kammermusiksaal

Two modern concert halls
(see pp38–41) in the Kulturforum
were designed by Hans Scharoun
in 1961 and 1987 respectively – the
Kammermusiksaal (chamber music
hall) was completed after Scharoun's
death in 1972 according to his plans
by his pupil Edgar Wisniewski. Both
buildings are renowned for their
excellent acoustics as well as for
their tent-like roof structures.

6 Hauptbahnhof

MAP J2 ■ Hauptbahnhof

Europe's largest train station sits
on the site of the historic Lehrter
Bahnhof. This impressive glass
and steel structure doubles as
a retail and hospitality hub.

7 Quartiere 205–207 Friedrichstraße

The Galeries Lafayettes and the
Friedrichstadtpassagen are based
within these three office blocks
(see p87) designed by architects
Nouvel, Pei and Ungers.

8 Nordische Botschaften

MAP N6 ■ Rauchstr.
■ Gallery: open 10am–7pm Mon–Fri,
11am–4pm Sat & Sun ■ www.
nordicembassies.org

No other embassy building has
caused as much of a stir as this
one housing five embassies of
the Nordic countries: its green
shutters open and close depending
on the available light. Art exhibitions are held here regularly and
there's a canteen and coffee bar.

9 DZ Bank on Pariser Platz

This elegant building (see p12) by
Frank Owen Gehry combines Prussian
and modern architecture. The giant
dome inside is remarkable.

Spectacular interior of the DZ Bank

10 Kant-Dreieck

MAP N4 ■ Kantstr. 155

The enormous "shark fin" on top
of the KapHag-Group's headquarters, built by Josef Paul Kleihues
in 1992–5, has become a symbol
of the new Berlin. The aluminium
weather vane is designed to turn in
the wind like a sail. Originally, the
structure, known as the "Kant
Triangle", was to be built one-third
higher than it is now, but the plans
were vetoed by the Berlin Senate.

🔟 Museums

Exhibit at the Pergamonmuseum

1 Pergamonmuseum
This impressive museum (see p26) on the Museuminsel is a vast treasure trove of antiquities. It is undergoing extensive renovations and will remain closed until 2027.

2 Ägyptisches Museum
MAP K5 ■ Museumsinsel, Bodestr. 1 ■ (030) 266 424 242 ■ Open 10am–6pm daily (until 8pm Thu) ■ Adm ■ www.smb.museum
The star exhibit in the Egyptian Museum (see pp24–5), part of the Neues Museum, is the bust of Nefertiti, wife of Akhenaton. The limestone bust, excavated in 1912, was copied all over ancient Egypt. Also worth seeing is the "Berlin Green Head", a small bust from the 4th century BCE. The museum also holds numerous mummies, sarcophagi, murals and sculptures.

3 Deutsches Historisches Museum
Germany's largest history museum (see pp16–19) uses unique exhibits, documents and films to take the visitor on a journey through German history, from the Middle Ages to the present day.

4 Museum Europäischer Kulturen
This museum (see p151) specializes in European folk art, lifestyle, tradition and culture, and, with some 280,000 objects, is one of the largest of its kind in the world. It hosts long-running as well as temporary exhibitions, often in conjunction with museums from other European countries. Among the vast collection of exhibits on display are earthenware items, costumes, handicrafts, jewellery, toys and tools.

5 Jüdisches Museum Berlin
The Jewish Museum, housed in a spectacular building (see p42) designed by Daniel Libeskind, documents the German–Jewish relationship through the centuries. There are special exhibitions on the influence of Berlin Jews on the town's cultural life, and on the life of the Enlightenment philosopher Moses Mendelssohn. An empty room commemorates the loss of Jewish culture. There is also an excellent programme of special events. The core exhibition opened in 2020.

A Junkers Ju 52 plane on display at the Deutsches Technikmuseum

6 Deutsches Technikmuseum

The fascinating German Museum of Technology (see p129), built on the site of a former railway goods yard, has some exciting hands-on displays on the history of technology.

7 Kunstgewerbemuseum

MAP L1 ■ Matthäikirchplatz ■ (030) 266 424 242 ■ Open 10am–6pm Tue–Fri, 11am–6pm Sat & Sun ■ Adm ■ www.smb.museum

European crafts spanning over five centuries are on display at the Museum of Decorative Arts (see p38). Its most valuable exhibits are the treasure of the Guelphs from Braunschweig and the silver treasure of the town council in Lüneburg. The museum also holds Italian tin-glazed earthenware, Renaissance faïence and German Baroque glass and ceramics. Popular displays show Neo-Classical porcelain and furniture, Jugendstil art and Tiffany vases.

8 Haus am Checkpoint Charlie

This museum (see p129) is set at the former Allied checkpoint and hosts an exhibition documenting events at the Berlin Wall. It screens documentaries relating to the exhibition theme throughout the day. In front of the museum is the famous sign that reads, "You are now leaving the American sector", written in English, Russian, French and German.

9 Museum für Naturkunde

With over 30 million specimens in its collection, the Natural History Museum (see p96) is one of the largest of its kind in the world. One of the star features is the world's largest dinosaur skeleton, a Giraffatitan found in Tanzania in 1909. There are six more dinosaur skeletons as well as a variety of fossils. It is also worth making a visit to the glittering exhibition of meteorites and minerals.

10 Musikinstrumenten-Museum

MAP L2 ■ Ben-Gurion-Str. 1 ■ (030) 25 48 10 ■ Open 2pm–7pm Tue–Sun ■ Adm ■ www.sim.spk-berlin.de

Some 800 musical instruments can be heard in this museum (see p39), including Frederick the Great's harpsichord. Don't miss the silent film organ which still works. Saturdays at noon is the best time to visit.

Eighteenth-century hunting horn

🔟 Art Galleries

Johannes Vermeer's *The Glass of Wine*

1 Gemäldegalerie

Berlin's best art museum, the Gemäldegalerie *(see pp38–41)* holds European art of the 13th–19th centuries, including Vermeer's *The Glass of Wine* and *The Adoration of the Shepherds* by Hugo van der Goes, as well as works by Rembrandt, Dürer, Caravaggio and Rubens.

2 Brücke-Museum
Bussardsteig 9 ■ Open 11am–5pm Wed–Mon ■ Adm ■ www.bruecke-museum.de

Must-see collection of German Expressionist works by the Brücke (bridge) movement, including Kirchner, Schmidt-Rottluff, Nolde, and Pechstein. Many Brücke works were labelled "degenerate" by the Nazis and destroyed.

3 Alte Nationalgalerie

The Old National Gallery *(see p24)*, built by Friedrich August Stüler in 1866–76, holds a collection of 19th-century, mainly German paintings, including works by Max Liebermann, Wilhelm Leibl, Adolf von Menzel and Arnold Böcklin. It also houses sculptures by Schadow, Rauch and Reinhold Begas, and is one of the many museums set on Museuminsel *(see p86)*, an island in the Spree River.

The façade of Martin-Gropius-Bau

4 Martin-Gropius-Bau
MAP F4 ■ Niederkirchnerstr.7 ■ (030) 25 48 60 ■ Open 11am–7pm, Mon & Wed–Fri, 10am–7pm Sat & Sun ■ Adm

Named after its architect Martin Gropius (1824–80), the building hosts temporary art exhibitions.

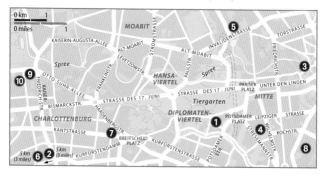

Interior of Hamburger Bahnhof

5 Hamburger Bahnhof

The historic Hamburg Station (*see p114*) houses modern paintings, installations and multimedia art. Former dispatch warehouses were converted and linked to the old railway building, forming the Rieckhallen, and doubling the exhibition space. A highlight is the Erich Marx Collection, with works by Joseph Beuys. Apart from famous artists like Andy Warhol, Jeff Koons and Robert Rauschenberg, it also owns works by Anselm Kiefer, Sandro Chiao and others.

6 Kunsthaus Dahlem

MAP N6 ▪ Käuzchensteig 8 ▪ Open 11am–5pm Wed–Mon ▪ Adm ▪ www.kunsthaus-dahlem.de

This exhibition venue for postwar German Modernism from East and West Germany was built during 1939–42 for sculptor Arno Breker. The building was used by US Information Control Division after the war and later became a workspace for artists.

7 C/O Berlin

MAP N4 ▪ Amerika-Haus, Hardenbergstr. 22–24 ▪ Open 11am–8pm daily ▪ www.co-berlin.org

Located in the former Amerika-Haus, this gallery hosts regularly changing exhibitions, lectures and historic and contemporary photography events.

8 Berlinische Galerie

MAP G5 ▪ Alte Jakobstr. 124–128 ▪ Open 10am–6pm Wed–Mon ▪ Adm ▪ www.berlinischegalerie.de

On display here are huge collections of German, east European and Russian painters, photographers, graphic designers and architects from the 20th century.

9 Sammlung Scharf-Gerstenberg

MAP B3 ▪ Schlossstr. 70 ▪ Open 10am–6pm Tue–Sun ▪ Adm ▪ www.smb.museum

This gallery has rare works by surrealists and their forerunners, such as Goya, Klee, Dalí, Max Ernst and Man Ray.

10 Bröhan-Museum

MAP B3 ▪ Schlossstr. 1a ▪ Open 10am–6pm Tue–Sun ▪ Adm (free 1st Wed of month) ▪ www.broehan-museum.de

Jugendstil and Art Deco objects from around Europe, and paintings by Berlin artists, are on display in this design and art museum.

Impressive exterior of the Bröhan-Museum

🔟 Famous Berliners

Actress Marlene Dietrich

① Marlene Dietrich

Born in Schöneberg, this famous filmstar (1901–92) began her career in Berlin in the 1920s. Her breakthrough came with the film *The Blue Angel* (1931). She lies buried in the Friedenau cemetery in Steglitz. Many of her personal possessions are exhibited in the Deutsche Kinemathek *(see p22)*.

② Albert Einstein

Albert Einstein (1879–1955) became the director of the Kaiser Wilhelm-Institute for Physics in 1914, and was awarded the Nobel Prize for Physics in 1921. He is now better known for his Theory of Relativity, first developed in 1905. Einstein mostly lived and worked in Potsdam, but was connected with Berlin through his lectures and teaching activity. In 1933 Einstein, who was Jewish, emigrated to the USA, where he stayed until his death.

③ Bertolt Brecht

Born in Augsburg, Bavaria, Bertolt Brecht (1898–1956) wrote some of his greatest works, such as the *Threepenny Opera*, in a small apartment in Charlottenburg. During the Third Reich, he emigrated to the US, and returned to Germany after the war and founded the Berliner Ensemble in East Berlin in 1949. He lived in Chausseestraße with his wife, Helene Weigel, until his death. His renovated apartment is now a museum.

④ Robert Koch

Like few other physicians and microbiologists of his day, Robert Koch (1843–1910) laid the foundations of modern medicine with his pioneering discoveries. The Director of the Institute for Infectious Diseases, Koch also taught and researched at the Charité Hospital. In 1905 he received the Nobel Prize for Medicine for his pioneering discoveries in the field of tuberculosis research.

⑤ Herbert von Karajan

Known as "Circus Karajani", this famous Austrian conductor (1908–1989) was head of the Berlin Philharmonic Orchestra from 1954 to 1989. During this time he helped create the orchestra's unique sound, which remains legendary until this day. Herbert von Karajan was both revered and feared by musicians due to his genius and fiery temperament.

Conductor Herbert von Karajan

⑥ Käthe Kollwitz

The sculptor and painter Käthe Kollwitz (1867–1945) portrayed the social problems of the poor, and her work provides a powerful, haunting commentary on human suffering. She spent most of her life in a modest abode in the square that is now named after her, in the Prenzlauer Berg district. A monument now celebrates her works and an enlarged reproduction of her Pietà now adorns the Neue Wache (see p17) war memorial.

7 Theodor Fontane

A Huguenot, Fontane (1819–98) was one of the most influential 19th-century novelists and poets in Germany. He also worked as a journalist and critic, penning many of his articles and essays in the Café Josty on Potsdamer Platz. Fontane is particularly well known for his novel *Effi Briest* and five-volume travelogue *Wanderungen durch die Mark Brandenburg (Ramblings through the March of Brandenburg)*.

Theodor Fontane

8 Jacob and Wilhelm Grimm

The brothers Jacob (1785–1863) and Wilhelm (1786–1859) Grimm are known for their classic fairy tales – *Little Red Riding Hood*, *Hansel and Gretel* and *Rumpelstiltskin*. Their linguistic output was equally important. Their *German Grammar* and *German Dictionary* are standard reference works even today.

9 Georg Wilhelm Hegel

The influential philosopher Hegel (1770–1831) taught at Humboldt University from 1818 until his death.

10 Nina Hagen

Singer, songwriter and actress, Nina Hagen was born in East Berlin in 1955. Known for her eccentric, theatrical style, she was at the forefront of the punk movement in the late 70s and early 80s. She still remains a beloved icon of her time.

TOP 10 INNOVATORS

1 Johann Gottfried Moritz (b 1777) and Wilhelm Wieprecht (b 1802)
Wieprecht and Moritz created the bass tuba and secured a patent for it in 1835.

2 Katharina (Käthe) Paulus (b 1868)
The first professional balloon pilot in Germany. She won a patent for creating the first collapsable parachute in 1921.

3 Otto Lilienthal (b 1848)
A German aviation pioneer who made over 2,000 glider flights and started the first standard production of an aircraft.

4 Ernst Litfaß (b 1816)
This publisher invented the *litfaßsäule*, a free-standing cylindrical advertising column which still bears his name today.

5 Friedrich von Hefner-Alteneck (b 1845)
While at Siemens, this engineer created a drum armature which played a huge role in the invention of the electric tram.

6 Reinhold Burger (b 1866)
In 1904 Burger patented the Thermos vacuum flask, which was a development of the work of Sir James Dewar (b 1842).

7 Oskar Picht (b 1871)
Director of a school for the visually impaired, Picht developed one of the first braille writers in the world.

8 Maximilian Negwer (b 1872)
This entrepreneur invented comfortable ear protection made using wax, vaseline and cotton wool.

9 Konrad Zuse (b 1910)
Zuse is known for creating Z1, the first programmable computer.

10 Herta Heuwer (b 1913)
In 1949, Heuwer created currywurst (sausage with curry sauce) at her kiosk.

Portrait of Otto Lilienthal

🔟 Parks and Gardens

① Großer Tiergarten
MAP E4 ■ Tiergarten

The Tiergarten – the green lungs of Berlin – is the most famous park (see p113) in the city. Set in the centre of town, the park covers more than 2 sq km (1 sq mile). Originally designed in 1833–40 by Peter Joseph Lenné as a hunting estate for the Elector, in the latter half of the 19th century the park became a recreation ground for all Berliners. It attracts cyclists, joggers, sunbathers and families having picnics, especially on weekends.

② Schlosspark Charlottenburg
MAP B3 ■ Schloss Charlottenburg, Spandauer Damm ■ Open sunrise–sunset daily ■ www.spsg.de

The Palace Park is one of the most attractive and charming green spaces in Germany. Immediately behind Schloss Charlottenburg (see pp34–7) is a small but magnificent Baroque garden, and beyond this extends a vast park, dating back to the early 19th century. It was landscaped in the English style and features artificial lake and river landscapes, small hidden buildings and idyllic shaded groves on the banks of ponds and streams. The park is ideal for strolling, and it is also a favourite place for sunseekers.

Charlottenburg park in autumn

③ Grunewald and Teufelsberg

The Grunewald, or "green forest", is the public woods (see pp150–55) in the southwest of Berlin. It is the least built-up area of woodland in the city. Parts of Grunewald are very quiet and isolated, and there are wild boar in the woods – which can be a nuisance to people who have gardens nearby. Grunewald is also home to Teufelsberg, the Cold War era listening tower.

The folly at Pfaueninsel

④ Pfaueninsel
Peacock Island, an island (see p151) in the middle of Großer Wannsee that can be reached only by ferry, is a romantic spot and a leisurely getaway outside of the centre. In the 19th century, the island served as a love nest for King Friedrich Wilhelm II. His charming folly of a palace ruin is undergoing renovation and will be closed to public until 2024. Visitors can enjoy green spaces, home to dozens of peacocks.

⑤ Botanischer Garten
Königin-Luise-Str. 6–8 ■ (030) 83 85 01 00 ■ Garden: open 9am–sunset daily ■ Museum: open 10am–6pm daily ■ Adm ■ www.bgbm.org/en

The 19th-century Botanical Garden is a paradise of flowers and plants in the southwest of the city. The vast area with 15 greenhouses was built in the late 19th century around gentle hills and picturesque ponds.

The Great Palm House by Alfred Koerner has spectacular 26-m (85-ft) high giant bamboo from Southeast Asia. The museum introduces visitors to the world of microbiology.

6 Viktoriapark and Kreuzberg

The old municipal park *(see p131)*, originally designed in 1888–94 as a recreation area for local workers, is a popular sunset spot. The meadows around Kreuzberg, which rise to 30 m (98 ft), are great for sunbathing. On top of the hill, a monument recalls the Prussian Wars of Liberation.

7 Volkspark Friedrichshain

Berlin's oldest park (1840) is an artificial landscape *(see p146)* of lakes and meadows and two wooded mounds, one of which is nicknamed "Mont Klamott", which means "mount rubble". There is also a fountain with statues of the most popular fairytale characters.

Fountain statue

8 Tierpark Berlin

Founded in 1955, the second largest zoo in Berlin *(see p147)* is set in the palace park of Friedrichsfelde, and houses some 860 animal species.

9 Treptower Park

The 19th-century park and garden *(see p146)* on the banks of the Spree is famous for the Soviet Memorial, which stands next to the graves of 7,000 Red Army soldiers.

10 Britzer Schloss and Park

Alt-Britz 73 ▪ (030) 60 97 92 30 ▪ Palace: open 11am–6pm Tue–Sun ▪ Garden: open 9am–sunset daily ▪ Adm ▪ www.schlossbritz.de

The palace in Britz, dating from 1706 and situated in a lovely park, has been meticulously refurbished with historical furniture from the Gründerzeit period after 1871.

TOP 10 LAKES, RIVERS AND CANALS

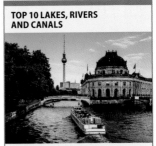

Boat ride on the Spree River

1 Spree River
MAP K1–K6 ▪ Mitte, Tiergarten
Guided boat tours, romantic evening cruises and riverside walks are on offer.

2 Teufelssee, Grunewald
One of Berlin's cleanest and most relaxed lakes – nudists and dog lovers enjoy the peaceful banks.

3 Großer Müggelsee
Thousands congregate at Berlin's largest lake in summer to swim, row, sail or surf *(see p146)*.

4 Schlachtensee
After Wannsee, this small lake is the second most popular. Avoid the crowds by going during the week.

5 Großer Wannsee
Europe's largest inland beach is beautifully white *(see p152)*.

6 Lietzensee
MAP A4 ▪ Am Kaiserdamm
Not suitable for swimming, but the surrounding meadows are idyllic.

7 Krumme Lanke, Fischerhüttenweg
Although many consider the lake not clean enough for bathing, it seems cleaner (but colder) than Schlachtensee.

8 Landwehrkanal
MAP M5–N5 ▪ Lützowplatz
Take a boat trip along the canal to see some of Berlin's most attractive bridges, or rent a boat to explore on your own.

9 Tegeler See, Alt-Tegel
The Greenwich Promenade, from Tegeler Hafen (harbour) to Schwarzer Weg, is an attractive walk.

10 Neuer See
MAP M3 ▪ Großer Tiergarten
This tranquil lake is hidden in the vast Großer Tiergarten park. On its banks is the Café am Neuen See *(see p117)*.

🔟 Off the Beaten Track

① Bearpit Karaoke
MAP G1 ▪ Topsstraße 28
▪ Open May–Oct: 3–5pm Sun
▪ www.bearpitkaraoke.com

Sunday afternoon karaoke sessions in the Mauerpark's "bearpit" amphitheatre are extremely popular. The show host, Joe Hatchiban, arrives on a fancy bicycle equipped with loudspeaker and laptop. Crowds of up to 2,000 gather to watch hopefuls take turns belting out oldies.

② Unterwelten Museum
MAP G1 ▪ Brunnenstraße 105
▪ (030) 49 91 05 18 ▪ English tours Apr–Oct: 11am, 1pm & 3pm ▪ Adm
▪ www.berliner-unterwelten.de

Did you know the Nazis made aircrafts underground? Or that Cold War nuclear bunkers were largely futile? Find out on guided tours of bomb shelters, tunnels and vaults going back to the 19th century. Exhibits include an Enigma encryption machine, armaments and atmospheric living quarters.

③ Boros Collection
MAP J3 ▪ Reinhardtstraße 20 ▪ English tours at 11am & 1pm daily (by reservation only) ▪ Adm
▪ www.sammlung-boros.de

This World War II air-raid shelter is now a contemporary art gallery owned by the advertising mogul Christian Boros (see p98). Originally built for the staff of nearby Friedrichstrasse railway station, this concrete behemoth has also served as a prison, a larder for

Boros Collection

produce, and a club. Visits can be made only on 90-minute private tours; book online well in advance.

The Badeschiff in the Spree

④ Badeschiff
Eichenstraße 4 ▪ (030) 533 20 30 ▪ Open May–Sep: 8am–midnight daily ▪ Adm ▪ www.arena-berlin.de

A shimmering island of blue, this old cargo container in the Spree is the city's coolest place for a dip. The pool is reached via a pier from a sandy beach. After sunset DJs spin vinyl and guests migrate to a nightclub boat, *Hoppetosse*, moored alongside.

⑤ Schwerbelastungs- körper
MAP E6 ▪ General-Pape-Straße
▪ (030) 533 20 30 ▪ Open Apr–Oct: 2–4pm Tue–Wed, 10am–6pm Thu, 1–3pm Sun ▪ www.schwerbelastungskoerper.de

Hitler and Albert Speer, the Führer's chief architect, planned to transform Berlin into a "world capital" called Welthauptstadt Germania. To test the feasibility of building a huge triumphal arch on the area's soft ground, they commissioned the Schwerbelastungskörper, a concrete cylinder weighing 12,650 metric tons. The Welthauptstadt was never built but the cylinder houses a historical exhibition.

6 Monsterkabinett

MAP J5 ■ Rosenthaler Straße 39 ■ (0152) 12 59 86 87 ■ Open 4–10pm Fri & Sat ■ Adm ■ www.monsterkabinett.de

Run by the Dead Chickens art collective, this installation features robots that interact with visitors. The 20-minute tour with heavy metal soundtrack and lightshow ends with a blast of anti-monster spray that blows the head off one creature.

7 Mount Mitte

MAP F2 ■ Caroline-Michaelis-Straße 8 ■ Open 2pm–sunset Mon–Fri, 10am–sunset Sat & Sun ■ Adm ■ www.beachmitte.de

Don a helmet, strap on a security line and wiggle your way through Berlin's oddest high-rope climbing course, tackling wooden barrels, surfboards and old East German Trabant cars suspended in midair.

8 Admiralbrücke

MAP H5 ■ Fraenkelufer 25

This lacy, wrought-iron bridge was built in 1882 in Jugendstil style, spanning one of the prettiest stretches on the Landwehrkanal. On balmy summer nights it fills up with beer-drinking revellers listening to street musicians playing their hearts out.

9 Museum der Illusionen

MAP G3 ■ Karl-Liebknecht-Straße 9 ■ (030) 25 78 41 17 ■ Open 10am–8pm daily ■ Adm

Set near Alexanderplatz and the TV Tower, this museum promises "to trick your senses and amaze you while doing it". It has specially constructed rooms, which aim to make visitors

believe that they are, for example, stuck to the ceiling or are the size of a dwarf. Scientific explanations accompany each illusion. You are encouraged to take photos of yourself and your companions in the midst of the optical and haptic illusions.

10 Tieranatomisches Theater

MAP J3 ■ Philippstraße 12 ■ (030) 209 346 625 ■ Open 2–6pm Tue–Sat ■ www.kulturtechnik.hu-berlin.de

Nestled in a university courtyard, the Veterinary Anatomical Theatre is Berlin's oldest surviving academic building, erected in 1789-90. Wander through the historical exhibition to the circular lecture hall with dissection table and spectator galleries.

Tieranatomisches Theater

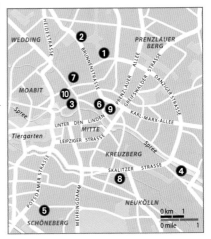

Children's Attractions

Deutsches Technikmuseum

1 Deutsches Technikmuseum

The technology museum (see p129) is a giant playground for children, excellent for learning through play. There are locomotives to clamber over, windmills to play with and the Science Center Spectrum, where older children can conduct their own physics and technology experiments.

2 Labyrinth Kindermuseum

Osloer Str. 12 ■ Open 1–6pm Thu & Fri (from 11am Sat & Sun) ■ Adm ■ www.labyrinth-kinder museum.de

Berlin's Museum for Children is particularly suitable for children at the preschool stage and in the early school years. Three or four themed exhibitions each year deal with subjects in a child-friendly and entertaining way – for example the "Pots and Pans Orchestra". Every exhibition is interactive, allowing children to join in and experiment. See website for details of special exhibitions and events.

Labyrinth Kindermuseum

3 Grips-Theater

MAP D3 ■ Altonaer Str. 22 ■ Check website for performance times ■ Adm ■ www.grips-theater.de

This famous Berlin theatre for children has been showing the hit musical *Linie 1* since 1986. The play, which is best suited to older children and adolescents, uses a U-Bahn line running from Kreuzberg to the Ku'damm as a metaphor for life in the big city. All shows are in German.

4 Museum für Naturkunde

Berlin's museum of natural history (see p55) has the biggest dinosaur skeleton on show anywhere in the world. The collections here are well presented.

Museum für Naturkunde

5 Zoologischer Garten

If you are visiting Berlin with children you should not miss out on the zoo (see p119). Particular favourites are the Monkey House (with baby gorillas and chimpanzees) and the Baby Zoo, where kids are allowed to touch and feed the young animals.

6 Zeiss-Großplanetarium

Artificial stars, planets and nebulae take you to faraway galaxies under the silvery dome of the planetarium (see p140).

LEGOLAND® Discovery Centre

⑦ LEGOLAND® Discovery Centre

Apart from the 4D cinema and rides at the world's first indoor LEGOLAND® *(see p21)*, thousands of LEGO® bricks are turned into replicas of sights around Berlin.

⑧ Filmpark Babelsberg

Exciting shoot-outs, a walk-on film set with a U-boat and a Wild West town are the film park's most popular attractions – and not just with the children. A tour of the former UFA-Film studios *(see p160)* takes you behind the scenes: younger visitors can see costumes or admire the Little Sandman (Sandmännchen), a TV figure popular with children in East Germany since 1959. These studios were among the world's most prestigious when they were in operation here in

The Little Sandman

Babelsberg from 1917 to 1945. Everywhere in the park are figures and props from well-known German films. A stunt show features fight scenes, car chases and pyrotechnics like those seen in *Inglourious Basterds*, *Valkyrie* and *Anonymous*, which were all shot here.

⑨ Puppentheater-Museum
MAP H6 ■ Karl-Marx-Str. 135 ■ (030) 687 81 32 ■ Open 9am–3pm Mon–Fri, 11am–4pm Sun ■ Adm

At the small but excellent Puppet Museum, children are allowed to perform their own puppet shows and have a go at being puppet theatre directors.

⑩ Futurium
Alexanderufer 2 ■ (030) 40 81 89 777 ■ Open 10am–6pm Wed–Mon

Opened in 2019, Futurium's eye-catching modern building at the River Spree houses a fantastic educational undertaking that explores the question: "How do we want to live in the future?" The interactive exhibition, which is divided into three main sections – nature, man and technology – is especially worth a visit for those travelling with children.

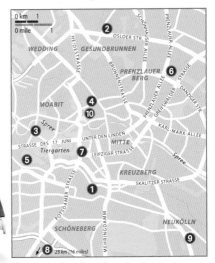

Performing Arts Venues

① Staatsoper Unter den Linden

Both the theatre troupe and the orchestra of the venerable Berlin Opera enjoy top reputations (see p16). This is the place to see the stars of the classical music scene. After a seven-year period of major renovation and modernization, the opera house reopened in October 2017.

② Philharmonie

Germany's temple (see pp38–9) of classical music still presents the best performers in the world. Designed by Scharoun, the concert hall has unique acoustics, much appreciated by artists and audience alike. Concerts by the Berlin Philharmonic Orchestra are very popular and are often sold out for weeks ahead.

③ Deutsche Oper

Berlin's most modern opera house (see p124) has an elegant retro design. It was built in 1961 on the site of the former Deutsches Opernhaus, which was destroyed during World War II. The controversial 88 slabs of washed-out concrete, chosen by architect Fritz Bornemann for the main façade, replaced the classic columned portico that once stood here,

Performance at the Deutsche Oper

leading critics to describe the building as lacking artistic formation. Concerts and opera and ballet performances are held here, along with an extensive children's programme.

④ Chamäleon-Varieté

MAP J5 ■ Rosenthaler Str. 40–1, Hackesche Höfe ■ (030) 400 05 90 ■ Check website for show timings ■ Closed Mon ■ www. chamaeleon.com/en

Established in 2004, the small, alternative Chamäleon stage is renowned for its innovative and unique programme. The lack of technology is more than made up for with much wit and ingenuity. If you are seated in the front row, you are likely to get pulled onto the stage.

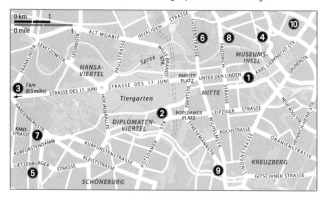

5 Bar jeder Vernunft

MAP C5 ▪ Schaperstr. 24 (car park Freie Volksbühne) ▪ (030) 883 15 82 ▪ Box office: open noon–7pm Mon–Sat, 3–7pm Sun & hols ▪ www.bar-jeder-vernunft.de/en

This venue, whose name means "devoid of all reason", is a popular comedy theatre. The cabaret offers a humorous and, at times, romantic programme of songs, *chansons*, reviews, cabaret, slapstick and comedy, all under an amazing mirror tent dating from the 1920s. Many stars of the international and German cabaret scene can be seen regularly among the performers here, including Tim Fischer, Georgette Dee, the Pfister Sisters and Gayle Tufts, as well as older stars such as Otto Sander.

6 Deutsches Theater

Performances at the German Theatre – one of the best – include mainly classic plays in the tradition of stage and screen actor and director Max Reinhardt who once worked here (see p98). Experimental theatre by young playwrights is performed at the DT Baracke.

7 Theater des Westens

In addition to producing its own shows, such as *La Cage aux Folles*, this theatre (see p124) also shows guest productions such as *Blue Man Group* and *Mamma Mia*.

8 Friedrichstadt-Palast

MAP J4 ▪ Friedrichstr. 107 ▪ www.palast.berlin/en

Shiny glass tiles and a white, plumed neon sign adorn the eyecatching façade of the Friedrichstadt-Palast, whose long-legged dancers are as popular today as they

Friedrichstadt-Palast

were in the 1920s. The original venue was damaged during World War II and replaced in the 1980s. Long celebrated as being among the world's best revues, the performances have become even more spirited and entertaining today.

9 Hebbel am Ufer

MAP F5 ▪ Hallesches Ufer 32 ▪ (030) 25 90 04 27 ▪ Performances daily ▪ www.hebbel-am-ufer.de/en

The Hebbel am Ufer has attained cult status in Berlin, thanks to its modern and varied programme of concerts, dance, music and theatre events. The best performers from around the world appear here.

10 Volksbühne

MAP H2 ▪ Rosa-Luxemburg-Platz ▪ (030) 24 06 57 77 ▪ www.volksbuehne-berlin.de

Opened in 1914 as a "theatre of the people", the iconic, avant-garde Volksbühne offers cosmopolitan theatre, dance and musical performances, and contemporary visual art.

Theater des Westens

☰🔟 LGBTQ+ Berlin

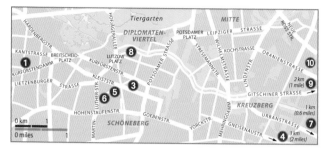

① Christopher Street Day

Every summer, Germany's largest pride festival, Christopher Street Day, transforms Berlin into a giant street party. Thousands of people walk in a parade (see p80) to celebrate the LGBTQ+ community. The parade route winds from Kurfürstendamm down the Straße des 17. Juni to Siegessäule (Victory Column). At night, the party continues in the city's many queer clubs and bars.

Christopher Street Day parade

② Siegessäule

Free in LGBTQ+ cafés and shops ▪ www.siegessaeule.de
Berlin's oldest and best-selling gay magazine is named after the Victory Column. This monthly magazine includes useful information, a round-up of what's on, small ads and interviews from the city's gay scene.

③ Mann-o-Meter

MAP E5 ▪ Bülowstr. 106 ▪ (030) 216 80 08 ▪ Open 5–10pm Tue–Fri, 4–8pm Sat & Sun ▪ www.mann-o-meter.de
Berlin's best-known advice centre for gay and bisexual men that offers all kinds of help. Apart from psychological support relating to AIDS, safe sex and coming out, its counsellors offer help in finding accommodation, give support to those in troubled relationships and provide legal advice. Mann-o-Meter is also a good starting point for gay visitors to Berlin who wish to find out about the gay scene. There is also a café.

④ SchwuZ

Rollbergstr. 26 ▪ (030) 57 70 22 70 ▪ Open from 11pm Wed, Fri and Sat ▪ Adm ▪ www.schwuz.de
Located in an ex-brewery in Neukölln, this queer club has been running since 1977 and is one of the best venues for parties for the LGBTQ+ community in Berlin, drawing a lively crowd. The parties are often themed, and details can be found in magazines such as *Siegessäule* or on the club's Facebook page.

⑤ Tom's Bar

MAP D5 ▪ Motzstr. 19 ▪ (030) 213 45 70 ▪ Open from 10pm daily ▪ www.tomsbar.de
One of the traditional pubs in Berlin, in the centre of the city's gay heart in Motzstraße, this popular, grungey hangout is not for those who are

shy and timid – Tom's is a well-known pick-up joint. Below the (rather dark and dingy) Kneipe is a darkroom.

6 Prinz-Eisenherz-Buchhandlung

MAP D5 ▪ Motzstr. 23 ▪ (030) 313 99 36 ▪ Open 10am–8pm Mon–Sat

Once Germany's first openly gay bookstore, this place now stocks the entire range of German and international publications relating to the LGBTQ+ community. Its knowledgeable bookshop assistants will track down rare or out-of-stock titles at your request. The bookshop also hosts frequent literary readings.

7 SilverFuture

MAP H6 ▪ Weserstr. 206 ▪ (030) 75 63 49 87 ▪ Open 5pm–2am Sun–Thu (until 3am Fri & Sat) ▪ www.silverfuture.net

This queer bar welcomes a mixed crowd. It is widely known as a safe, discrimination-free space for all.

8 Schwules Museum

MAP E4 ▪ Lützowstr. 73 ▪ (030) 69 59 90 50 ▪ Open 2–6pm Mon, Wed, Fri & Sun (until 8pm Thu, until 7pm Sat) ▪ Adm ▪ www.schwulesmuseum.de

Situated in Tiergarten, this small Gay Museum documents, through a variety of temporary exhibitions, the high and low points of LGBTQ+ life since the 19th century. The museum was first conceptualized in 1984. Next to the museum is an archive, a small library and a venue for cultural events.

9 Stueck

MAP H5 ▪ Schlesische Str.16, 10997 Berlin–Kreuzberg ▪ Open from 7pm Mon–Sat

Stueck is located where the famous queer bar Barbie Deinhoff once stood. The history of the bar survives in Stueck's fresh new interior. The bar continues to be popular for its two-for-one Tuesdays. Thursdays are reserved for women, trans and non-binary guests.

Band flyers and posters, SO36

10 SO36

A Kreuzberg classic, this famous – and infamous – dance venue (see p134) has been very popular for many years and attracts a mixed crowd. The Sunday night club "Café Fatal", when old German chart hits and dance tunes are played, is legendary.

Galleries at the small Schwules Museum

TOP 10 Lounges and Clubs

1 Tresor Club
MAP H4 ▪ Köpenicker Str. 70 ▪ (030) 62 90 87 50 ▪ Open 11pm–6am Wed–Sat ▪ www.tresorberlin.com

Berlin's first techno club, Tresor opened in 1991 in the vaults of the former Wertheim department store. Today, it is sited in the basement and industrial halls of a giant former power station and continues to deliver the latest in electronic music with a full programme of visiting musicians and DJ sets.

2 Kater Blau
MAP H4 ▪ Holzmarktstraße 25 ▪ Check website for events ▪ www.katerblau.de

A techno club with two dance floors, Kater Blau is famous for its dance parties which start at midnight and last until the following afternoon on Fridays and weekends. The outdoor area overlooks the river which features 'Agnes', an anchored ship.

3 House of Weekend
MAP J6 ▪ Alexanderstr. 7 ▪ (0152) 24 29 31 40 ▪ Open from 11pm Thu–Sat

This rooftop club in an old Soviet block with great views of the glittering high-rises on Alexanderplatz is a young, trendy and surprisingly down-to-earth house, techno and electro pop club, frequented by a young, fashionable crowd.

4 SilverWings Club
Housed in the former Tempelhof Airport building (see p134), this 1950s US-Air Force Officers Club (see p134) is ideal for dance and events. It hosts legendary theme parties on Saturday nights, which draw a crowd that prefers Rock 'n' Roll, Soul and New Wave music.

5 Spindler & Klatt
Köpenicker Str. 16 ▪ (030) 319 881 860 ▪ Restaurant: open from 7pm daily ▪ Club: open from 11pm Fri & Sat

This event space doubles as a regular lounge with a pan-Asian restaurant, but it is famous for hosting special events.

6 Sage Club
MAP H4 ▪ Brückenstr. 1 ▪ (030) 27 89 83 20 ▪ Open from 7pm Thu ▪ Kit Kat Club: open from 11pm Sat & Sun

Dating from 1997, this is one of the city's oldest and most successful clubs. With a stylish interior and an impressive state-of-the-art sound system, the Sage Club is a sure

The fabulous rooftop location of House of Weekend

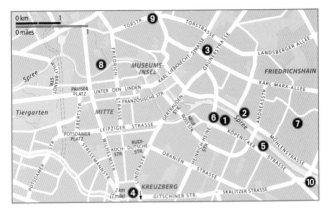

bet for a thrilling night out. On weekends it hosts the notorious, clothing-optional Kit Kat Club events (check website for event details). The club is also known for the eccentric bands it books and the various DJs who spin a range of tracks on its three different dance floors.

7 Berghain

Set inside an East-German-era power station, this (see p148) is Berlin's hottest bastion of electronic music. Some of the world's top DJs spin to spectacular light shows, and the bouncers are notoriously picky, so be prepared to wait (or not get in at all). Hardcore partiers spend entire weekends here with no sleep. The venue is due to become a temporary art gallery. The Panorama Bar on the top floor affords a fantastic view over the Spree River, while the Berghain Garden hosts events in the summer.

8 Tausend

A great alternative to techno and house-dominated clubs, this chic bar (see p93) is hidden under the S-Bahn tracks and has live music. It also plays soul, jazz and pop music from the 1970s and 80s. Tausend has an affiliated cantina and serves excellent mixed cocktails.

9 Mein Haus am See

A former bookshop, this club (see p100) offers the most comfortable seats for guests to sit back and relax. Open 24 hours, this place is also great for a coffee during the day. Note that the bar and club can get crowded on weekends. There is a minimum spend of €12.90 per person until 9pm and €19.90 per person after 9pm.

The bar at Mein Haus am See

10 Watergate

Falckensteinstr. 49 ■ (030) 61 28 03 94 ■ Open from midnight Wed, Fri & Sat

Located on the Spree River with beautiful views of the illuminated Oberbaumbrücke, the Watergate is one of Berlin's cutting-edge clubs, featuring the latest in house, techno, and drum 'n' bass styles, plus an LED dance floor.

⏫ Kneipen (Pubs) and Bars

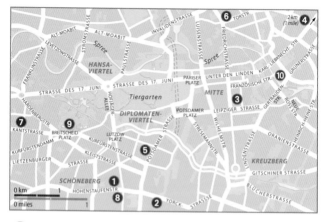

① Green Door

This Berlin classic (see p134) never goes out of style. The interiors of this intimate speakeasy bar are well-hidden from the outside. Green Door attracts a young urban crowd that comes here for the cocktails and to mingle at the minimalist retro-style bar as well as along the curved, green walls. There's an outdoor bell, but the door policy is pretty liberal as long as you look sober.

② E & M Leydicke

This slightly dated winery (see p134) is still a big hit with tourists as well as groups of pupils and students. It regularly hosts concerts and parties featuring swing, blues, jazz and rock 'n' roll bands. Try the sweetish strawberry and raspberry wines.

③ Newton Bar

To see and be seen is the name of the game at this elegant venue (see p92). The service here is charming, and in summer there's even a fold-down bar on the pavement outside. Heavy leather armchairs make for comfortable sitting, and the walls are adorned with enlarged photographs of nudes by Helmut Newton, after whom the bar is named. Don't miss out on the Caribbean and Latin-American cocktails.

The atmospheric Beckett's Kopf

④ Beckett's Kopf

MAP H1 ▪ Pappelallee 64
▪ (030) 44 03 58 80 ▪ Open 8pm–3am Wed–Sat

One of Berlin's finest cocktail bars, Beckett's Kopf has a portrait of writer Samuel Beckett in its window. Its dark interior is hung with heavy velvet curtains, as if to keep the secret recipes from prying eyes. The superb concoctions include the "Mother-in-Law", with fruity notes, and the "Prince of Wales", said to be a favourite indulgence of King Edward VII.

The retro ambience of Berlin's Victoria Bar

5 Victoria Bar
MAP E5 ■ Potsdamer Str. 102 ■ (030) 25 75 99 77 ■ Open 6pm–3am Mon–Thu, 6pm–4am Fri & Sat (until 2am Sun)

This cosy bar, with its understated 1960s ambience, subdued lighting and sophisticated lounge music is a great place for a relaxing drink and has become a firm favourite among the well-to-do artsy crowd. The cocktails are mixed by the renowned barman Stefan Weber.

6 Weinbar Rutz
Berlin's best (but pricey) wine bar and shop (see p100) is found downstairs from the award-winning Michelin-star restaurant of the same name (see p75). It offers over 1,000 wines, but sommelier Billy Wagner is on hand to assist you. It offers an excellent selection of food.

7 Zwiebelfisch
MAP N3 ■ Savignyplatz 7–8 ■ (030) 312 73 63 ■ Open noon–6am daily

A classic venue reflecting the somewhat ageing Charlottenburg scene, this place is where the last survivors of the 1968 student revolt generation come to reminisce. Photographs of artists, once patrons of this establishment, are hung on the walls. In the summer, there are tables outdoors.

8 Café M
MAP E5 ■ Goltzstr. 33 ■ (030) 216 70 92 ■ Open 10am–late daily (from noon Sat & Sun)

Noisy yet laid-back, the Café M Kneipe in Schöneberg is (in)famous. Little has changed since it opened more than 40 years ago.

9 Monkey Bar
MAP D4–D5 ■ Budapester Str. 40 ■ (030) 120 22 12 10 ■ Open noon–2am daily

For beer or cocktails, come to this popular rooftop bar offering views of the neighbouring Berlin Zoo. It hosts regular DJ and live music events.

10 Zum Nußbaum
One of only a few traditional Kneipen in the historic Nikolaiviertel quarter worth checking out, the Nußbaum (see p108) serves draught beer and traditional Berlin food.

The traditional Zum Nußbaum pub

🔟 **Best Places to Eat**

The stylish Restaurant Tim Raue

1 Restaurant Tim Raue

With a well-lit interior and casual vibe, this upscale dining room *(see p135)* is located on the ground floor of a five-storey historical building around the corner from Checkpoint Charlie. Its high ceilings and modern artwork are reminiscent of the art gallery that this restaurant replaced. The Asian fusion menu is craftily created by blending Japanese, Thai and Chinese culinary methods. All dairy products used here are lactose-free. The dishes are artfully prepared by acclaimed German chef Tim Raue.

2 Vox

The exquisite food in this elegant restaurant *(see p117)* at the Grand Hyatt is a sleek and modern fusion of Asian and international dishes, with an emphasis on Japanese (sushi) dishes and French-Italian fare. In summer, reserve one of the tables on the terrace outside. It is open for breakfast, too.

3 Hugos

The Michelin-starred Hugos *(see p117)* at Hotel Intercontinental Berlin *(see p172)* is the city's most affable gourmet restaurant, with impeccable service and stunning views. Wood panelling and plush leather set the tone, while the international cuisine reveals the light touch of German chef Eberhard Lange. The wine list is extensive, and private dining rooms are also available.

4 Bocca di Bacco

This hip Italian restaurant *(see p93)* offers fresh fish and exceptional meat creations such as

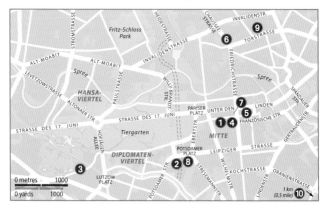

bresaola di cavallo (cured horse meat served with salad and nuts). The seasonal menu is assessed and revised daily. This is also an excellent *enoteca* with a good wine list.

5 Borchardt
Everyone of importance, including German chancellors, dines at Borchardt *(see p93)*. The historic room is furnished in Wilhelminian style (featuring tall columns, wall mosaics and tile flooring) – a stunning setting for the modern French cooking and schnitzel served here. Without a reservation, however, even celebrities can't get a table.

Courtyard dining at Facil

8 Facil
Set in a green oasis in the courtyard of the Mandala Hotel *(see p173)*, this Michelin-starred restaurant *(see p117)* is a study in understated elegance. During the summer months, patrons can dine alfresco or amidst the bamboo gardens. Chef Michael Kempf creates stylish Mediterranean dishes with a French accent.

The simple interiors of Borchardt

6 Rutz
This rising star *(see p101)* in Berlin's gourmet scene has slowly worked towards its second, well-deserved Michelin star by offering consistently high-quality fish and hearty meat dishes based on local recipes, but served with a creative twist. Rutz is cosy and informal, with a prodigious wine list of over 1,000 wines *(see p73)*.

7 Cookies Cream
Located between Komische Oper *(see p90)* and the Westin Grand Hotel *(see p173)*, this trendy Michelin-starred restaurant *(see p93)* is hidden behind a service alley. The excellent dishes at this vegetarian fine-dining restaurant are presented in such an interesting manner that it comes highly recommended for vegetarians and non-vegetarians alike. Cocktails are available at the bar near the entrance.

9 Bandol sur Mer
Offering modern French cuisine, this Michelin-starred restaurant *(see p101)* seats 20 people in a relaxed, intimate setting. Diners can watch as chefs prepare and plate their meals in the bistro-style open kitchen. The ambitious menu changes with the seasons, and comprises creatively plated meat and fish dishes and clever wine pairings.

10 Horváth
The culinary inventiveness of chef Sebastian Frank helped earn this restaurant *(see p135)* its second Michelin star in 2015. On offer here are dishes that creatively play on traditional Austrian cuisine. Diners should allow themselves at least three hours to enjoy the seven-course menu and the accompanying wine. The candle-lit interior, complete with wood furnishings, has a warm feel to it.

🔟 Shops and Markets

Façade of Kaufhaus des Westens

1 Kaufhaus des Westens (KaDeWe)

MAP P5 ▪ Tauentzienstr. 21–24 ▪ (030) 212 10 ▪ Open 10am–8pm Mon–Thu & Sat (until 9pm Fri)

Whatever you are looking for, you will find it here. Over its eight floors, the venerable Kaufhaus des Westens ("department store of the West"), affectionately called KaDeWe, offers more than three million products. On its gourmet floor, West Berlin's former "shop window", you can choose from 1,800 cheeses, 1,400 breads and pastries and 2,000 cold meats. The window displays and inner courtyards are also worth a visit in themselves.

2 Antik- und Flohmarkt Straße des 17. Juni

MAP M4 ▪ Str. des 17. Juni ▪ Open 10am–5pm Sat & Sun

Berlin's largest art and antiques market specializes in antique furnishings and fittings, cutlery and porcelain, books, paintings, clothing and jewellery. The traders are professionals and demand high prices, but in return you are assured of buying something truly special. With its street artists and buskers, the market is an ideal weekend spot for browsing and people-watching.

3 Galeries Lafayette

Located within Quartier 207, this small branch *(see p91)* of the luxury French department store specializes in classic womens- and menswear on one level, and young fashion upstairs. French delicacies are sold in the food department.

4 Art and Fashion House Quartier 206

MAP L4 ▪ Friedrichstr. 71 ▪ (030) 20 94 60 00 ▪ Open 10:30am–7:30pm Mon–Sat

This renowned shopping centre features stunning Art Deco interiors, with mosaic flooring and a marble staircase. Luxury labels such as Moschino, Etro and Bally offer stylish designer clothing and accessories, while the elegant basement and first-floor cafés provide a welcome taste of Berlin coffee culture.

Art and Fashion House Quartier 206

5 Stilwerk KantGaragen

In 2022, this exclusive design and lifestyle store *(see p125)* moved into the premises of the oldest preserved elevated garage in Europe. There are food spots and shops on the ground floor, and artwork is showcased on the spiral ramps and the upper four floors.

6 Gipsformerei Staatliche Museen

MAP A3 ■ Sophie-Charlotten-Str. 17–18 ■ (030) 326 76 90 ■ Open 9am–4pm Mon–Fri (until 6pm Wed)

If you fancy a Schinkel statue for your home or an elegant Prussian sculpture from the Charlottenburg Palace gardens, you'll find moulded plaster reproduction here.

7 Königliche Porzellan-Manufaktur (KPM)

MAP M4 ■ Wegelystr. 1 ■ (030) 39 00 90 ■ Open 10am–6pm Mon–Sat

Prussia's glory and splendour to take away – traditional KPM porcelain for your dining table at home. Apart from elegant porcelain dinner services, figures and accessories made in the Berlin factory are also on sale here.

8 Winterfeldtmarkt

The trendiest and also the most attractive weekly food and clothing market *(see p133)* in Berlin has developed into something of a hotspot with the Schöneberg crowd.

Shoppers at Winterfeldtmarkt

On sale are a wide variety of high-quality goods and produce. This is the place for meeting up on Saturday mornings.

9 Türkenmarkt am Maybachufer

Berlin's largest weekday Turkish market *(see p133)* is held on Tuesdays and Fridays on the Landwehrkanal. Pick up a few picnic supplies from the market, and find a shady waterside spot to have lunch while taking in the sun.

10 Antik- und Buchmarkt am Bode-Museum

MAP J4 ■ Am Kupfergraben 1 ■ (030) 208 26 45 ■ Open 11am–5pm Sat & Sun

Numerous stalls for antiques and souvenirs are scattered along the Kupfergraben in front of the Bode-Museum. Much of it is overpriced, but occasionally browsers will find a bargain.

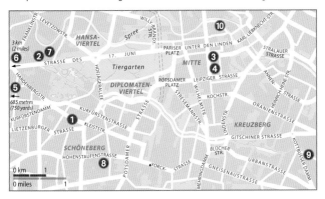

🔟 Berlin for Free

View from the Reichstag dome

1 Reichstag

Berlin's biggest freebie *(see pp14–15)* happens to be a must-see attraction. There's no topping the fabulous 360° view of the city skyline that you get from Lord Norman Foster's beautiful modern dome. Guided tours take in the plenary hall and graffiti left by Russian soldiers in 1945. You have to register in advance and will need your passport to enter.

2 Tempelhofer Feld

Tempelhof Flughafen was Germany's biggest airport when it was built in 1939. A powerful symbol of the new Berlin, the grounds of this historic airport were turned into an enormous public green space *(see p132)*. You will find urban gardeners, cyclists, in-line skaters, go-karters, and people barbequeing, doing T'ai Chi, flying kites and playing baseball.

3 Open Monument Day

Sep ▪ www.visitberlin.de
Beautiful private gardens, interiors of historic monuments, and the hallowed halls of government ministries, scattered throughout the city, are opened to the public for a few days every year. All events are free of charge.

4 Free Concerts

MAP L2 ▪ Herbert-von-Karajan-Str. 1 ▪ (030) 25 48 89 99 ▪ Open Sep–Jun ▪ www.berliner-philharmoniker.de
Churches, universities and even renowned classical orchestras give free concerts. The Berliner Philharmoniker's gratis lunchtime concerts *(see pp38–9)*, usually with small ensembles, are held every Tuesday at 1pm.

5 East Side Gallery

The biggest remaining stretch *(see p146)* of Berlin Wall is now an artistic statement on Germany's division from 1961 to 1989. Famous murals include a Trabant busting through the masonry, *Heads with Big Lips* by Thierry Noir, and Brezhnev and Honecker kissing.

Mural on the Berlin Wall

6 Gedenkstätte Berliner Mauer

MAP 2F ▪ Bernauer Str. 111 ▪ (030) 46 79 86 66 ▪ Centre: open 9:30am–8pm Tue–Sun ▪ www.berliner-mauer-gedenkstaette.de
The Berlin Wall Memorial is well worth a visit for its recreated "death strip", excellent documentary centre and dramatic stories of how East Germans escaped over (or under) the hated barrier. Listening stations and displays are spread along the former border.

7 Free Walking Tours

Daily, year-round ■ Check websites for times and departure points ■ www.alternativeberlin.com, www.brewersberlintours.com, www.newberlintours.com

Join a guided walking tour of the city run by Alternative Berlin Tours, Brewer's Berlin Tours and New Berlin Tours. They're free of charge, although tips are encouraged.

8 Museums

Many museums and galleries, including the Alliiertenmuseum (see p152) and Knoblauchhaus (see p104) have no admission charge. Some of Berlin's most prestigious museums, such as Gemäldegalerie (see pp38–40), the Pergamonmuseum (see pp24–6) and Alte Nationalgalerie (see p56) are free to visitors under 18.

9 Holocaust-Denkmal

Designed by New York architect Peter Eisenman, the striking Memorial to the Murdered Jews of Europe consists of 2,711 concrete pillars placed on undulating ground (see p87). The underground Information Centre offers a moving introduction to the horrors that took place during the Holocaust.

10 Schlosspark Sanssouci

For those who fancy a stroll through a Romantic landscape paint-ing, the Schlosspark Sanssouci is a must-visit. Just a half-hour from Berlin by commuter train, these gar-dens in Potsdam are strewn with ponds and whimsical follies, including an Orangerie, Roman Baths modelled on an Italian villa and a Rococo-style Chinese house (see p158).

The charming Schlosspark Sanssouci

TOP 10 MONEY-SAVING TIPS

Bode-Museum, Museumsinsel

1 The city's public museums, including the comprehensive complex on the Museumsinsel, are covered by the pop-ular Berlin Museum Pass (€29). This offers free entry at participating institutions on three consecutive days.

2 Many of Berlin's neighbourhoods are perfect for a leisurely walk, and you will be surprised by how quick and easy it is to travel between the city's main sights on foot.

3 Theatres and opera houses sell reduced tickets at the door on the day of the performance.

4 Go gallery-hopping in the arty Mitte district. Here, Auguststrasse and Linienstrasse teem with collections open to the public.

5 Buy a drink from a *Späti* (late-night convenience store) and do as the locals do: sit in a park or by the canal for a break any time the sun shines.

6 Buy discounted public transport tickets (such as a 4-pack or a day pass) or hire a bicycle to get around and see the city like a local.

7 Bus lines 100 and 200 take in Berlin's best sights for the price of a single fare.

8 Take advantage of the good-value set meals in cafés and restaurants, particularly at lunchtime.

9 Comb through the vast Mauerpark flea market for unique vintage and retro finds. The market runs all day on Sundays (see p140).

10 If you are a visitor from outside the EU and are leaving the EU with purchased goods, remember to get a refund on Germany's 19 per cent sales tax. Ask sales staff at stores for an *Ausfuhrbescheinigung* (export papers).

Festivals and Fairs

1 Fashion Week
Various venues ■ Jan & Jul ■ Adm ■ www.fashion-week-berlin.com/en

Top designers and local talent present their new collections.

2 Grüne Woche
MAP A4 ■ Messe Berlin ■ 2nd half of Jan ■ Adm ■ www.gruenewoche.de/en

The largest gourmet feast in the world, Green Week is a tasty agri-cultural and gastronomical fair for everyone. Nowhere else can you enjoy a culinary journey around the world in such a condensed space.

3 Berliner Filmfestspiele
MAP L2 ■ Berlinale Palast and various cinemas throughout the city ■ 2nd & 3rd week in Feb ■ www.berlinale.de

The Berlinale is the top German film festival, and is attended by Hollywood and German stars alike. Until 1999, the film festival took place around the Zoo-Palast cinema; today the area around Potsdamer Platz takes centre stage for the festivities.

4 Internationale Tourismus Börse (ITB)
MAP A5 ■ CityCube Berlin ■ Mar ■ Adm ■ www.itb.com/en

The world's largest tourism fair offers up-to-date travel information to the general public, often at elaborately designed stalls. The night-time shows put on by many of the exhibiting countries are especially popular.

5 Karneval der Kulturen
MAP G/H5/6 ■ Kreuzberg ■ Whitsun (varying date in May or early Jun)

Multicultural Berlin celebrates for three days in the colourful Kreuzberg district in a street carnival parade.

6 Christopher Street Day
MAP P3/4 ■ Kurfürstendamm and Straße des 17. Juni ■ Jul ■ www.csd-berlin.de/en

This colourful pride parade (see p68) on Christopher Street Day celebrates sexual diversity. Up to 500,000 people from all around the world boisterously celebrate as they drink and dance in the streets of Central Berlin.

Crowds surround the red carpet at the Berliner Filmfestspiele

7 Lange Nacht der Museen

Berlin museums ▪ (030) 24 74 97 00 ▪ Last weekend Aug ▪ Adm ▪ www.lange-nacht-der-museen.de

For one night, one ticket gives access to all the city's museums until well after midnight, offering visitors an unusual experience. Many institutions also put on special events, and street artists and sellers entertain the patiently queueing public.

8 Pop-Kultur

Various venues ▪ End Aug/early Sep ▪ www.pop-kultur.berlin

As a successor of the Berlin Music Week, this new festival for bands, musicians, artists, producers, labels and audiences is held at various venues in Kulturbrauerei in the Prenzlauer Berg district.

A crowded pavilion at the IFA

9 Internationale Funkausstellung (IFA)

MAP A4 ▪ Messe Berlin ▪ Every year in early Sep ▪ Adm ▪ www.b2b.ifa-berlin.com/en

The latest in high-tech toys and entertainment technology are on show from over 1,500 global exhibitors at the IFA (International Broadcasting Exhibition).

10 Festival of Lights

Various venues ▪ Oct ▪ www.festival-of-lights.de

For 10 days, dozens of Berlin's most popular landmarks are illuminated using light installations created by a number of artists.

TOP 10 SPORTS HIGHLIGHTS

Kite festival at Tempelhofer Feld

1 Tempelhofer Feld
MAP F6 ▪ Open daily
Berlin's largest sports ground (see p132).

2 Berliner Neujahrslauf
MAP K3 ▪ Brandenburger Tor ▪ 1st Jan
A New Year's Day Run in the cold.

3 Sechstagerennen
Velodrom ▪ 2nd half of Jan ▪ www.sixday.com/en
The Six-Day Race is one of Berlin's most venerable sports events.

4 Velocity Cycling Races
MAP C3 ▪ Mercedes Benz Arena ▪ End of Jun/early Jul ▪ www.velocity.berlin
A cycling race that passes through seven Berlin districts.

5 DFB-Pokalfinale
Olympiastadion ▪ May
Germany's second-most important soccer cup final is played here.

6 Skate by Night
Mercedes Benz Platz ▪ Jun–Aug: Sun evening
Skaters meet for night-time "blading".

7 Berlin Triathlon
Treptower Park ▪ Early Jun ▪ www.berlin-triathlon.de
Amateurs can register online for this.

8 Internationales Stadionfest (ISTAF) and ISTAF Indoor
Mercedes Benz Arena and Olympiastadion ▪ Feb and early Sep
Germany's biggest athletics festivals.

9 Berlin Marathon
Str. des 17. Juni ▪ 3rd/4th Sun in Sep ▪ www.bmw-berlin-marathon.com/en
Attracts thousands of runners.

10 Deutsches Traberderby
Trabrennbahn Mariendorf ▪ 1st week in Aug
The derby for professional trotter races.

Berlin
Area by Area

Nikolaiviertel and Rotes Rathaus with the Berliner
Dom and Fernsehturm in the background

TOP 10 Central Berlin: Unter den Linden

The boulevard of Unter den Linden is the heart of historic Mitte. Many of Berlin's sights are set along this avenue and around Bebelplatz, creating a picture of Prussian and German history from the early 18th century onwards. To the south is the Neo-Classical Gendarmenmarkt, one of Europe's most attractive squares; around it are elegant restaurants and cafés. Nearby Friedrichstraße is lined with luxury stores and modern offices and apartments.

Statue, Unter den Linden

CENTRAL BERLIN: UNTER DEN LINDEN

1 Brandenburger Tor
MAP K3 ■ Pariser Platz

Berlin's best-known landmark on Pariser Platz leads through to Unter den Linden (see pp12–13).

2 Humboldt Forum
MAP K5 ■ Schloßplatz
■ Open 10am–8pm Mon, Wed, Thu & Sun (until 10pm Fri & Sat)
■ www.humboldtforum.com

Designed by Franco Stella and opened in 2021, this museum and cultural complex features a rooftop terrace offering spectacular views. The exhibits on show here include artifacts from sub-Saharan Africa, Asia, Oceania and the Americas.

The historical Alte Bibliothek

3 Forum Fridericianum
MAP K4 ■ Unter den Linden and Bebelplatz

The historic structures of this complex are among some of the city's finest. In 1740, Frederick the Great commissioned architect von Knobelsdorff to design and construct the prestigious Neo-Classical buildings for the area around today's Bebelplatz. Frederick personally influenced their designs of Deutsche Staatsoper, Prinz-Heinrich-Palais, Alte Bibliothek and the Catholic St.-Hedwigs-Kathedrale, and later the Humboldt University. The opera house was the first to be built. A memorial set into the ground in 1995 at Bebelplatz recalls its dark past – in 1933, it was the site of the Nazi book burning. Frederick's successors commissioned the Altes Palais and a statue of "Old Fritz", surrounded by "his" buildings. Christian Daniel Rauch created the bronze figure in 1840, portraying Frederick wearing his trademark tricorn hat and coronation mantle. The statue has always faced west but wags claim that the East German government mistakenly placed the figure the wrong way around.

FREDERICK AS ARCHITECT

Forum Fridericianum was not only Frederick the Great's memorial to himself, it also ensured that Unter den Linden became one of the greatest boulevards in Europe. The king, who favoured a Neo-Classical style, drew up plans for the buildings himself, and Knobelsdorff executed his ideas.

Museumsinsel's Bode-Museum, with the Fernsehturm in the background

④ Museumsinsel

MAP J5 ■ Pergamonmuseum: Bodestr. 1–3; (030) 266 424 242; closed for renovation until 2027 ■ Alte Nationalgalerie: Bodestr. 1–3; (030) 266 424 242; open 10am–6pm Tue–Sun (until 8pm Thu); adm ■ www.smb.museum

Museum Island (see pp24–7), a UNESCO World Heritage Site, is one of the most significant complexes of museums in the world, holding major arts collections and imposing, full-scale ancient structures. Based here are the Pergamonmuseum, the Bode-Museum, the Alte Nationalgalerie and the Altes and Neues Museums, including the famous Ägyptisches Museum.

⑤ Gendarmenmarkt

MAP L4 ■ Mitte ■ Konzerthaus: Gendarmenmarkt 2; (030) 203 092 101; open Apr–Oct: 11am–6pm; tours 3:30pm Mon–Fri, 1pm Sun; en.konzerthaus.de

This square, whose strict layout is reminiscent of an Italian Renaissance piazza, is probably the most beautiful in Berlin. Named after a regiment of gens d'armes stationed nearby, Gendarmenmarkt was built at the end of the 17th century as a market square. The Schauspielhaus (theatre) on the west side of the square was reopened as the Konzerthaus (concert hall) in 1984 (see p50). A statue of the playwright Friedrich Schiller stands in front of the building. To the left and right of the Konzerthaus stand the twin towers of the Deutscher and Französischer Doms (German and French cathedrals), dating back to the late 18th century. Französischer Dom, to its north, is a prestigious late Baroque building (see p49); concealed behind it is the Französische Friedrichstadtkirche, a church serving Berlin's Huguenot community. The Deutscher Dom opposite, built in 1708 on the south side of the square for the Reformed Protestant Church, did not receive its first tower until 1785. An exhibition on democracy in Germany is on display here.

THE HUGUENOTS IN BERLIN

In 1685, the Great Elector issued the famous Edict of Potsdam, granting asylum in Berlin to around 20,000 Huguenots, who were persecuted in their native France because of their Protestant faith. Skilled academics and crafters, they moulded Berlin's social and cultural life and enriched it with the French art of living. Today, the city's French community still worships at the Friedrichstadtkirche, part of the Französischer Dom complex.

6 Friedrichstraße
MAP J4–L4 ■ Mitte

Friedrichstraße has regained some of the glamour and vibrancy it possessed before World War II. Today, Berlin's Fifth Avenue is once again home to elegant shops and upmarket restaurants and cafés. Especially worth visiting are the three Quartiers 205, 206 and 207 (the latter designed by architect Jean Nouvel) within the Friedrich-stadtpassagen, containing the Galeries Lafayette store (see p91) and Art and Fashion House Quartier 206 (see p76). At the northern end of the street is the famous Dussmann store (books, music, events), S-Bahn station Friedrichstraße and the former entertainment district, which includes the Friedrichstadt-Palast (see p67) and the impressive Admiralspalast (see p90).

Concrete steles, Holocaust-Denkmal

7 Holocaust-Denkmal
MAP L3 ■ Ebertstr. ■ (06) 26 39 43 36 ■ Information Centre: open 10am–6pm Tue–Sun ■ www.stiftung-denkmal.de

The Memorial to the Murdered Jews of Europe serves as Germany's national Holocaust memorial (see p79). After years of debate, US star architect Peter Eisenman completed the monument in 2005. It consists of a large field with dark grey steles of varying heights up to 2 m (6 ft) high, which symbolize the six million Jews and others murdered by the Nazis in concentration camps between 1933 and 1945. Below the memorial, an information centre explains the causes and history of the genocide.

HISTORIC MITTE WALK

Hotel Adlon Kempinski
Wilhelm-strasse
The Square
Galeries Lafayette
Borchardt
Holocaust-Denkmal
Friedrich-strasse
Gendarmen-markt
Vossstrasse
Anton-Wilhelm-Amo Strasse
Federal Ministry of Finance

▶ MORNING

Turn back the clock on **Wilhelmstraße** (see p88), Berlin's political nerve centre until 1945. Starting at **Hotel Adlon Kempinski**, head south past the bold modern British Embassy. Turn right at Behrensstraße to visit the **Holocaust-Denkmal**, then carry on along Wilhelmstraße, where signs point out the old ministries. The Prussian State Council was in the Neo-Classical building at No. 54; its last president was Konrad Adenauer, who became West Germany's first chancellor. At the corner of **Vossstraße** were Hitler's main offices in the Neue Reichskanzlei. Continue down to No. 97, the giant structure of the former Ministry of Aviation. Today the **Federal Ministry of Finance** is based here. Retrace your steps north, turn right into **Anton-Wilhelm-Amo Straße** then left into **Friedrichstraße**. Head to **Galeries Lafayette** (see p91), whose gourmet food department is perfect for a snack lunch.

AFTERNOON

After lunch, head for the shops at Galeries Lafayette and the concept store **The Square** (see p91) just down the street. Then head to the **Gendarmenmarkt** square nearby. Take some time to admire its Konzerthaus and the imposing Deutscher and Französischer Domes. The latter holds regular classical music concerts – check their website for the schedule. Round off your day with a hearty meal at the historic **Borchardt** (see p52) on Französische Straße.

See map on pp84–5 ←

British Embassy, Wilhelmstraße

8 Wilhelmstraße
MAP L3 ■ Between Unter den Linden and Leipziger Str.

In imperial Berlin, the centre of the German Empire's governmental power was based in Wilhelmstraße. Around 100 years later, nothing remains of the prestigious historic buildings which represented the equivalent of No. 10 Downing Street in London or Quai d'Orsay in Paris. All political decisions were made at Wilhelmstraße: both Chancellor (at No. 77) and President (No. 73) of the German Reich lived here in old town houses. Their gardens became known as "ministerial gardens". Adolf Hitler had the street system-atically developed into the nerve centre of Nazi power. The Neue Reichskanzlei (the Chancellor's office) was built in 1937–9 to plans by Albert Speer, at the corner of Vossstraße and Wilhelmstraße. It was blown up in 1945. Behind the Reichskanzlei was the so-called "Führerbunker" where Adolf Hitler committed suicide on 30 April 1945. It is now a car park. Of the historic buildings, only the former Ministry of Aviation (Reichsluftfahrtministerium) remains. Today, Wilhelmstraße is lined by modern residential and office buildings; the British Embassy, built in 2000 by Michael Wilford, creates a link with the international importance of this street.

9 Schlossplatz
MAP K5 ■ Mitte

Once the Stadtschloss (town residence) of the Hohenzollerns stood here. It was blown up by the East German government in 1950–51, and today just a few historic fragments of the original can be seen. Remains include the façade of the doorway where Karl Liebknecht supposedly proclaimed the Socialist Republic in 1918. The portal has been incorporated into the former Staatsratsgebäude (State Council Building) on the south side of the square. On its eastern side, the square used to be bordered by the Palast der Republik (Palace of the Republic), the former seat of the East German parliament demolished in 2008.

NAZI ARCHITECTURE

One of few surviving examples of the monumental architectural style favoured by the Nazis is the former Reichsluftfahrtministerium (Ministry of Aviation), commissioned by Hermann Göring in 1935–6 from Ernst Sagebiel. The sandstone office block was the world's largest and most modern, strengthened against attack by steel girders. After reunification, the Treuhandanstalt (privatisation agency) was based here; today it houses the Federal Ministry of Finance.

The Humboldt-Forum cultural centre (see p85) was opened in 2021 and is set in the reconstructed Berlin Palace. It features a façade reminiscent of the old Hohenzollern Palace (see p151) and a library. The non-European collections of the former Dahlem Museums (of Asian Art and of Ethnology) are housed in the building.

The former State Council Building

⑩ Museum für Kommunikation

MAP L4 ▪ Leipziger Str. 16 ▪ (030) 20 29 40 ▪ Open 9am–5pm Tue–Fri (until 8pm Tue), 10am–6pm Sat & Sun ▪ Adm ▪ www.mfk-berlin.de

The world's largest Post Office Museum opened in 1872. Its excellent displays document the history of communication from the first postage stamps of the Middle Ages to today's satellite technology. Particularly worth seeing are a blue and a red stamp from Mauritius, one of the first telephone installations (dating back to 1863) and three talking robots who interact with the visitors. Younger visitors always enjoy the Computer-galerie, where they can learn and gain new insights while playing.

Historic letterbox

A DAY OF CULTURE

Grill Royal
Museumsinsel
Berliner Dom
Brandenburger Tor
Café Felix at Staatsbibliothek
Humboldt Forum
Einstein Unter den Linden
Schloss-platz
Pariser Platz
Russian Embassy
Palais Populaire
Forum Fridericianum
Bocca di Bacco

▶ **MORNING**

Start your stroll on Unter den Linden, which begins in front of the **Brandenburger Tor** on **Pariser Platz** (see pp12–13). This was Berlin's prestigious royal avenue, and the rich and famous still promenade here today. For breakfast, pop into **Einstein Unter den Linden** (see p92). Afterwards continue east along the boulevard; you will pass the **Russian Embassy** built in 1952. From here you can already see the 13.5-m (44-ft) high equestrian statue of Frederick the Great at **Forum Fridericianum** (see p85). This area and Bebelplatz are right in the centre of old Berlin, with the Staatsoper, Altes Palais, St.-Hedwigs-Kathedrale and Humboldt-Universität around them. Stop for an early lunch at **Palais Populaire** (Unter den Linden 5) or **Café Felix at Staatsbibliothek** (Unter den Linden 8).

AFTERNOON

In the early afternoon continue east along Unter den Linden. At the end of the street lies the **Museumsinsel** (see pp24–7). Cross the Schloßbrücke to explore the wealth of treasures in the island's museums. If you have time, visit the **Berliner Dom** (see p48). Opposite the impressive cathedral you will see **Schlossplatz**, with the **Humboldt-Forum** (see p85). Return along Unter den Linden to **Bocca di Bacco** (see p93) or **Grill Royal** (see p93) in Mitte and end your day with a delicious meal.

The Best of the Rest

Trabant at the DDR Museum

1 DDR Museum
MAP K5 ▪ Karl-Liebknecht-Str. 1 ▪ Open 9am–9pm daily ▪ www.ddr-museum.de/en

This museum of everyday life in East Germany recreates socialist-era interiors and displays examples of East German design, including a Trabant car visitors can sit in.

2 Lustgarten
MAP K5 ▪ Unter den Linden 1

A former parade ground for the German Democratic Republic, Lustgarten (Pleasure Garden) is now a popular park on the Museuminsel. It is a pleasant place for a break.

3 WMF-Haus
MAP L3 ▪ Leipziger Str., corner Mauerstr.

The former headquarters of the porcelain and cutlery manufacturer WMF has remarkable façades decorated with beautiful mosaics.

4 Alte Kommandantur
MAP K5 ▪ Unter den Linden 1

Rebuilt with the original Classicist façade, this impressive building houses the Berlin offices of the media giant Bertelsmann.

5 Maxim-Gorki-Theater
MAP K4 ▪ Am Festungsgraben 2 ▪ www.gorki.de

This renowned theatre was once Berlin's Singakademie, or singing school. Paganini and Liszt, among others, performed here.

6 S-Bahnhof Friedrichstraße
MAP J4 ▪ Friedrichstr.

Remodelled several times, this has always been one of Berlin's most famous stations. Between 1961 and 1989, it was the principal crossing point between East and West.

7 Komische Oper
MAP K4 ▪ Behrenstr. 55–57 ▪ english.komische-oper-berlin.de

One of Germany's most magnificent opera houses, dating from 1892; it's closed for renovation until 2025.

8 Palais am Festungsgraben
MAP K4 ▪ Am Festungsgraben 1 ▪ (030) 208 40 00

The 1753 Baroque palace has retained its original elegant interior and magnificent ceiling frescoes.

9 Admiralspalast
MAP J4 ▪ Friedrichstr. 101 ▪ (030) 22 50 70 00 ▪ Hours vary, check website ▪ www.admirals palast.theater

Berlin's most legendary venue stages musicals and comedy shows.

Façade of the Admiralspalast

10 Cold War Museum
MAP K4 ▪ Unter den Linden 14 ▪ Open 10am–8pm Mon–Sun ▪ www.coldwarmuseu.de

Opened in 2022, this museum uses interactive displays to tell the story of the Cold War, which spanned over 40 years, and the conflict between capitalism and communism.

Shops

1 Galeries Lafayette
MAP L4 ■ Friedrichstr. 76–78
■ (030) 20 94 80 ■ Open 10am–8pm
Mon–Sat

Located within Quartier 207, this is the only German branch of the luxury French store (see p76). Here you will find elegant fashion, and gourmet foods on the lower level.

2 The Square
MAP G4 ■ Französiche Straße 40 ■ (030) 20 67 09 50

This trendy concept store offers newcomer fashion and luxury labels such as Christian Louboutin and Stella McCartney.

Interior of Mall of Berlin

3 Mall of Berlin
MAP L3 ■ Leipziger Platz 12
■ (030) 20 62 17 70

The Mall of Berlin occupies an entire block and connects Leipziger Straße and Wilhelmstraße with a passage. There are 270 shops and restaurants.

4 Bucherer
MAP L4 ■ Friedrichstr. 176–179 ■ (030) 204 10 49

A luxury outlet selling excellent quality watches and jewellery.

5 Karl Lagerfeld
MAP L4 ■ Friedrichstraße 172
■ (030) 20 63 33 22

Find refined, elegant accessories, shoes, bags and sunglasses at this luxury fashion label's store.

6 Stiche Düssel
MAP G4 ■ Charlottenstraße 53/54 ■ (030) 20 16 56 66

Visitors can rifle through a vast collection of over 10,000 antique prints from the 16th to the 19th century, including cityscapes, maps from all over the world, and decorative engravings.

7 Kulturkaufhaus Dussmann
MAP K4 ■ Friedrichstr. 90
■ (030) 20 25 11 11

A trove of books, movies and sheet music, Kulturkaufhaus Dussmann has a large section on classical music. The English-language section here is also excellent. It is open until mid-night on weekdays.

8 Ritter Sport Bunte Schokowelt
MAP K4 ■ Französische Str. 24
■ (030) 20 09 50 80

The chocolate-maker's flagship store has fun merchandise, a chocolate-themed exhibition and workshops.

9 Fassbender & Rausch
MAP L4 ■ Charlottenstr. 60
■ (030) 20 45 84 43

Giant chocolate sculptures of the Reichstag and Brandenburger Tor adorn the windows and tempt visitors into this shop. There is also a café on the upper floor where you can try some of the store's delicious creations.

10 Jack Wolfskin
MAP K4 ■ Behrenstr. 23
■ (030) 20 64 80 70

Make sure you stock up on apparel, equipment and footwear before setting out on any outdoor activities at this branch of Germany's famous outfitter.

See map on pp84–5

Pubs and Bars

1 Newton Bar
MAP L4 ■ Charlottenstr. 57
■ (030) 20 29 54 21 ■ Open 11am–
3am Thu–Sat (until 2am Sun–Wed)
One of the trendiest bars in town.
Sink into the deep leather armchairs
and sip your cocktails, surrounded
by enlarged photographs of nudes
by Helmut Newton (see p72).

2 Rooftop Hotel de Rome
MAP K4 ■ Behrenstr. 37 ■ (030)
460 60 90 ■ Open noon–11pm daily
The stylish bar on the roof of Hotel
de Rome offers spectacular views of
Bebelplatz and excellent Italian fare.

3 Zosch
MAP J4 ■ Tucholskystrasse
30 ■ (030) 280 76 64 ■ Open 4pm–
3am Mon–Sat
An old-fashioned pub in Mitte, Zosch
has an unpolished charm. Concerts
hosted in the brick vaulted cellar
range from folk to jazz music.

4 Sra Bua Bar
MAP K3 ■ Behrenstr. 72 ■ (030)
22 61 19 59 ■ Open 6–10:30pm Tue–
Fri (from 7pm Sat)
At the back of Hotel Adlon Kempinski,
this elegant bar specializes in Asian
cocktails and creative cuisine by the
team of star chef Tim Raue.

5 Café LebensArt
MAP K4 ■ Unter den Linden 69A
■ (030) 44 72 19 30 ■ Open 9am–11pm
Sun–Thu (until midnight Fri & Sat)
A café rather than a bar, LebensArt
offers breakfast and afternoon cakes.

6 Einstein Unter den Linden
MAP K4 ■ Unter den Linden 42
■ (030) 204 36 32 ■ Open 8am–
10pm Mon–Fri, 10am–10pm Sat
(until 6pm Sun)
This Viennese coffeehouse-inspired
bistro is popular with politicians,
artists and journalists. Excellent
wines and beer brands are on offer.

7 Ständige Vertretung
MAP J3 ■ Schiffbauerdamm 8
■ (030) 282 39 65 ■ Open 10am–
1am daily
The name harks back to the
permanent West German repre-
sentation in East Berlin. Ständige
Vertretung is famous for its Rhine
specialities, such as Kölsch beer.

8 Bellboy Bar
MAP L4 ■ Anton-Wilhelm-
Amo-Str. 30 ■ (030) 20 07 70 70
■ Open 6pm–3am Tue–Sun
Located on the ground floor of the
Hilton Berlin, this plush bar has a
wide range of food and drink.

9 Brauhaus Lemke
MAP J5 ■ Dircksenstr.
S-Bahn arch No. 143 ■ (030)
24 72 87 27 ■ Open noon–
midnight daily
Berlin's first craft brewery,
this pub has a relaxed ambience and a variety of beer.

10 Windhorst
MAP K3 ■ Dorotheen-
str. 65 ■ (030) 20 45 00 70
■ Open 6pm–1am Mon (until
2am Tue–Fri), 8pm–2am Sat
Sophisticated jazz bar with
bartenders whipping up
your cocktail of choice.

Wooden interiors of Sra Bua Bar

Restaurants

Waterfront seating at the Grill Royal

PRICE CATEGORIES

For a three-course meal for one with half a bottle of wine (or equivalent meal), taxes and charges included.

€ under €30   €€ €30–60   €€€ over €60

1 Grill Royal
MAP J4 ■ Friedrichstr. 105b ■ (030) 28 87 92 88 ■ Open 5pm–midnight daily ■ €€

Steak-lovers can choose from a range of cuts from around the world.

2 Crackers
MAP K4 ■ Friedrichstr. 158 ■ (030) 680 730 488 ■ Open 7pm–midnight daily ■ €€€

Head chef Stephan Hentschel serves up exceptional dishes at this stylish restaurant. An extravagant drinks menu makes Crackers a perfect spot for a late-night cocktail.

3 Bocca di Bacco
MAP K4 ■ Friedrichstr. 167–8 ■ (030) 20 67 28 28 ■ Open noon–3pm & 6:30–10pm Mon–Sat ■ €€€

A sophisticated Italian diner, Bocca di Bacco (see p74) offers a wide range of fresh fish and meat dishes. Their homemade pasta lunches are especially popular.

4 Liu Nudelhaus
MAP L4 ■ Kronenstr. 72 ■ (030) 17 86 68 45 72 ■ Open 11:30am–3pm daily & 5–7:30pm Wed–Fri ■ €€

The Sichuan noodles here are widely regarded as the best in the city. Expect to wait a while for a table.

5 Tausend Cantina
MAP J3 ■ Schiffbauerdamm 11 ■ (030) 27 58 20 70 ■ Open 7:30pm–late Tue–Sat ■ €€

Top-notch Asian and Ibero-American cuisine by celebrated chef Duc Ngo, a Berliner with Vietnamese roots.

6 Restaurant & Café 1687
MAP F3 ■ Mittelstr. 30 ■ (030) 20 63 06 11 ■ Open 8am–1am daily ■ €€€

Enjoy modern European cuisine with Franco-Mediterranean influences at this elegant restaurant. There is also an extensive wine list on offer.

7 Borchardt
MAP K4 ■ Französische Str. 47 ■ (030) 81 88 62 62 ■ Open 11:30am–midnight daily ■ €€€

This beautiful high-ceilinged restaurant (see p71) has a nice court-yard. Try the tender weiner schnitzel.

8 Cookies Cream
MAP K4 ■ Behrenstr. 55 ■ (030) 27 49 29 40 ■ Open 5–11pm Tue–Sat ■ €€

The only vegetarian restaurant with a Michelin star in Germany, Cookies Cream (see p75) is a popular choice.

9 Rotes Kamel
MAP L3 ■ Hannah-Arendt-Str. 4 ■ Open 3–11pm daily ■ €€

Fresh, satisfying meals and tasting plates, with flavours inspired from the Middle East, are on offer here.

10 Hugo & Notte
MAP K4 ■ Gendarmenmarkt 5 ■ 52 68 02 17 30 ■ Open noon–10pm Tue–Sun ■ €€

Enjoy French cuisine at this restaurant on the premises of the French Dome.

See map on pp84–5
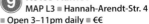

📘 Central Berlin: Scheunenviertel

Richly decorated Postfuhramt building

From the mid-19th-century onwards, the Scheunenviertel ("barn quarter") was home to thousands of poor Jewish migrants. After World War II the area was entirely neglected and fell into decay. It has been rejuvenated in recent decades and many historic merchants' yards and narrow side streets have been restored, reviving the quarter's unique and lively character. With its new restaurants, galleries and shops, the district has become fashionable. The tragic history of its former inhabitants, however, remains unforgotten.

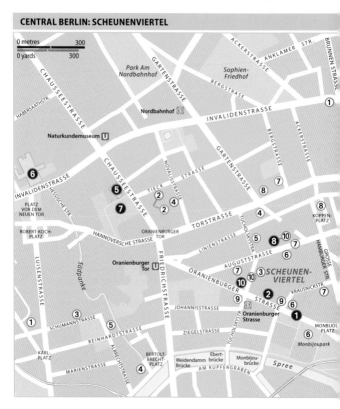

CENTRAL BERLIN: SCHEUNENVIERTEL

1 Oranienburger Straße
MAP J4 ■ Mitte, between Friedrichstr. and Rosenthaler Str.

Located in the centre of old Scheunenviertel, Oranienburger Straße symbolizes the rise and fall of Jewish culture in Berlin like no other street does. Traces of its Jewish past are visible at the Neue Synagoge and several Jewish cafés and restaurants *(see p101)*. Some 18th- and 19th-century buildings attest to the street's former splendour – the Postfuhramt *(see p97)* with its ornate façade, for example, or the house at No. 71–72, built in 1789 by Christian Friedrich Becherer for the Grand Lodge of the German Freemasons. The area is also great for a night out – visit one of the many bars and restaurants *(see p100)* lining the street.

Striking dome of the Neue Synagoge

2 Neue Synagoge
MAP J4 ■ Oranienburger Str. 28–30 ■ Open 10am–8pm Sun & Mon (until 6pm Tue–Thu, until 5pm Fri) ■ Adm ■ www.cjudaicum.de

Once the largest in Europe, the New Synagogue *(see p49)* was opened in 1866. In 1938, it survived Kristallnacht thanks to a brave guard, but it was damaged by bombs during World War II. Behind the splendid Moorish façades are a prayer room and the Centrum Judaicum.

3 Hackesche Höfe
MAP J5 ■ Rosenthaler Str. 40–41

Berlin's largest and most attractive group of restored commercial buildings, Hackesche Höfe extends from Oranienburger Straße to Rosenthaler Straße. The complex, comprising eight interconnecting courtyards, was designed around the turn of the 20th century by August Endell and Kurt Berndt, two leading exponents of the Jugendstil. The first courtyard especially has elements typical of the style: geometric motifs on vibrant glazed tiles cover the building. The complex has been carefully restored and is a popular centre of nightlife.

4 Sophienstraße
MAP J5 ■ Große Hamburger Str. 29

Narrow Sophienstraße has been beautifully restored and looks just as it did in the late 18th century. The buildings and courtyards now host shops and arts and crafts workshops. The Baroque Sophienkirche (see p98) nearby, the first Protestant parish church, was founded by Queen Sophie Luise in 1712. Next to it is a cemetery with some tombs dating back to the 18th century.

5 Brecht-Weigel-Gedenkstätte
MAP F2 ■ Chausseestr. 125 ■ (030) 200 571 844 ■ Open 10am–noon & 2–3:30pm Tue, 10–11:30am Wed & Fri, 10am–noon & 5–6:30pm Thu, 10am–3:30pm Sat, 11am–6pm Sun ■ Adm ■ www.adk.de/en/archive

Bertolt Brecht, one of the greatest playwrights of the 20th century, lived here with his wife, Helene Weigel, between 1953 and 1956. On display are original furnishings, documents and photographs.

Exhibit at Museum für Naturkunde

6 Museum für Naturkunde
MAP F2 ■ Invalidenstr. 43 ■ (030) 20 93 85 91 ■ Open 9:30am–6pm Tue–Fri (from 10am Sat & Sun) ■ Adm ■ www.naturkunde museum-berlin.de

The Museum of Natural History (see p55) is one of the largest of its kind and houses the world's largest dinosaur skeleton to have ever been discovered: a Giraffatitan found in Tanzania. Also on display are taxidermist Alfred Keller's insect models, various types of fossils, meteorites and minerals.

7 Dorotheenstädtischer Friedhof
MAP F2 ■ Chausseestr. 126 ■ Open summer: 8am–8pm daily (winter: until sunset)

This is a striking cemetery dating back to 1762. To the left of the entrance are the graves of Heinrich Mann (1871–1950) and Bertolt Brecht (1898–1956); further along are the pillar-like tombstones of Johann Gottlieb Fichte (1762–1814) and Georg Wilhelm Friedrich Hegel (1770–1831). On Birkenallee (left off the main path) are the graves of Karl Friedrich Schinkel (1781–1841), Friedrich August Stüler (1800–65) and Johann Gottfried Schadow (1764–1850).

JEWISH BERLIN

In the 19th century, Berlin had a population of 200,000 Jews, the largest such community in Germany. Apart from the wealthier Jews who lived in the west of the city, it included many Jewish migrants from Eastern Europe. They settled in Spandauer Vorstadt, primarily in Scheunenviertel, an impoverished part of the district that had the reputation of being a criminal red-light area. Later, Nazi propaganda used that name to denote the whole area to tarnish all Jews by association. Nazi stigmatization of Jews also included the enforced public wearing of a Star of David. The Jewish quarter is still known as Scheunenviertel, but very few Jews live here now. Only some 5,000 Jewish Berliners survived the 1933–45 persecution.

8 KW Institute for Contemporary Art

MAP G2 ▪ Auguststr. 69 ▪ (030) 243 45 90 ▪ Open 11am–7pm Wed–Mon (until 9pm Thu) ▪ www.kw-berlin.de

Housed in a former margarine factory, this gallery displays works by established as well as up-and-coming artists.

9 Gedenkstätte Große Hamburger Straße

MAP J5 ▪ Große Hamburger Str. ▪ www.jg-berlin.org/en.html

Before 1939, this was a thoroughly Jewish street, with Jewish schools, the oldest Jewish cemetery in Berlin and an old people's home. The latter achieved tragic fame during the Nazi period – the SS used it as a detention centre for Berlin's Jews before transporting them to concentration camps. A monument commemorates the thousands who were sent to their death from here. To the left of the home is a Jewish school, on the site of an earlier school founded in 1778 by the Enlightenment philosopher Moses Mendelssohn (1729–86). To the right is the Alter Jüdischer Friedhof (old Jewish cemetery), where some 12,000 of Berlin's Jews were buried between 1672 and 1827. It was destroyed by the Nazis in 1943,

Moses Mendelssohn

and in 1945 it was converted into a park. Only a few Baroque tombstones or *masebas* survived. The spot thought to be Mendelssohn's tomb is marked by a *maseba*.

10 Postfuhramt

MAP J4 ▪ Oranienburger Straße 35

The richly ornamented Postfuhramt (post office transport department) dates from the 19th century. The building houses the head office of a medical technology firm.

A DAY IN SCHEUNENVIERTEL

▶ MORNING

Take the S-Bahn to Berlin's former entertainment district at Friedrichstraße and explore this vibrant, glamorous street. Then walk north up to Reinhardtstraße, opposite the Friedrichstadt-Palast, and turn left here towards Bertolt-Brecht-Platz. Continue south to Albrechtstraße to the **Berliner Ensemble** (see p98). Admire the theatre where Bertolt Brecht used to work, then make a detour to visit his home, the **Brecht-Weigel-Gedenkstätte**. Return to Friedrichstraße and walk north to Chausseestraße. Then retrace your steps and turn left into **Oranienburger Straße** (see p95) to get to the heart of fashionable Scheunenviertel. About a 7-minute walk down the street will bring the dome of the **Neue Synagoge** (see p95) into view.

AFTERNOON

Walk down Tucholskystraße and turn right into Auguststraße for some refreshments at **Strandbad Mitte** (Kleine Hamburger Straße 16). After lunch return to Auguststraße. Some of the most picturesque courtyards are to be found here, such as the old-world **Schulhof** (see p99) at No. 21. Just across the street is the **KW Institute for Contemporary Art**. Continue along Auguststraße then turn right for the **Gedenkstätte Große Hamburger Straße** and the **Hackesche Höfe** (see p95). Shop a little, then round off your tour of Scheunenviertel with an evening meal at one of its restaurants.

See map on pp94–5 ←

The Best of the Rest

Exhibit at the Charité museum

1 Charité
MAP J3 ■ Schumannstr. 20–21 ■ (030) 450 536 156 ■ Medizinhistorisches Museum: open 10am–5pm Tue, Thu, Fri, Sun, 10am–7pm Wed & Sat

Many renowned physicians, such as Rudolf Virchow and Robert Koch, worked and taught at this world-famous hospital, founded in 1710. The Museum of Medical History has some 750 remarkable exhibits on display.

2 Alte and Neue Schönhauser Straße
MAP J5 ■ Hackescher Markt

Alte Schönhauser Straße is one of the oldest streets in Spandauer Vorstadt. It is characterized by a colourful jumble of traditional and new fashion shops.

3 Deutsches Theater
MAP J3 ■ Schumannstr. 13A ■ (030) 28 44 12 25 ■ www.deutschestheater.de/english

Once the place of work (see p67) of Max Reinhardt, this theatre – widely considered the best German-language theatre – shows mainly German classics, often in new interpretations.

4 Berliner Ensemble
MAP J3 ■ Bertolt-Brecht-Platz 1 ■ (030) 28 40 81 55

This theatre, established in 1891–2 by Heinrich Seeling, was the main venue for Bertolt Brecht's plays.

5 Hochbunker
MAP J3 ■ Reinhardtstr 20 ■ www.sammlung-boros.de

One of the last surviving World War II bunkers in Berlin, the imposing Hochbunker now houses the Boros Collection gallery (see p62).

6 Monbijoupark
MAP J5 ■ Oranienburger Str./Spree

A small park, in which once stood the little Monbijou palace, Monbijoupark is a great spot for a break.

7 Auguststraße
MAP G2 ■ Between Oranienburger Str. & Rosenthaler Str.

The area round this road harks back to old Scheunenviertel, with courtyards and art galleries.

8 Koppenplatz
MAP G2 ■ Near Auguststr.

In this small square, a monument of a table and upturned chair recall the expulsion of the Jews.

9 Sophienkirche
MAP G3 ■ Große Hamburger Str. 29

This parish church, built in 1712, has managed to preserve its traditional old Berlin charm. Be sure not to miss the Baroque pulpit.

The imposing Baroque Sophienkirche

10 Tucholskystraße
MAP J4

This narrow street is typical of the transformation of Scheunenviertel – trendy shops next to both decaying and beautifully renovated façades.

Old Courtyards

Sophie-Gips-Höfe
MAP G3 ■ Sophienstr. 21–22

Famous for the Hoffman art collection, which is based here, this former sewing machine factory is a popular meeting place.

2 Sophienhöfe
MAP G3 ■ Sophienstr. 17–18

The 19th-century red-brick artisans' workshops have been transformed into artists' studios and a theatre.

Courtyards of Heckmann-Höfe

3 Heckmann-Höfe
MAP G3 ■ Between Oranienburger Str. 32 and Auguststraße 9

These lavishly restored yards in a candy factory attract visitors with a restaurant and fashionable shops.

4 Sophienstr. 22 and 22A
MAP G3

Two small inner courtyards, partially planted, are surrounded by yellow and red-brick walls.

5 Rosenthaler Straße 37
MAP J5

This green-tiled courtyard is unique. Once part of the Wertheim department store, it now houses a boutique and tapas bar. The 1775 townhouse through which it is accessed has a beautiful wooden staircase.

6 Schulhof
MAP G2 ■ Auguststr. 21

Time seems to have stood still around 1900 in this courtyard, which houses an elementary school.

7 Hof Auguststraße 5A
MAP G3

The extensive courtyard of the former Postfuhramt permits a glimpse of the original façade of the building.

8 Rosenthaler Straße 39
MAP J5

Berlin's post-Wall subculture of edgy art collectives is still alive and well in this unrenovated courtyard.

9 Kunsthof
MAP J4 ■ Oranienburger Str. 27

A courtyard full of nooks and crannies, which is today occupied by a number of workshops, offices and cafés. Take a look at the richly ornamented staircases.

10 Kunst-Werke (KW)
MAP G2 ■ Auguststr. 69

Large-scale installations by the resident artists are regularly on display at this well-known centre for contemporary art; artists-in-residence have included Susan Sontag. The courtyard has a café designed by US artist and curator Dan Graham in the conservatory.

The Kunst-Werke courtyard

See map on pp94–5

Pubs, Bars and Nightclubs

Buck and Breck
MAP G2 ▪ Brunnenstr. 177
▪ Open from 6pm daily

A bar with an intimate setting, this place specializes in fine cocktails.

2 Weinbar Rutz
MAP F2 ▪ Chausseestr. 8 ▪ (030) 24 62 87 60 ▪ Open 4–11pm Tue–Sat

Taste the best wines from the wine list offered here (see p73).

3 B-flat
MAP G3 ▪ Dircksenstr. 40 ▪ (030) 283 31 23 ▪ Open from 8pm Sun, Wed & Thu (from 6:30pm Fri & Sat)

Live jazz, and occasionally dancing, are on offer at this small venue.

4 Reingold
MAP F2 ▪ Novalistr. 11 ▪ (030) 28 38 7676 ▪ Open 8pm–2am Wed & Thu (until 5am Fri & Sat)

A relaxed bar with a 1920s ambience, Reingold is perfect for a nightcap.

5 Hackbarth's
MAP G2 ▪ Auguststr. 49A ▪ (030) 282 77 04 ▪ Open 10am–4am daily

This breakfast café transforms into a bar by sun down, serving beer on tap.

6 Mr. Susan
MAP J4 ▪ Krausnickstraße 1 ▪ Open from 6pm Wed–Sat ▪ www.mrsusan.com

A modern cocktail bar serving creative drinks. It hosts occasional brunch pop-up events as well.

7 Anna Koschke
MAP J2 ▪ Krausnickstr. 11 ▪ (030) 283 55 38 ▪ Open 5pm–1am Mon–Thu, 5pm–3am Fri & Sat

This neighbourhood pub is popular with locals and students. The *boulletten* (meat balls) here are legendary.

8 Yosoy
MAP J5 ▪ Rosenthaler Str. 37 ▪ (030) 28 39 12 13 ▪ Open from 11am daily

Tasty tapas, good wines and exciting cocktails are served at this attractively furnished Spanish restaurant – which is why it is usually crowded late into the night.

9 Mein Haus am See
MAP G2 ▪ Brunnenstr. 197-198 ▪ (030) 27 59 08 73 ▪ www.mein-haus-am-see.club

Open 24 hours a day, this café and bar (see p71) is popular with locals, especially on weekends. Reservations should be made online, in advance.

10 Oxymoron
MAP J5 ▪ Rosenthaler Str. 40–41 ▪ (030) 28 39 18 86 ▪ Open from 10am daily

This small bar, club and restaurant in popular and lively Hackesche Höfe (see p95) features chintz decoration and serves light German and international meals.

The vibrant interior of Mr. Susan

Restaurants

PRICE CATEGORIES
For a three-course meal for one with half
a bottle of wine (or equivalent meal),
taxes and charges included.

€ under €30 €€ €30–60 €€€ over €60

1 Chen Che
MAP G2 ▪ Rosenthaler Str. 13
▪ (030) 28 88 42 82 ▪ Open noon–
midnight daily ▪ €€

This Vietnamese teahouse-style
restaurant offers fresh food and
has a tranquil bamboo garden.

2 Rutz
MAP F2 ▪ Chausseestr. 8
▪ (030) 24 62 87 60 ▪ Open 6:30–
10pm Tue–Sat ▪ €€€

Enjoy exceptional dishes created
using local ingredients at this cosy
restaurant (see p75).

3 Monsieur Vuong
MAP G2 ▪ Alte Schönhauser
Str. 46 ▪ (030) 99 29 69 24 ▪ Open
noon–midnight daily ▪ €

This tiny Vietnamese snack joint
serves delicious Asian dishes.

4 Frea
MAP G2 ▪ Torstr. 180, cnr. of
Kleine Hamburger Str. ▪ (030) 98 39
61 98 ▪ Open 5:30pm–midnight ▪ €€

This sustainable restaurant serves
organic, plant-based food made with
zero-waste practices.

5 Beth-Café
MAP G2 ▪ Tucholskystr. 40
▪ (030) 281 31 35 ▪ Open 11am–8pm
Sun–Thu (until 5pm Fri) ▪ No credit
cards ▪ €

Small Jewish café of the Adass-
Jisroel community, serving Jewish
snacks and kosher wines and beers.

6 Hackescher Hof
MAP J5 ▪ Rosenthaler Str. 40–41
▪ (030) 283 52 93 ▪ Open from 8am
Mon–Fri (from 9am Sat & Sun) ▪ €€

The best restaurant in Hackesche
Höfe serves delicious local produce.

Interior of Bandol Sur Mer

7 Bandol sur Mer
MAP G2 ▪ Torstraße 167
▪ (030) 67 30 20 51 ▪ Open 6–10pm
Thu–Mon ▪ €€€

A prestigious Michelin-starred
restaurant, Bandol sur Mer (see p75)
is casual with a bistro-style open
kitchen. They offer flavourful French
dishes which are beautifully plated.

8 Gärtnerei
MAP G2 ▪ Torstr. 179 ▪ (030) 24
63 14 50 ▪ Open 6pm–11:30pm daily
▪ €€€

A chic Michelin–starred restaurant,
Gärtnerei serves German dishes,
accompanied by predominantly
Austrian wines. The menu also
offers plenty of vegetarian options.

9 Kamala
MAP J4 ▪ Oranienburger
Str. 69 ▪ (030) 283 27 97 ▪ Open
noon–11:30pm daily ▪ €€

This hidden gem offers diners
traditional Thai cuisine alongside an impressive wine list.
Kamala is good value for money.

10 Coccodrillo
MAP G2 ▪ Veteranenstr. 9
▪ Open 11:45am–2:45pm & 5:30pm–
midnight Mon–Fri, 10:30am–1pm Sat
& Sun ▪ www.bigsquadra.com/en/
restaurants/coccodrillo-berlin ▪ €€

The all-Italian staff here serves
traditional Italian food in a gleaming
1950s-style setting.

See map on pp94–5

🔟 Central Berlin: Around Alexanderplatz

The area around Alexanderplatz – "Alex" to locals – is one of the city's oldest parts. It was here that the twin towns of Cölln and Berlin merged in the 13th century. The square defined the heartbeat of the city before World War II; after the ravages of war, it seemed vast and a little forlorn, but its vibrancy described by Alfred Döblin in his novel *Berlin Alexanderplatz* has slowly returned. A short walk away is the city's oldest coherent quarter – the 18th-century Nikolaiviertel – with its medieval Nikolaikirche.

Rotes Rathaus

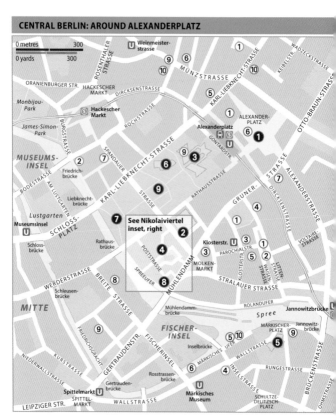

CENTRAL BERLIN: AROUND ALEXANDERPLATZ

0 metres 300
0 yards 300

Alexanderplatz's Neptunbrunnen with Marienkirche in the background

1 Alexanderplatz
MAP J6 ■ Mitte

The huge, largely desolate square in the centre of East Berlin, called "Alex" by Berliners, was one of the most vibrant places in Berlin before World War II. Alfred Döblin beautifully captured the rhythm of the city in his famous novel *Berlin Alexanderplatz* (1929). Not much remains today of the once frenzied atmosphere, although there is plenty of bustle around the Galeria department store *(see p107)*. Alexanderplatz was originally a cattle and wool market. Not many of the prewar buildings have survived – only Berolinahaus and Alexanderhaus remain, next to Alexanderplatz, the historic S-Bahn station, both dating back to 1929. The square was almost completely laid to waste in World War II, and most of the surrounding soulless tower blocks were built in the 1960s.

2 Rotes Rathaus
MAP K6 ■ Rathausstr. 15 ■ (030) 90 26 20 32 ■ Open 9am–6pm Mon–Fri

Berlin's proud town hall *(see p50)*, the office of the Governing Mayor, is the political centre of power in Greater Berlin. It was built in 1861–9 to a design by Hermann Friedrich Waesemann on the site of an older town hall. The Rathaus was meant to demonstrate the power and the glory of Berlin, and the architect took his inspiration for the new building from Italian Renaissance *palazzi*. The building is known as the *Rotes Rathaus* (Red Town Hall) – not a reference to its Socialist past, but to the red bricks from Brandenburg province with which it is built.

3 Berliner Fernsehturm

MAP J6 ▪ Panoramastr. 1a
▪ (030) 24 75 75 37 ▪ Open Mar–
Oct: 9am–midnight; Nov–Feb:
10am–midnight ▪ Adm ▪ www.
tv-turm.de/en

The 368-m- (1,207-ft-) high TV tower
is the tallest building in Berlin,
affording views of up to 40 km
(25 miles). There is a viewing
platform at 203 m (666 ft).
The Sphere restaurant above
rotates around its own axis
once every 30 minutes. The
tower, visible from afar, was
erected in 1965–9 by the
East German government
to signify the triumph of
their capital East Berlin.

4 Nikolaiviertel

MAP K6 ▪ Mitte
▪ Knoblauchhaus: Poststr.
23 ▪ Open 10am–6pm Tue–
Sun ▪ Adm ▪ www.en.
stadtmuseum.de

Märkisches Museum

Centred around the medieval
Nikolaikirche *(see p48)*, the
small Nikolaiviertel quarter with its
nooks and crannies, souvenir shops
and old Berlin restaurants is one of
the most charming parts of the city.
The area extending between the
banks of the Spree River and
Mühlendamm was razed to the
ground in World War II. East
Germany restored it after the war,
unfortunately not always

successfully: some houses were
covered in prefabricated façades.
Knoblauchhaus was one of few to
escape wartime destruction. Dating
from 1835, it was the former home
of the Knoblauch family (Neue
Synagoge was designed by architect
Eduard Knoblauch). Today it houses
a museum depicting everyday life
in Berlin, and includes a fully
furnished apartment in the
Biedermeier style.

5 Märkisches Museum

MAP L6 ▪ Am Köllnischen
Park 5 ▪ (030) 24 00 21 62
▪ Closed for renovation
until 2026 ▪ www.en.
stadtmuseum.de

Berlin's municipal museum
holds artifacts relating to
the city's culture and history, including architectural
treasures such as doorways
and the head of one of the
horses from the top of
the Brandenburg Gate. There
is also a Gothic Chapel room with a
collection of medieval sculptures.

6 Marienkirche

MAP J6 ▪ Karl-Liebknecht-Str. 8
▪ (030) 242 44 67 ▪ Open 10am–6pm
Mon–Sat, noon–6pm Sun

Originally built in 1270, Marienkirche
(see p48) was extensively remodelled
in the 15th century. Thanks to its
Baroque church tower, it is one of
Berlin's loveliest churches. Inside, the
alabaster pulpit by Andreas Schlüter
(1703) and the main altar (1762) are
highlights. The 15th-century Gothic
font and a 22-m (72-ft) long fresco
from 1485, *Der Totentanz* (The Dance
of Death), are its two oldest treasures.
The church is now the only reminder
of the once densely built-up historic
city core here.

7 Marx-Engels-Forum

MAP K5

This public park was founded by
East German authorities shortly
after German reunification in 1989.
The words "Next time it will all be

Buildings in the Nikolaiviertel

different" were scrawled onto the bronze monument to Friedrich Engels and Karl Marx, the fathers of Socialism, erected in 1986.

8 Ephraim-Palais

MAP K6 ■ Poststr. 16 ■ (030) 24 00 21 62 ■ Open 10am–6pm Tue–Sun ■ Adm ■ www.en.stadt museum.de

This Rococo palace, built in 1766 for the merchant, court jeweller and mint master Nathan Veitel Heinrich Ephraim, was once regarded as the city's most beautiful spot. Rebuilt using original elements after the old palace was demolished, it houses a museum on Berlin art history.

9 Neptunbrunnen

MAP K6 ■ Am Rathaus

The green Neo-Baroque fountain, dating from 1895, depicts the sea god Neptune. He is surrounded by four female figures, symbolizing Prussia's main rivers at the time: the Rhine, Weichsel, Oder and Elbe.

Neptunbrunnen, Alexanderplatz

10 Karl-Marx-Allee and Frankfurter Allee

MAP H3 ■ Mitte/Friedrichshain

This avenue, lined by Soviet-style buildings, was built as a showpiece for Socialism in 1949–55. Known then as "Stalinallee", it provided ultra-modern apartments that are again in high demand today.

A DAY AROUND ALEXANDERPLATZ

> ### MORNING

Start your day at Strausberger Platz where you can admire the products of Socialist architecture lining Frankfurter Allee and **Karl-Marx-Allee**. Then take the U-Bahn (or continue on foot) to the vast **Alexanderplatz** (see p103) where you can indulge in a bit of people-watching or shopping before heading to the beautiful **Marienkirche**. Step back outside to admire the lovely **Neptunbrunnen** fountain a few steps away, then walk to the **Berliner Fernsehturm** and – if the weather is nice – take the lift up to the viewing platform. Afterwards, stroll past **Rotes Rathaus** (see p103) towards **Marx-Engels-Forum**, which houses statues of the two revolutionaries, and head to the Schlüterhof. For lunch with a view, pop into **Zillestube** (see p109); the outdoor seating here is a particular draw.

AFTERNOON

After lunch, cross **Schloßlatz** (see p88) to walk along the canal and Friedrichsgracht and turn left into Gertraudenstraße and Petriplatz until you find **Brüderstraße** (see p106), which features two historic townhouses. Continue on Breite Straße, turn left to Grunerstraße and cross the Spree River at Mühlendammbrücke. To the left is the old **Nikolaiviertel** quarter, with its narrow alleyways and nooks. The Nikolaikirche museum is especially worth a visit. Round off your day with a meal at **Zur Gerichtslaube** (see p109).

See map on pp102–3

The Best of the Rest

① Franziskaner-Klosterkirche

MAP K6 ▪ Klosterstr. 74
▪ Open 10am–6pm daily

Remnants of a 13th-century Franciscan abbey, these ruins are surrounded by lawns, making this a picturesque spot for a break.

Detail, Parochialkirche

② Stadtmauer

MAP K6 ▪ Waisenstr.

A fragment of the 13th–14th-century town wall that once surrounded the twin towns of Berlin and Cölln.

③ Palais Podewil

MAP K6 ▪ Klosterstr. 68
▪ (030) 24 74 96

The light yellow Baroque palace, built in 1701–4, has been transformed into Podewil, a cultural centre, and a subsidiary of the Grips-Theater (see p64).

④ Stadtgericht

MAP K6 ▪ Littenstr. 13–15
▪ Open 9am–1pm Mon–Fri

The imposing municipal courts building features extravagant stairs in the lobby area, with curved balustrades and elegant columns.

Decorative balustrades at Stadtgericht

⑤ Parochialkirche

MAP K6 ▪ Klosterstr. 67
▪ Open 9am–3:30pm Mon–Fri

This church, by Johann Arnold Nering and Martin Grünberg, was one of Berlin's most charming Baroque churches, but the interior and bell tower were destroyed in World War II. In 2016, a replica of the tower was mounted, bearing a new carillon with 52 bells.

⑥ Märkisches Ufer

MAP L6

This picturesque riverside promenade gives a good impression of the city in the late 18th century. Look out for No. 12, a typical Berlin Baroque house that was initially built on Fischerinsel in 1740 and transplanted here in 1969.

⑦ Heilig-Geist-Kapelle

MAP J5 ▪ Spandauer Str. 1

A beautiful example of Gothic brick architecture, this hospital church was built around 1300.

⑧ Ribbeckhaus

MAP K5 ▪ Breite Str. 36

The only Renaissance house in central Berlin, with a remarkable, lavishly ornamented façade.

⑨ Brüderstraße

MAP L5

This little street behind Petriplatz has a rich historic past. Two of the few surviving 17th-century Berlin town houses are located here. Palais Happe at Brüderstraße 10 now houses the art gallery Kewenig.

⑩ Historischer Hafen

MAP L6 ▪ Märkisches Ufer
▪ (030) 21 47 32 57 ▪ Museum: open May–Sep: 1–6pm Sat & Sun

Moored at this port are barges and tugboats that once operated on the Spree. The *Renate-Angelika* hosts a historical display on inland shipping.

Shops and Markets

Vast interiors of the Galeria Kaufhof

1 Galeria
MAP J6 ■ Alexanderplatz 9
■ (030) 24 74 30 ■ Open 9:30am–
8pm Mon–Sat
The largest department store in
eastern Berlin stocks everything
your heart could desire. Its food
department entices with a range
of international gourmet foods.

2 Die Puppenstube
MAP K6 ■ Propststr. 4
■ (030) 242 39 67 ■ Open 9am–
6:30pm Mon–Sat, 11am–6pm Sun
Adorable dolls made from
porcelain and other materials
await, as do mountains of cute
fluffy teddy bears.

3 Teddy's
MAP K6 ■ Propststr. 4
■ (030) 247 82 44 ■ Open
10am–6pm daily
An old-fashioned toy store
with probably the city's best
selection of teddy bears,
including brands like Steiff.
They also have bear clothing
and accessories.

4 TeeGschwendner
MAP K6 ■ Propststr. 3
■ (030) 242 32 55 ■ Open
10am–7pm Mon–Sat
A charming specialist tea shop
opposite Nikolaikirche, full of
delicious scents. They carry
more than 300 varieties of tea.

5 Ausberlin
MAP J6 ■ Karl-Liebknecht
Str. 9 ■ (030) 97 00 56 40 ■ Open
10am–8pm Mon–Sat
Whimsical stock, with a fashion
focus, all created in Berlin. Exclusive
designer items include Breath of
Berlin perfume, bags and T-shirts.

6 U- and S-Bahnhof Alexanderplatz
MAP J6 ■ Alexanderplatz
This bustling area has a selection
of shops for daily needs, plus late-
opening fast food outlets and
German *imbisse* (food stands).

7 Alexa
MAP K6 ■ Am Alexanderplatz,
Grunerstr. 20 ■ (030) 269 34 00
■ Open 10am–9pm Mon–Sat
This mall houses some 180 retail
outlets, such as Build-a-Bear
Workshop, where kids assemble
their own teddy, and LOXX, the
world's largest digitally operated
model train set.

8 Erzgebirgischer Weihnachtsmarkt
MAP K6 ■ Propststr. 8 ■ (030) 241
12 29 ■ Open 11am–6pm Mon–Sun
A vast array of stalls laden with a
range of German handicrafts,
including traditional wooden
nutcrackers and Plauen lace.

Wooden nutcracker

9 Münzstraße
MAP J6
This tiny street, just
off Alexanderplatz, is
full of original fashion
boutiques and designer
stores. A real hotspot for
fashion aficionados.

10 Wood Wood
MAP J6 ■ Rochstr.
3/4 ■ (030) 28 04 78 77
■ Open noon–6pm Mon–Sat
This flagship store stocks highly
curated men's and women's
designer wear, plus its own line.

See map on pp102–3

Pubs, Cafés and Beer Gardens

1 Zur letzten Instanz
MAP K6 ▪ Waisenstr. 14–16 ▪ (030) 242 55 28 ▪ Open noon–midnight Tue–Sun

Berlin's oldest pub dates back to 1621, and former guests include Napoleon, Beethoven, German artist Heinrich Zille, former Soviet leader Mikhael Gorbachev and Angela Merkel.

2 Zum Nußbaum
MAP K6 ▪ Am Nußbaum 3 ▪ (030) 242 30 95 ▪ Open noon–midnight

This charming historic pub (see p73) in Nikolaiviertel serves draught beers and Berliner Weiße in summer.

3 The Greens
MAP H3 ▪ Am Molkenmarkt 2 ▪ Open 10am–6pm Mon–Fri, noon–6pm Sat & Sun ▪ www.the-greens-berlin.de

A hidden café which offers coffee, tea and snacks amidst potted plants.

4 Brauhaus Georgbräu
MAP K6 ▪ Spreeufer 4 ▪ (030) 242 42 44 ▪ Open summer: 10am–midnight daily; winter: from noon daily

Attracting both Bavarians and tourists, this beer garden offers rustic fare and beer from both Berlin and Munich.

German pub food at Zur letzten Instanz

5 Hafenbar-Fischerinsel
MAP H4 ▪ Märkisches Ufer 28 ▪ (030) 21 79 14 04 ▪ Open May–Oct: noon–11pm Wed–Sun

This restaurant is on the deck of a historical tugboat, the *Renate-Angelika*. Enjoy a beer here, alongside their famous potato salad.

6 Café Oliv
MAP J6 ▪ Münzstr. 8 ▪ (030) 89 20 65 40 ▪ Open 8:30am–6pm Mon–Fri, 9:30am–7pm Sat, 10am–6pm Sun

Trendy Berliners get their organic sandwiches, flat whites and home-baked cakes from this sleek venue.

7 Café Ephraim's
MAP K6 ▪ Spreeufer 1 ▪ (030) 24 72 59 47 ▪ Open noon–11pm daily ▪ No credit cards

Hearty German food and excellent coffee and cakes added to the great views of the Spree River attract both locals and tourists.

8 tigertörtchen
MAP K6 ▪ Spandauer Str. 25 ▪ (030) 67 96 90 51 ▪ Open 8am–6pm Thu–Tue

Come here for inventive cupcake creations such as date and walnut or crab and dill.

9 Marinehaus
MAP L6 ▪ Märkisches Ufer 48–50 ▪ (030) 279 32 46 ▪ Open noon–late daily

Traditional pub with maritime decor, serving German food.

10 Hofbräu Wirtshaus
MAP H3 ▪ Karl-Liebknecht-Straße 30 ▪ (030) 679 66 55 20 ▪ Open noon–11pm Mon–Fri, 10pm–midnight Sat & Sun

Enjoy southern German dishes at this Bavarian beer garden.

Interior, Brauhaus Georgbräu

Restaurants

PRICE CATEGORIES
For a three-course meal for one with half
a bottle of wine (or equivalent meal),
taxes and charges included.

€ under €30   €€ €30–60   €€€ over €60

 The Grand
MAP J6 ■ Hirtenstrasse 4
■ (030) 278 909 95 55 ■ Open from
7pm daily ■ €€
The lavish restaurant at The Grand
is famous for its outstanding steaks.

 **Alois Moser –
Alpenküche**
MAP K5 ■ Anna-Luise-Karsch-Straße 2
■ (030) 30 87 77 517 ■ Open 10am–
10pm Mon–Sun ■ €€
Cosy restaurant with an Austrian
menu and views of the Museum
Island and the Berliner Dom.

 Zur Gerichtslaube
MAP K6 ■ Poststr. 28 ■ (030)
241 56 98 ■ Open 11:30am–1am
daily ■ €€
The former court building is a stylish
setting for traditional Berlin specialities such as Prussian sausages.

 **MAMMAM Street
Food Mitte**
MAP L6 ■ Inselstr. 8 ■ (030) 247 223
655 ■ Open 11am–9pm daily ■ €€
Sample street-food-inspired dishes
from Vietnam and Thailand at this
cosy spot.

 Zum Paddenwirt
MAP K6 ■ Nikolaikirchplatz
6 ■ (030) 242 63 82 ■ Open from
noon daily ■ No credit cards ■ €€
A must for fans of traditional Berlin
food, including fried herrings and
brawn, and a strong beer.

 Zillestube
MAP K6 ■ Propststr. 9
■ (030) 242 52 47 ■ Open from
11am daily ■ €
Named after the 19th-century Berlin
illustrator and photographer

The simple interior of Zillestube

Heinrich Zille, this rustic pub serves
hearty Berlin food and beers.

 Fischer & Lustig
MAP K5 ■ Poststr. 26 ■ (030)
56 82 99 90 ■ Open noon–midnight
■ www.fischerundlustig.de ■ €€
With a a large menu of fish dishes,
Fischer & Lustig serves regional
cuisine made with locally sourced
ingredients. The courtyard tables are
especially popular during summer.

 Balthasar Spreeufer 2
MAP K6 ■ Spreeufer 2
■ (030) 30 88 21 56 ■ Open
noon–10pm daily ■ €€
Enjoy German and international
cuisine with fusion dishes such as
tagliatelle with a ginger and tomato
sauce, and many more meat- and
fish-based mains.

 Fernsehturm Sphere
MAP J6 ■ Panoramastr. 1a
■ (030) 242 59 22 ■ Open 10am–
midnight daily ■ €€
This revolving restaurant in the TV
Tower offers superb views and Berlin-
Brandenburg specialities, including
cod with beetroot and potato purée.

 Mutter Hoppe
MAP K6 ■ Rathausstr. 21
■ (030) 241 56 25 ■ Open from
11:30am daily ■ €€
Gigantic portions of delicious German
food make up for the brusque service.

See map on pp102–3 ←

ⓉⓄⓅ10 The Tiergarten and Federal District

In 1999, Berlin's green centre became the government district. Around the Tiergarten, Berlin's largest park, stand the Reichstag, the Bundeskanzleramt and Schloss Bellevue, official residence of the President of the Federal Republic of Germany. The sprawling Tiergarten itself is a great place for strolling and cycling, and it also offers access to the Landwehrkanal, the Neuer See, the Spree River and Berlin's zoo. In summer, its lawns are used for picnics, sunbathing and casual sports.

Sowjetisches Ehrenmal

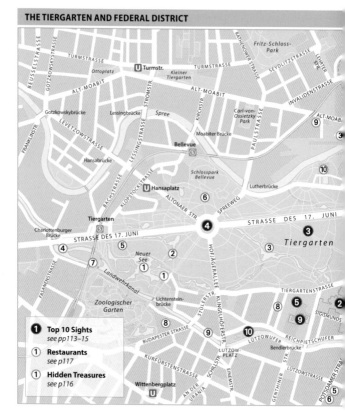

THE TIERGARTEN AND FEDERAL DISTRICT

1 Top 10 Sights
see pp113–15

1 Restaurants
see p117

1 Hidden Treasures
see p116

Previous pages Early summer in the lovely wooded environs of Berlin's Großer Tiergarten

The majestic Reichstag with its beautiful modern dome

1 Reichstag

More than any of the other landmarks in Berlin, the Reichstag (see pp14–15), the seat of the German parliament, has come to symbolize German history.

2 Kulturforum

This unique complex (see pp38–41) of modern buildings features the best museums and concert halls in western Berlin.

3 Großer Tiergarten
MAP E4 ▪ Tiergarten

The Großer Tiergarten (see p60) is Berlin's largest park, straddling an area of 200 hectares (494 acres) between the eastern and western parts of the town. Formerly the Elector's hunting grounds, it was redesigned in the 1830s as a park by Peter Joseph Lenné. At the end of the 19th century, the Siegesallee was established in the east of the park, more than 500 m (1,640 ft) in length, lined by statues of monarchs and politicians. After World War II, the starving and freezing population chopped down nearly all the trees for firewood and dug up the lawns to grow food. Thanks to reforestation since the 1950s, the Tiergarten, today, is one of Berlin's favourite green spaces and the lungs of the city.

4 Siegessäule
MAP M6 ▪ Großer Stern ▪ Adm

In the middle of the Tiergarten stands the 62-m- (203-ft-) high Victory Column (see p51), erected to commemorate Prussian victory against Denmark in the war of 1864. After victory over Austria in 1866 and France 1871, the structure was crowned by a 35-ton gilded statue of the goddess Victoria. There are great views from the viewing platform, 285 steps up.

PETER JOSEPH LENNÉ

Lenné (1789–1866), one of Germany's most influential landscape architects, was born into a family of gardeners in Bonn. He studied in Paris and joined the Royal Gardens in Potsdam as an apprentice in 1816. There he met Schinkel and together they set out to design the parks of Berlin and Potsdam in the harmonious style of the time.

The Sowjetisches Ehrenmal

⑤ Diplomatenviertel

MAP E4 ■ Between Stauffenbergstr. and Lichtensteinallee as well as along Tiergartenstr.

In the late 19th century, an embassy district sprang up. Most structures were destroyed during World War II, and the buildings were left to decay until German reunification. After the government moved back to Berlin from Bonn in 1999, new life was breathed into the diplomats' quarter and, thanks to its adventurous architecture, it is now one of Berlin's most interesting areas. Especially worth seeing are the Austrian and Indian embassies on Tiergartenstraße, the Nordic embassies (see p53) on Rauchstraße and the Mexican embassy on Klingelhöferstraße.

⑥ Hamburger Bahnhof

MAP F2 ■ Invalidenstr. 50–51 ■ Open 10am–6pm Tue–Fri (until 8pm Thu), 11am–6pm Sat & Sun ■ Adm ■ www.smb.museum

This former railway station (see p57) is now the Museum für Gegenwart (Museum of the Present Day) and holds contemporary works of art. One of the highlights is the private collection of Erich Marx, with works by Beuys and others.

⑦ Sowjetisches Ehrenmal

MAP K2 ■ Str. des 17. Juni

The Soviet Memorial was opened on 7 November 1945, the anniversary of the Russian October Revolution. It is flanked by two tanks, supposedly the first to reach Berlin. The memorial commemorates the 300,000 Red Army soldiers who died during World War II in the fight to liberate Berlin. A legend persists that the large column was made from the marble blocks of Hitler's Reich Chancellery. Designed by Nicolai Sergijevski, the column is crowned by a bronze statue by Lev Kerbel. Behind the memorial, 2,500 Russian soldiers are buried.

⑧ Potsdamer Platz

MAP F4

Ravaged by World War II, Potsdamer Platz (see pp20–23) remained a wasteland for the succeeding 40 years. In the 1990s, Europe's largest construction site created this hub, taking five years to build. Today, it is one of the busiest squares in Berlin. Adjoined to the east is the Leipziger Platz, featuring the Mall of Berlin. To the southwest is the Kulturforum, where you can find the Berlin Philharmonic and the Gemäldegalerie.

Wall exhibit at Hamburger Bahnhof

9 Gedenkstätte Deutscher Widerstand

MAP E4 ▪ Stauffenbergstr. 13–14
▪ (030) 26 99 50 00 ▪ Open 9am–
6pm Mon–Wed & Fri (until 8pm Thu),
10am–6pm Sat & Sun ▪ www.gdw-
berlin.de/en

Today known as Bendlerblock, this
1930s complex lies behind the former
Prussian Ministry of War. During
World War II it served as army headquarters. It was here that a group of
officers planned the assassination
of Adolf Hitler. The attempt failed
on 20 July 1944 and Claus Schenk
Count von Stauffenberg and others
were arrested. Many of them were
shot in the courtyard during the
night. A memorial, created by Richard
Scheibe in 1953, commemorates
these events. On the upper floor is
a small exhibition documenting the
German resistance against the Nazi
regime. The Bendlerblock has been
incorporated into the Berlin branch
of the Federal Ministry of Defence.

Gedenkstätte Deutscher Widerstand

10 Villa von der Heydt

MAP E4 ▪ Von-der-Heydt-Str.
18 ▪ www.preussischer-kulturbesitz.
de/en

This late Neo-Classical villa, built
in 1860–61 by architects Hermann
Ende and G A Linke for one of the
city's most elegant residential areas
at the time, is one of the few extant
examples of the architectural villa
style typical of the Tiergarten. The
Prussian Heritage Foundation now
has its headquarters here.

A DAY OUT AROUND TIERGARTEN

▶ MORNING

Start your tour of the
Tiergarten near the **Reichstag**
(see pp14–15). Explore the government district starting with the
Bundeskanzleramt (Federal
Chancellor's Office). Stop at **Käfer
im Reichstag** (see p117) in the
Reichstag building for breakfast.
Via John-Foster-Dulles-Allee you
will pass the **Carillon** (see p116)
and the Haus der Kulturen der
Welt on the way to **Großer
Tiergarten** (see p113). Continue
along one of the paths into the
park, directly opposite the old
Kongresshalle, until you reach
Straße des 17. Juni. Turn right
to go towards **Siegessäule** (see
p113). From there continue along
Fasanerieallee in a southwesterly
direction until you reach **Café am
Neuen See** (see p117) for lunch.

AFTERNOON

After lunch, take a stroll through
the Diplomatenviertel. From
Neuer See, it is only a few steps
east along Lichtensteinallee and
Thomas-Dehler-Straße until
you get to Rauchstraße with its
Scandinavian embassies. On
Tiergartenstraße you will pass,
among others, the embassies
of Japan, Italy, India and Austria.
Head towards the **Kulturforum**
(see pp38–41), then walk along
Reichpietschufer and the canal
until you reach the **Neue Nationalgalerie** (see p38) to view works
by artists such as Edvard Munch,
Gerhard Richter and Andy Warhol.
There is a café at the gallery. Stop
for a meal at the Michelin-starred
Vox (see p74) at the Grand Hyatt.

See map on pp112–13

Hidden Treasures

① Neuer See
MAP M5 ■ S-Bahn station Tiergarten

Shimmering in a mysterious emerald green, the largest lake in the Tiergarten is perfect for rowing. Afterwards you can recover in the Café am Neuen See.

② Löwenbrücke
MAP M5 ■ Großer Weg

The Lion Bridge, which leads across a small stream near Neuer See, was built in 1838 and is "suspended" from the sculptures of four lions. This idyllic spot is a favourite meeting point in Berlin.

③ Lortzing-Denkmal
MAP L1 ■ Östlicher Großer Weg

There are 70 statues of philosophers, poets and statesmen in Tiergarten. The statue of the composer Lortzing, at one end of Neuer See, is one of the most beautiful.

④ Houseboats
MAP M4 ■ Str. des 17. Juni, Tiergartenufer

Docked on the banks of the Spree River are some of the few remaining houseboats in Berlin – an idyllic haven in the middle of the city's bustle.

⑤ Gaslights in Tiergarten
MAP M5 ■ At S-Bahn station Tiergarten

With 80 beautiful historic gaslights from different cities illuminating the paths, an evening stroll in the Tiergarten can be a romantic affair.

⑥ Englischer Garten
MAP P3 ■ An der Klopstockstr.

The lovely English-style landscaped garden near Schloss Bellevue is ideal for strolling or relaxing at the Teehaus with coffee and cake.

⑦ Locks
MAP M5 ■ At the Zoo, S-Bahn station Tiergarten

The two Landwehrkanal locks and the quirky Schleusenkrug beer garden (next to the eponymous lock) are very popular with locals and visitors.

Beer garden on the canal

⑧ Estonian Embassy
MAP E4 ■ Hildebrandstr. 5

In a street next to the ruined Greek Embassy, this building is characteristic of the diplomats' quarter.

⑨ Landwehrkanal
MAP M/N5/6 ■ Corneliusstr.

The grassy banks of the 11-km (7-mile) long Landwehrkanal are ideal for chilling out.

⑩ Carillon
MAP K1 ■ John-Foster-Dulles-Allee (Haus der Kulturen der Welt) ■ Open May–Sep: 3pm Sun (open-air concerts)

The *carillon*, officially dedicated in 1987, is the largest of its kind in Europe. The 68 bells are rung every day at noon and 6pm in the 42-m-(138-ft-) high black tower.

The *carillon* tower

Restaurants

PRICE CATEGORIES

For a three-course meal for one with half a bottle of wine (or equivalent meal), taxes and charges included.

€ under €30 ■ €€ €30–60 ■ €€€ over €60

The tastefully decorated Vox

 Café am Neuen See

MAP M5 ■ Tiergarten, Neuer See, Lichtensteinallee 2 ■ (030) 254 49 30 ■ Open Mar–Oct: 9am–11pm daily; Nov–Feb: 10am–8pm Sat & Sun ■ €

On the shore of the lake, this is a restaurant, café and beer garden. The "Italian breakfast" is delicious.

2 Schleusenkrug

MAP M5 ■ Tiergarten-Schleuse ■ (030) 313 99 09 ■ Open noon–midnight Mon–Sat, from 11am Sun (until 7pm winter) ■ No credit cards ■ €

This café, next to a lock, has a beer garden and is popular with students.

3 Zollpackhof

MAP J1 ■ Elisabeth-Abegg-Straße 1 ■ (030) 33 09 97 20 ■ Open noon–11pm daily ■ €€

Huge beer garden under old chestnut trees with views of the Spree River, serving German-Austrian food and Bavarian beer.

4 Käfer im Reichstag

MAP K2 ■ Platz der Republik ■ (030) 22 62 99 35 ■ Open 9am–1pm & 7–11pm Thu–Sat, 9am–1pm Sun ■ €€

An ambitious restaurant, better known for its view than its food.

5 Joseph-Roth-Diele

MAP E5 ■ Potsdamer Str. 75 ■ (030) 26 36 98 84 ■ Open 10am–midnight Mon–Fri ■ €

Popular restaurant/bar serving traditional German food. Cash only.

6 Panama

MAP E5 ■ Potsdamer Straße 91 ■ (030) 983 20 84 35 ■ Open 6–11pm Wed–Fri (from 4pm Sat & Sun) ■ €€

The innovative dishes at Panama are perfect for tapas-style sharing.

7 Vox

MAP F4 ■ Marlene-Dietrich-Platz 2 ■ (030) 25 53 17 72 ■ Open 6:30–11pm daily ■ €€

An elegant restaurant in the Grand Hyatt Hotel, Vox *(see p74)* serves a modern fusion of Asian and international dishes. Do not miss the sushi.

8 Hugos

MAP N5 ■ Budapester Str. 2 ■ (030) 26 02 12 63 ■ Open 6:30–9:30pm Tue–Sat ■ €€€

Excellent gourmet food, stellar views and superb service combine to make Hugos *(see p74)* one of the best. There's also a wine bar and private dining rooms available.

9 Paris-Moskau

MAP J1 ■ Alt-Moabit 141 ■ (030) 394 20 81 ■ Open noon–3pm & 6pm–midnight Mon–Fri (6–10pm Sat) ■ €€

A classic restaurant serving seasonal dishes with an emphasis on game and seafood.

10 Facil

MAP L2 ■ Potsdamer Str. 3 ■ (030) 590 051 234 ■ Open noon–3pm & 7–11pm Mon–Fri ■ €€€

This two-Michelin-starred gourmet restaurant focuses on Mediterranean cuisine. The rooftop dining area is surrounded by bamboo gardens.

See map on pp112–13

TOP 10 Charlottenburg and Spandau

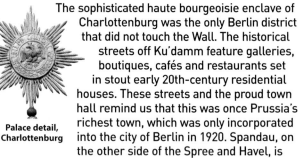

The sophisticated haute bourgeoisie enclave of Charlottenburg was the only Berlin district that did not touch the Wall. The historical streets off Ku'damm feature galleries, boutiques, cafés and restaurants set in stout early 20th-century residential houses. These streets and the proud town hall remind us that this was once Prussia's richest town, which was only incorporated into the city of Berlin in 1920. Spandau, on the other side of the Spree and Havel, is almost rural in comparison, with a Late Medieval core and citadel that make it seem like a small independent town.

Palace detail, Charlottenburg

1 Kurfürstendamm
This famous Berlin boulevard (see pp30–31) was frequented by writers, directors and painters in the interwar years. Today it is a lively avenue lined with designer stores and elegant cafés.

2 Schloss Charlottenburg
The Baroque and English-style gardens of this Hohenzollern summer residence (see pp34–7) are perfect for a stroll. The palace's restored interiors are stunning.

SPANDAU AND BERLIN

Berliners consider the Spandauers to be rather different sorts of people, provincial and rough, and not "real" Berliners at all. But the Spandauers can reassure themselves that Spandau is 60 years older than Berlin, and proudly point to their independent history. The mutual mistrust is not just a result of Spandau's geographical location, isolated from the remainder of the city by the Havel and Spree Rivers. It is also due to the fact that Spandau was only incorporated into Berlin in 1920. Spandauers today still say they are going "to Berlin", even though the city centre is only a few U-bahn stops away.

CHARLOTTENBURG AND SPANDAU

0 metres 500
0 yards 500

3 Zoologischer Garten
MAP N5 ▪ Hardenbergplatz 8
& Budapester Str. 34 ▪ (030) 25 40 10
▪ Open mid-Mar–Sep: 9am–7pm daily
(winter: until 5pm daily) ▪ Adm
▪ www.zoo-berlin.de
Founded in 1844, this is the country's
most prominent zoological garden,
combined with an aquarium.

4 Zitadelle Spandau
Am Juliusturm ▪ (030) 354 94
40 ▪ Open 10am–5pm daily ▪ Adm
▪ www.zitadelle-berlin.de
This citadel, built in 1560 by
Francesco Chiaramella de Gandino,
is sited at the strategic confluence of
the Havel and Spree. The Juliusturm,
a remnant of a fortress that stood
here as early as the 12th century,
was used as a prison in the 19th
century. Later, the reparations paid

The imposing Zitadelle Spandau

by France after its defeat in the
Franco-Prussian War of 1870–71
were kept here. The City History
Museum of Spandau is located in
the former arsenal of the citadel.

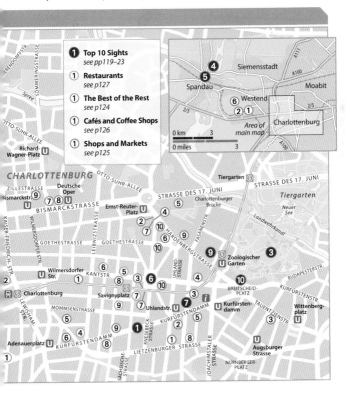

Exterior of the 15th-century Gotisches Haus in Spandau's Altstadt

⑤ Spandau Old Town
Breite Str., Spandau

When walking around Spandau's pedestrianized Old Town (Altstadt), it is easy to forget that you are still in Berlin. The narrow alleyways and nooks and crannies around the 13th-century Nikolaikirche are lined by Late Medieval houses, a reminder that Spandau was founded in 1197 and is older than Berlin itself. The Gotisches Haus – the oldest house in Berlin, dating back to the late 15th century – stands at Breite Straße 32. It was built of stone at a time when most houses were made of wood. It is now the Visitor Information Centre, and some of its rooms are used to showcase finds from the house and other artifacts of the period.

Savignyplatz at night

⑥ Savignyplatz
MAP N3 ■ An der Kantstr.

One of Berlin's stunning squares is right in the heart of Charlottenburg. Savignyplatz, named after a 19th-century German legal scholar, is known as a district for artists and intellectuals as well as for dining out and entertainment. The square has two green spaces, either side of Kantstraße. It was built in the 1920s as part of an effort to create parks in the centre of town. Small paths, benches and pergolas make it a pleasant place for a rest. Dotted all around Savignyplatz are street cafés, restaurants and shops, especially in Grolman-, Knesebeck-, and Carmerstraße, all three of which cross the square. Many have lost their way here after a night out, which is why the area is jokingly known as the "Savignydreieck" (the Savigny Triangle). In the north, you can explore some of the most attractive streets in Charlottenburg, including Knesebeck-, Schlüter- and Goethestraße. This is still a thriving Charlottenburg community; the shops, bookshops, and cafés are always busy, especially on Saturdays. South of the square, the red-tiled S-Bahn arches lure visitors with their shops, cafés and bars, particularly the Savignypassage near Bleibtreustraße and the small passageway between Grolman- and Uhlandstraße on the opposite side of the square.

⑦ Fasanenstraße
MAP N/P4 ■ Charlottenburg

This elegant street is the most attractive and trendiest street off Kurfürstendamm. Designer shops, galleries and restaurants are tucked away in Fasanenstraße along with a retail strip catering to the masses. The junction of Fasanenstraße and Ku´damm is one of the liveliest spots in Berlin. One of the best known places is the Hotel Bristol Berlin, formerly known as the Kempinski, at the northern end of Fasanenstraße. The former bank opposite cleverly combines a historic building with a modern structure. Next to it is the Jüdisches Gemeindehaus (see p124), the Jewish community house and a little further along, at the junction with Kantstraße, is the Kant-Dreieck (see p53). The Berliner Börse (stock exchange), based in the ultra-modern Ludwig-Erhard-Haus (see p53), is just above, at the corner of Hardenbergstraße. The southern end of the street is dominated by residential villas, some of which may seem a little pompous, as well as the Literaturhaus, Villa Grisebach, one of the oldest art auction houses in Berlin. There are also some very expensive fashion stores here, as well as a few cosy restaurants. At its southern end, the street leads to picturesque Fasanenplatz, where many artists lived before 1933.

Antiques store on Fasanenstraße

A DAY IN CHARLOTTENBURG

Stilwerk KantGaragen 270 metres (295 yards)

Ashoka

Carmerstrasse

Museum für Fotographie

Theater des Westens

Breitscheidplatz

Der Kuchenladen

Savignyplatz

Kempinski Hotel Bristol Berlin

Café Wintergarten

Kurfürstendamm

Fasanenstrasse

Mommsenstrasse

▶ MORNING

Begin your tour of Charlottenburg at Breitscheidplatz and head west along **Kurfürstendamm** (see pp30–31). At **Fasanenstraße** turn left to visit the Literaturhaus. You could stop for a mid-morning breakfast at the lovely **Café Wintergarten** (see p126) in the Literaturhaus, before going back up Fasanenstraße in a northerly direction. You will pass the **Hotel Bristol Berlin** (see p172) on the left, and on the right you can see the Jüdisches Gemeindehaus and the Ludwig-Erhard-Haus. Diagonally opposite across Kantstraße stands the **Theater des Westens** (see p67). Turn left and head west along Kantstraße until you reach **Savignyplatz**. Explore the small streets around the square, such as Knesebeck-, Bleibtreu- and Mommsenstraße. Browse the shops for unique gifts. Northwest of the square is the Indian restaurant **Ashoka** (Grolmanstraße 51), which is a great place for lunch. Alternatively, head further west along Kanststraße and lunch at one of the many restaurants there.

AFTERNOON

Carry on west along Kantstraße until you reach **Stilwerk Kant-Garagen** (see p125), an interior design shop and art gallery set in a converted garage. On your way back, visit **Der Kuchenladen** (Kantstraße 138) for some cake and coffee. Head up Kantstraße and Jebensstraße to end your tour at the **Museum für Fotografie** (see p123) where you can marvel at Helmut Newton's iconic Big Nudes.

See map on pp118–19 ←

The Funkturm rising above the old ICC building at the Messegelände

⑧ Funkturm and Messegelände

MAP A4/5 ■ Messedamm 22 ■ (030) 303 80 ■ Open 10am–8pm Mon; tower: open 10am–11pm Tue–Sun ■ Adm ■ www.messe-berlin.de/en

The 150-m-(492-ft-) high Funkturm (TV tower), reminiscent of the Eiffel Tower in Paris, is one of the landmarks of Berlin that can be seen from afar. Built in 1924 to plans by Heinrich Straumer, it served as an aerial and as an air-traffic control tower. The viewing platform at 125 m (410 ft) provides magnificent views, while the restaurant, situated at 55 m (180 ft), overlooks the oldest part of the complex, the exhibition centre and the surrounding pavilions. The giant building in the east is the Hall of Honour built to designs by Richard Ermisch in 1936, in the colossal Fascist architectural style. On the opposite side rises the shiny silver ICC, the International Congress Centrum, built in 1975–9 by Ralf Schüler and Ursulina Schüler-Witte. Once considered one of the world's most advanced conference centres, it has fallen into disrepair and may be demolished. Nearby is the two-tier CityCube, Berlin's new trade fair and conference facility. The ExpoCenter grounds (160,000 sq m/40 acres) around it host International Grüne Woche (Green Week, an agricultural fair), Internationale Tourismus Börse (ITB, a tourism fair) and Internationale Funkausstellung (IFA, the consumer electronics fair).

THE HISTORY OF CHARLOTTENBURG

The magnificent Charlottenburger Rathaus (town hall) on Otto-Suhr-Allee is a reminder of the time when this district of 200,000 people was an independent town. The town, named after the eponymous palace, arose in 1705 from the medieval settlement of Lietzow. Towards the end of the 19th century, Charlottenburg – then the wealthiest town in Prussia – enjoyed a meteoric rise following the construction of the Westend colony of villas and of Kurfürstendamm. Thanks to its numerous theatres, the opera and the Technical University, the district developed into Berlin's west end during the 1920s.

⑨ Museum für Fotografie

MAP N4 ▪ Jebensstr. 2 ▪ Open 10am– 6pm Tue–Sun (until 8pm Thu) ▪ Adm ▪ www.smb.museum

Helmut Newton (1931–2004), the world-famous photographer, has finally returned to his home city. This museum presents changing exhibitions of his early fashion and nude photography, as well as his photos of the famous, rich and beautiful, artfully captured since 1947.

Façade of the Museum für Fotografie

⑩ Kaiser-Wilhelm-Gedächtnis-Kirche

MAP C4

Commonly known as "hollow tooth", this landmark church (see pp32–3) in west Berlin is also an anti-war memorial. The original western tower was the only building left standing on Breitscheidplatz, after the 1943 air raids. Efforts have been made over the years to preserve this grand ruin.

A SPANDAU AND WESTEND WALK

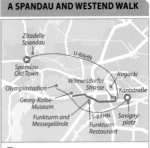

▶ **MORNING**

Start with a journey on the U-Bahn. From the centre of town, take a U2 train in the direction of Ruhleben, and at Bismarckstraße station change to the U7 train in the direction of Rathaus Spandau. Ten minutes later you will have reached the centre of **Spandau Old Town** (see p120), where you can visit Breite Straße and Nikolaikirche. Before returning to Charlottenburg, visit the **Zitadelle Spandau** (see p119). Return by U-Bahn, getting off at the Wilmersdorfer Straße station, one of the few pedestrianized areas in Berlin. This is a particularly good area for shopaholics and bargain hunters. Stop for a fish lunch and a glass of Riesling at the iconic **Rogacki** (see p124).

AFTERNOON

From Wilmersdorfer Straße a 30-minute walk west along Neue Kantstraße will take you to the **Funkturm and Messegelände** with the "Ehrenhalle". Have a well-earned coffee break high above the city's rooftops at the **Funkturm-Restaurant** and enjoy the magnificent views from the observation deck. The Haus des Rundfunks (broadcasting house) nearby and the **Georg-Kolbe-Museum** (see p124), a 25-minute walk away, are worth visiting. Then, take the S-Bahn to the **Olympiastadion** (see p124). In the evening, return to Savignyplatz by S75 from S-Olympiastadion. End your day at one of the many acclaimed Asian restaurants on Kantstraße.

See map on pp118–19 ←

The Best of the Rest

The Fascist-style architecture of the Olympiastadion

1 Georg-Kolbe-Museum
Sensburger Allee 25 ▪ (030) 304
21 44 ▪ Open 10am–6pm daily ▪ Adm
▪ www.georg-kolbe-museum.de
Sculptures by Kolbe (1877–1947) are
exhibited in his home and workshop.

2 Le-Corbusier-Haus
Flatowallee 16
This innovative block was built for
the 1957 Interbau trade fair. French
architect Le Corbusier lived here.

3 Jüdisches Gemeindehaus
MAP P4 ▪ Fasanenstr. 79–80 ▪ (030)
88 02 82 06 ▪ www.jg-berlin.org
The Jewish community house stands
on the site of the Charlottenburg
synagogue. It was damaged during
Kristallnacht on 9 November 1938
and mostly destroyed during World
War II. Only the portal remains.

4 Theater des Westens
MAP N4 ▪ Kantstr. 12 ▪ (0180)
544 44 ▪ Ticket Office: open 1–7:30pm
Tue–Fri (from noon Sat & Sun)
Located in a building from 1895–6,
this theatre (see p67) is regarded
as one of Germany's best
musical theatres.

5 Technische Universität
MAP M4 ▪ Str. des 17. Juni
▪ (030) 31 40 ▪ www.tu.berlin/en
Berlin's Technical University
was founded in 1879.

6 Olympiastadion
Olympischer Platz ▪ (030) 25
00 23 22 ▪ Open mid-Mar–Oct:
9am–7pm daily (until 8pm Aug);
Nov–mid-Mar: 10am–4pm daily
Built for the 1936 Olympic Games,
the stadium is an example of Fascist
architecture favoured by the Nazis.

7 Deutsche Oper
MAP B4 ▪ Bismarckstr. 34–37
▪ (030) 34 38 43 43 ▪ Adm ▪ www.
deutscheoperberlin.de
This opera house (see p66) specializes in Italian and German classics.

8 Denkmal Benno Ohnesorg
MAP B4 ▪ Bismarckstr.
Alfred Hrdlicka's 1971 sculpture
honours student Benno Ohnesorg,
who was shot dead here in
April 1967.

9 Universität der Künste
MAP N4 ▪ Hardenbergstr.
32–33 ▪ (030) 318 50 ▪ www.udk.de
The School of Art is one of the best
German universities for the fine
arts, architecture and design.

10 Renaissance Theater
MAP M3 ▪ Knesebeckstr. 100
▪ (030) 315 97 30 ▪ Tickets: (030) 312
42 02 ▪ www.renaissance-theater.de
A gem of Art Deco architecture,
this little venue has been run as
an actors' theatre since the 1920s.

Shops and Markets

① Stilwerk KantGaragen
MAP N2 ■ Kantstr. 127
■ (030) 315 15 01 ■ Open 10am–
7pm Mon–Sat

A design and lifestyle store located in a converted parking garage *(see p77)*.

Exterior of Manufactum Store

② Manufactum Store
MAP M3 ■ Hardenbergstr. 4-5,
■ (030) 24 03 38 44 ■ Open 10am–
8pm Mon–Fri (until 6pm Sat) ■ www.
manufactum.com

A unique store with a selection of classic textiles, furniture, garden tools, lamps and office supplies.

③ Peek & Cloppenburg
MAP P5 ■ Tauentzienstr. 19
■ (0800) 555 90 50 ■ Open 10am–
8pm Mon–Sat

Offering five floors of men's, women's and children's clothing, this is one of Berlin's most popular stores.

④ Suarezstraße
MAP A4/B5 ■ Schlüterstra. 37
■ www.suarezstrasse.com

To the west of Charlottenburg, this street is lined by around 30 antique stores. Visitors can find furniture, textiles, art objects and more.

⑤ TITUS Berlin Zoopreme
MAP P4 ■ Meinekestr. 2
■ (030) 32 59 32 39 ■ Open 10am–
8pm Mon–Sat

The latest must-have labels are stocked at this streetwear store.

⑥ Veronica Pohle
MAP P2 ■ Kurfürstendamm 64
■ (030) 883 37 31 ■ Open 11am–6pm
Mon–Sat

This multi-label store specializes in evening and party dresses.

⑦ Bücherbogen
MAP N3 ■ Stadtbahnbogen 593
■ (030) 31 86 95 11 ■ Open 11am–
6pm Mon–Thu (until 7pm Fri & Sun)

Berlin's leading arts and photography bookseller, it is situated under the S-Bahn viaduct at Savignyplatz.

⑧ Patrick Hellmann
MAP P2 ■ Bleibtreustr. 36
■ (030) 88 48 77 16/19 ■ Open
10am–7pm Mon–Sat

Gentlemen's fashions made from the best materials, including Hellmann's own collection and clothes from well-known designers can be found here.

⑨ Rogacki
MAP P4 ■ Wilmersdorfer Str.
145/6 ■ (030) 343 82 50 ■ Open
10am–6pm Tue–Thu, 9am–6pm Fri,
8am–2pm Sat ■ www.rogacki.de

Established in 1935, Roogacki is a famous seafood delicatessen.

⑩ Lindner
MAP N3 ■ Knesebeckstr. 92
■ (030) 313 53 75 ■ Open 8am–6pm
Mon–Fri (until 1:30pm Sat)

This traditional store specializes in fresh delicatessen products.

Lindner store and deli

See map on pp118–19

Cafés and Coffee Shops

A variety of coffee beans on display at Berliner Kaffeerösterei

1 Berliner Kaffeerösterei
MAP P4 ■ Uhlandstraße 173 ■ (030) 88 67 79 20 ■ Open 9am–8pm Mon–Sat, 10am–7pm Sun

A cosy mix of a café and coffee bar, this place offers coffee beans from around the world, cakes and snacks.

2 Café Wintergarten im Literaturhaus
MAP P4 ■ Fasanenstr. 23 ■ (030) 882 54 14 ■ Open 9am–midnight daily

One of Berlin's most beautiful cafés, this is based in the conservatory of an old city mansion. In summer guests can sit outside in the garden.

3 Einstein Café Savignyplatz
MAP N3 ■ Stadtbahnbogen 596 ■ (030) 33 93 09 25 ■ Open 7am–8pm Mon–Fri, 8am–8pm Sat (from 9am Sun) ■ €€

This branch of the Berlin café chain is located under the arches of the Savignyplatz S-Bahn station viaduct.

4 Manufactum Brot und Butter
MAP N3 ■ Hardenbergstrasse 4-5 ■ (030) 26 30 03 46 ■ Open 8am–7pm Mon–Fri (until 6pm Sat) ■ €€

A bakery-café on the ground floor of the Manufactum department store.

5 Café Maitre Münch
MAP P2 ■ Giesebrechtstr. 16 ■ Open 11am–6pm Tue–Fri (from 10am Sat) ■ www.cafe-maitre-muench.de ■ €€

Expect homemade desserts such as cakes and macaroons, and a small but hearty mains menu at this cosy spot.

6 Café Hardenberg
MAP N3 ■ Hardenbergstr. 10 ■ (030) 312 26 44 ■ Open 9am–1am daily ■ No credit cards

A favourite of students and artists since the 1850s, this café has a great atmosphere and reasonable prices.

7 Balzac Coffee
MAP M3 ■ Knesebeckstraße 1–2 ■ Open 7am–8pm Mon–Fri, 8am–8pm Sat (until 7pm Sun) ■ No credit cards

A German gourmet coffee chain serving speciality drinks and snacks.

8 Der Kuchenladen
MAP N3 ■ Kantstr. 138 ■ (030) 31 01 84 24 ■ Open 10am–6:30pm daily ■ No credit cards

Enjoy lemon tart and other delicious homemade delights at this tiny café.

9 Café Kleine Orangerie
MAP A3 ■ Spandauer Damm 20 ■ (030) 322 20 21 ■ Open 10am–6pm Tue–Sun

A small, pleasant garden café at the Charlottenburg Palace.

10 Schwarzes Café
MAP N3 ■ Kantstr. 148 ■ (030) 313 80 38 ■ Open 24 hours

This alternative rock café offers excellent all-day breakfasts and is often packed until dawn.

Restaurants

PRICE CATEGORIES

For a three-course meal for one with half
a bottle of wine (or equivalent meal),
taxes and charges included.

€ under €30   €€ €30–60   €€€ over €60

1 Francucci
MAP B5 ■ Kurfürstendamm
90 ■ (030) 323 33 18 ■ Open noon–
11pm Mon–Sat, 4–10pm Sun ■ €€

This popular Tuscan restaurant
serves excellent pizza, homemade pasta and creative meat
and fish dishes.

2 Lamazère Brasserie
MAP B4/5 ■ Stuttgarter Platz 18
■ (030) 31 80 07 12 ■ Open 6–11pm
Tue–Sun ■ €€

With interiors shaped like a tunnel,
this charming restaurant serves
typical French cuisine. Book ahead.

3 Eiffel
MAP B5 ■ Kurfürstendamm
105 ■ (030) 891 13 05 ■ Open 9am–
midnight daily ■ €€

A spacious and charming French
restaurant with outside tables and
some dishes traditional to Berlin
and the Mediterranean.

4 Die Nußbaumerin
MAP C5 ■ Leibnitzstr. 55
■ (030) 50 17 80 33 ■ Open
5–11:30pm Mon–Fri ■ €€

Michelin-starred chef Johanna
Nußbaum's menu features a variety
of good value Austrian delicacies
such as *Tafelspitz* (a hearty boiled
beef broth) and *Kaiserschmarrn*
(sweet scrambled pancake).

5 Kuchi
MAP N3 ■ Kantstr. 30
■ (030) 31 50 78 16 ■ Open noon–
11pm daily ■ No credit cards ■ €€

Thanks mainly to its exquisite sushi
and mixed Asian hot dishes, this
minimalist restaurant has a loyal
clientele and ranks among the
best sushi bars in town.

6 Lon Men's Noodle House
MAP N3 ■ Kanstr. 33 ■ (030)
31 51 96 78 ■ Open noon–10pm
Wed–Mon ■ €€

The wait is worth it at this Taiwanese
restaurant, which serves some of the
best noodles in town.

7 Lubitsch
MAP N3 ■ Bleibtreustr. 47 ■ (030)
882 37 56 ■ Open 10am–midnight
Mon–Sat, 6pm–midnight Sun ■ €€

A small, elegant restaurant,
serving fresh, regional cuisine.

Outdoor seating at Lubitsch

8 Mine Restaurant
MAP P4 ■ Meinekestr. 10
■ (030) 88 92 63 63 ■ Open 6pm–
midnight Tue–Sat ■ €€

Enjoy contemporary Italian dishes,
complemented by a terrific wine list
and delicious desserts.

9 Marjellchen
MAP P3 ■ Mommsenstr. 9
■ (030) 883 26 76 ■ Open 5pm–
midnight daily ■ €€

This delightful restaurant serves
hearty dishes from East Prussia,
Pomerania and Silesia.

10 Bruderherz
MAP N1 ■ Leonhardstr. 6
■ (030) 33 85 20 77 ■ Open noon–
midnight Tue–Sat ■ €

A relaxed restaurant run by two
Polish brothers, serving excellent
pasta and other Italian food.

See map on pp118–19

🔟 Kreuzberg, Schöneberg and Neukölln

Checkpoint Charlie

Before the Wall fell, Kreuzberg was a hotbed of squatters, hippies and anarchists. Despite rapid gentrification it is still the city's most colourful area. Here, a diverse community of professionals, artists and students harmoniously coexists in renovated petit-bourgeois flats. The adjacent Neukölln is Berlin's most trendy area for art galleries, grunge-hip bars and clubs, particularly along Weserstraße. Schöneberg is not as daring as Kreuzberg, but still evokes a free-minded spirit. Here, Winterfeldtplatz is lined with inviting pubs, and Nollendorfplatz is the nexus of Berlin's lively LGBTQ+ scene.

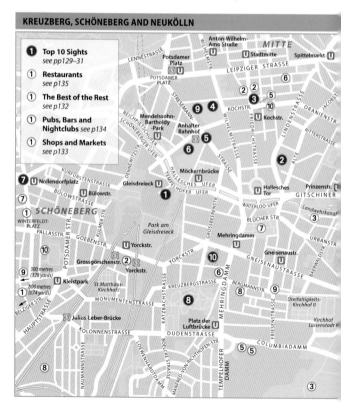

KREUZBERG, SCHÖNEBERG AND NEUKÖLLN

- ❶ **Top 10 Sights** see pp129–31
- ① **Restaurants** see p135
- ① **The Best of the Rest** see p132
- ① **Pubs, Bars and Nightclubs** see p134
- ① **Shops and Markets** see p133

1 Jüdisches Museum Berlin

The Jewish Museum's unique architecture and exhibitions (see pp42–3) aim to illustrate the repercussions of the Holocaust. Narrow, slanting galleries with zig-zag turns evoke a sense of dislocation, and are punctured by "voids" – empty spaces embodying the vacuum left behind by the destruction of Jewish life. Nearly 1,000 years of German-Jewish cultural history are documented here; a special exhibition evokes everyday Jewish life in Berlin from the end of the 19th century. Visitors can hear the sound of a shofar, and listen to ancient and modern Jewish music at the Music Room. After undergoing extensive renovation, a permanent exhibition opened in 2020.

Inside the Deutsches Technikmuseum

2 Deutsches Technikmuseum

MAP F5 ▪ Trebbiner Str. 9 ▪ (030) 90 25 40 ▪ Open 9am–5:30pm Tue–Fri, 10am–6pm Sat & Sun ▪ Adm (kids free after 3pm) ▪ www.sdtb.de

The history of technology and crafts is the theme of this museum (see p64), located in the grounds of a former railway goods yard. Visitors can learn about developments in aviation and admire 40 planes, including a Junkers Ju 52 and a "raisin bomber", the type of plane used or the Berlin airlift. Old ships and steam locomotives hark back to the Industrial Revolution. A must-visit is the Science Center Spectrum where you can perform any of the 150 experiments on offer.

3 Haus am Checkpoint Charlie

MAP G4 ▪ Friedrichstr. 43–45 ▪ (030) 253 72 50 ▪ Open 9am–10pm daily ▪ Adm ▪ www.mauermuseum.de

Founded shortly after the Wall was built, this museum (see p55) details the history of the Wall and the means people used to escape to West Berlin, from a hot-air balloon to a car with a false floor. Of the former border only a replica control hut remains.

④ Topographie des Terrors
MAP F4 ▪ Niederkirchnerstr.
8 ▪ (030) 254 50 90 ▪ Open
10am–6pm daily (until 8pm May–
Sep) ▪ www.topographie.de/en

Between 1933 and 1945, three Nazi
institutions of persecution and terror
were located in this area: the Secret
State Police Office; the SS leadership;
and the Reich Security main office.
After World War II, all the buildings
were bulldozed. A striking documentation centre, designed by Berlin
architect Ursula Wilms, was inaug-
urated in 2010 on this site, providing
information about the headquarters
of the National Socialist SS and police
state during the Third Reich and
showing the extent of the Nazi reign
of terror throughout Europe.

⑤ Anhalter Bahnhof
MAP F5 ▪ Askanischer Platz 6–7

Only pitiful fragments remain of
the railway station that was once the
largest in Europe. The giant structure
was erected in 1880 by architect Franz
Schwechten as a showcase station:
official visitors to the Empire were
meant to be impressed by the splendour and glory of the German capital.

The ruins of the Anhalter Bahnhof

TURKISH BERLIN

In the 1960s, thousands of Turkish
Gastarbeiter ("guest workers") came to
Berlin in response to a labour shortage.
Today the community numbers nearly
240,000 and it is their children and
grandchildren who leave their mark
on life in the city, with many Turkish
Berliners owning shops and businesses.
50 years after their arrival in Berlin,
many people of Turkish descent are
still plagued by social stagnation.
As neighbourhoods like Kreuzberg
or Neukölln, once popular amongst
Turkish families, gentrify, many are
forced into Berlin's outer boroughs.

In 1943 it was damaged by bombs
and in 1960 it was pulled down. The
waste ground behind the façade was
meant to become a park, but today
the Tempodrom is based here, hosting
concerts and cabaret shows.

⑥ Berlin Story Bunker
MAP F5 ▪ Schöneberger Str.
23A ▪ (030) 26 55 55 46 ▪ Open
10am–7pm daily ▪ Adm

Two exhibitions are installed in a
former air raid bunker near the
World War II ruins of Anhalter
Bahnhof. The "Hitler: How Could It
Happen" exhibition tells the story of
Hitler's rise to power, incorporating a
model of the infamous Führerbunker.

⑦ Nollendorfplatz
MAP E5

Nollendorfplatz and neighbouring
Winterfeldtplatz are right in the
centre of Schöneberg. The former
square has been a focal point for
Berlin's LGBTQ+ scene. A plaque at
the Nollendorfplatz U-Bahn station
honours the 5,000 homosexual

victims killed in concentration camps by the Nazis. Today, LGBTQ+ life is concentrated more in the surrounding streets than the square itself. Nollendorfplatz was a centre of entertainment before World War II. The Metropol-Theater, now a club, then was helmed by famed theatre director Erwin Piscator. The writer Christopher Isherwood, whose novel was the basis of *Cabaret*, the musical and film, lived next door.

⑧ Viktoriapark
MAP F6 ■ Kreuzbergstr.

This park *(see p61)* was set up as a recreational space for workers in Kreuzberg in 1888–94 to plans by Hermann Mächtig. It has an artificial waterfall, and the Neo-Gothic Schinkel memorial, 66 m (216 ft) high, commemorates Prussian victory in the Wars of Liberation against Napoleon.

⑨ Martin-Gropius-Bau

This ornamented former museum *(see p56)* of arts and crafts hosts contemporary and archaeological exhibitions.

Detail, Martin-Gropius-Bau

⑩ Riehmers Hofgarten
MAP F6 ■ Yorckstr. 83–86

Over 20 buildings make up this estate, which was built as officers' quarters in the Gründerzeit, following the founding of the German Empire in 1871. Restored in the 1970s, they include a pleasant hotel with restaurant.

A DAY IN KREUZBERG

▶ MORNING

Start at the ruins of **Anhalter Bahnhof**, which you can reach by S-Bahn. From here continue along Stresemannstraße in a northwesterly direction to the **Martin-Gropius-Bau**. Wander around the exhibitions for a few hours in this impressive building, then take a break in the museum café. Afterwards, a visit to the neighbouring **Topographie des Terrors** exhibition will bring you face to face with the dark Nazi past of this area. Continue along Niederkirchnerstraße, which will take you past an original section of the Berlin Wall. Cross Wilhelmstraße and stop at **Haus am Checkpoint Charlie** *(see p129)* at the former East–West border at Friedrichstrasse.

AFTERNOON

Have lunch at **Sale e Tabacchi** *(see p135)* in Rudi-Dutschke-Straße. Before you continue east, make a detour south on Lindenstraße to the **Jüdisches Museum Berlin** *(see p129)* and the **Berlinische Galerie** *(see p57)*. Then take the U6 from Hallesches Tor station to Platz der Luftbrücke. **Viktoriapark** nearby is a good place for a rest, or stroll up Bergmannstraße for shopping or a coffee break. At the end of the street, turn north into Baerwaldstraße and continue to Carl-Herz-Ufer, for a meal at the **Rutz Zollhaus** *(see p135)* on the Landwehrkanal. Walk west along Planufer, turn left and cross the Kottbusser Brücke bridge to explore pubs between Kottbusser Tor and Oranienstrasse in the Kreuzberg district.

See map on pp128–9

The Best of the Rest

 Rathaus Schöneberg
MAP D6 ▪ John-F-Kennedy-Platz

It was from this town hall in 1963 that US President John F Kennedy made his famous "I am a Berliner" speech, expressing his commitment to the freedom of West Berlin.

 Asisi's Wall Panorama
MAP F4 ▪ Friedrichstr. 205 ▪ Open 10am–7pm daily ▪ Adm ▪ www.die-mauer.de/en

This is a life-size reproduction of the Berlin Wall as it appeared in the early 1980s, with sound and light installations.

Cyclists at Tempelhofer Feld

 Tempelhofer Feld
MAP G6 ▪ Tempelhofer Damm 1 ▪ (030) 70 09 06 89 ▪ www.thf-berlin.de

Tempelhofer Feld (see p78) has existed as a public park since the airport here closed in 2008. The old terminal can be visited on a guided tour.

Mariannenplatz
MAP H5

This park-like square with old trees is dominated by a large Gothic-style building. The former hospital and nursing school, Bethanien, is now a protected landmark and is used by cultural and social initiatives.

Oberbaumbrücke
Warschauer/Skalitzer Str.

Pedestrians and cyclists can cross to the other side of the Spree River from Kreuzberg to Friedrichshain on this red-brick bridge, one of Berlin's loveliest, which was built in 1894–6. The bridge provides views of the TV Tower and the Molecular Man.

 Mosse-Haus
MAP G4 ▪ Schützenstrasse 25

One of Berlin's most influential publishing houses was based in this Jugendstil corner house in the former newspaper district.

 Friedhöfe Hallesches Tor
MAP G6 ▪ Mehringdamm

Many celebrities lie buried in these four cemeteries, including the composer Felix Mendelssohn Bartholdy and the writer E T A Hoffmann, whose work inspired Offenbach to compose his *opéra fantastique The Tales of Hoffmann*.

Gasometer Schöneberg
MAP E6 ▪ Torgauer Str. 12–15

Once a massive gas holder, this Schöneberg landmark was decommissioned in the 1990s and turned into a viewing platform.

Kottbusser Tor
MAP H5

Social diversity in Kreuzberg is tucked away in between 1970s prefabricated buildings in the Turkish heart of the district.

Kammergericht
MAP E6 ▪ Potsdamer Str. 186

From 1947 to 1990, this magnificent supreme court, built in 1909–13, was used as Allied Control Council.

The façade of Kammergericht

Shops and Markets

Fresh produce at Winterfeldtmarkt

1 Winterfeldtmarkt
MAP E5 ▪ Winterfeldtplatz
▪ Open 8am–4pm Sat (until 1pm Wed)

At Berlin's largest market *(see p77)*, located in Schöneberg, you can buy fresh fruit and vegetables, homeware, flowers and deli goods.

2 Türkenmarkt am Maybachufer
MAP H5 ▪ Maybachufer ▪ Open 11am–6:30pm Tue & Fri

This vibrant, sometimes chaotic, market *(see p77)* is the place to buy unleavened bread, fresh fruit and vegetables, and goat's cheese.

3 Wesen
Tellstraße 7 ▪ (030) 54 59 22 77 ▪ www.format-favourites.de ▪ Open 11am–7pm daily

Find ethically and locally produced jewels, bags or shoes here, manufactured by fair-trade fashion brands.

4 Oranienplatz and Oranienstraße
MAP H5 ▪ Oranienstr./corner Oranienplatz

Kreuzberg's main square and unofficial high street specialize in all things alternative.

5 Winterfeldt Schokoladen
MAP E5 ▪ Goltzstr. 23 ▪ (030) 23 62 32 56 ▪ Open 9am–8pm Mon–Fri (until 6pm Sat), midnight–7pm Sun

Choose from a variety of chocolates at this lovely store with an adjoining café.

6 Depot 2
MAP H5 ▪ Oranienstr. 9 ▪ (030) 611 46 55

This small boutique sells the latest streetwear, sneakers and hip-hop fashion of local labels.

7 Hard Wax
MAP H5 ▪ Paul-Lincke-Ufer 44a ▪ (030) 61 13 01 11 ▪ Open noon–8pm Mon–Sat

Hidden in a warehouse, this record store offers a carefully curated music collection. Find everything from dubstep and techno to reggae and disco.

8 Ararat
MAP G6 ▪ Bergmannstr. 99A ▪ (030) 693 50 80

One of Berlin's best-stocked and trendiest stationery, curiosity and gift shops, the colourful Ararat has many designer items for sale.

9 Marheineke-Markthalle
MAP G6 ▪ Marheinekeplatz ▪ Open 8am–8pm Mon–Fri (until 6pm Sat)

This is one of the last remaining market-halls in Berlin. It has colourful fruit and vegetable stores and a wide range of organic produce, as well as numerous snack bars.

Shoes on display at Overkill

10 Overkill
MAP H4 ▪ Köpenicker Straße 195A ▪ (030) 61 07 6 33 ▪ Open 11am–8pm Mon–Sat

With more than 500 pairs of sneakers in stock, this shop is a paradise for streetwear fans.

See map on pp128–9 ←

Pubs, Bars and Nightclubs

The bar at Ankerklause

1 Ankerklause
MAP H5 ■ Kottbusser Damm 104 ■ (030) 693 56 49

An informal and popular late-night bar and café on the Landwehrkanal.

2 E & M Leydicke
MAP E6 ■ Mansteinstr. 4 ■ (030) 216 29 73 ■ Open 7pm–1am daily

Enjoy the parties hosted by this popular family-run bar (see p72).

3 Max und Moritz
MAP H5 ■ Oranienstr. 162 ■ (030) 695 15 911 ■ Open 5–11pm Wed–Mon

A 120-year-old inn serving dishes such as *Königsberger Klopse* (braised meatballs with caper sauce) and rare local beers.

4 Van Loon
MAP G5 ■ Carl-Herz-Ufer 5–7 ■ (030) 692 62 93 ■ Open 10am–11pm daily

Enjoy a snack surrounded by nautical artifacts on this old barge moored in Urbanhafen.

5 SilverWings Club
MAP F6 ■ Columbiadamm 10 ■ (030) 69 50 92 11 ■ Open 10pm–5am Sat

Established in 1952, SilverWings (see p70) is one of the oldest nightclubs in Berlin. It hosts various events and parties featuring heart 'n' soul and rock music.

6 Rauschgold
MAP F6 ■ Mehringdamm 62 ■ (030) 92 27 41 78

Best visited late at night, this popular bar gets very crowded on weekends. It offers karaoke and themed nights with a mixed crowd.

7 Green Door
MAP E5 ■ Winterfeldstr. 50 ■ (030) 215 25 15 ■ Open 6pm–2am Sun–Thu (until 3am Fri & Sat)

Do not miss out on the extensive drinks menu offered here (see p72). Happy hours are from 6 to 8pm.

8 SO36
MAP H5 ■ Oranienstr. 190 ■ (030) 61 40 13 06 ■ www.so36.de

The SO36 (see p69) is a very lively alternative dance club.

9 Würgeengel
MAP H5 ■ Dresdener Str. 122 ■ (030) 615 55 60

The drinks at the "Angel of Death" are not lethal, but the bar staff and clientele are straight out of a Buñuel film.

10 Klunkerkranich
Karl-Marx-Str. 66 ■ freunde@ klunkerkranich.org

This rooftop bar overlooks the city and offers stunning views at sunset. Take the elevator to the top of Neukölln Arcaden, then walk the rest of the way through the parking lot.

The rooftop bar at Klunkerkranich

Restaurants

PRICE CATEGORIES
For a three-course meal for one with half
a bottle of wine (or equivalent meal),
taxes and charges included.
....
€ under €30 ■ €€ €30–60 ■ €€€ over €60

Elegant setting at Lavanderia Vecchia

1 Defne
MAP H5 ■ Planufer. 92c ■ (030)
81 79 71 11 ■ Open summer: 4pm–
midnight daily; winter: 5pm–midnight
daily ■ No credit cards ■ €

A restaurant with an intimate setting,
Defne serves modern Turkish food.

2 Entrecôte
MAP G4 ■ Schützenstr. 5
■ (030) 20 16 54 96 ■ Open 11:30am–
midnight Mon–Fri, 6pm–midnight
Sat, 5:30pm–midnight Sun ■ €€

Simple yet tasty meals are served at
this French brasserie, located close
to Checkpoint Charlie *(see p129)*.

3 Rutz Zollhaus
MAP G5 ■ Carl-Herz-Ufer 30
■ (030) 692 33 00 ■ Open from 4pm
Wed–Sat (from 1pm Sun) ■ €€

Formerly a border control point on
the banks of the Landwehrkanal, the
Altes Zollhaus serves international
and German fare. Be sure to try the
house speciality *Brandenburger
Landente aus dem Rohr* (roast duck).

4 Zola
MAP H5 ■ Paul-Lincke-Ufer 39
■ (030) 27 69 59 38 ■ Open noon–10pm
Sun–Thu (until 10:30pm Fri & Sat) ■ €

Excellent Neapolitan-style pizza draws
crowds to this quaint place with outdoor seating on the Landwehrkanal.

5 Restaurant Tim Raue
MAP G4 ■ Rudi-Dutschke-Str.
26 ■ (030) 25 93 79 30 ■ Open noon–
2pm & 7pm–midnight Tue–Sat ■ €€€

The tasting menus here *(see p74)*
explore interesting combinations such
as glazed partridge with Japanese
chestnut. The Obamas have also
dined at this two-Michelin-starred
restaurant. Reservations are a must.

6 Lavanderia Vecchia
MAP H6 ■ Flughafenstr. 46
■ (030) 62 72 21 52 ■ Open noon–
2:30pm & 7:30–11pm Tue–Fri,
7:30–11pm Sat ■ €€

Set in an old laundry, this Italian
restaurant excels in Roman tapas.

7 Long March Canteen
MAP H5 ■ Wrangelstr. 20
■ 0178 884 95 99 ■ Open 6–11pm
daily ■ €€

A hip dim sum restaurant with
communal tables and dim lighting,
like a real Chinese street kitchen.

8 Horváth
MAP H5 ■ Paul-Lincke-Ufer
44a ■ (030) 61 28 99 92 ■ Open 6:30–
10:30pm Wed–Sun ■ €€€

Graced with two Michelin stars, this
fine-dining restaurant *(see p75)* serves
elegantly presented Austrian dishes.

9 Lochner Weinwirtschaft
MAP D6 ■ Eisenacher Str. 86
■ (030) 23 00 52 20 ■ Open 4pm–
12:30am Tue–Sun ■ €€

Wine and dinner bar with an outside
terrace. Refined snacks also served.

10 Sale e Tabacchi
MAP G4 ■ Rudi-Dutschke-Str.
23 ■ (030) 252 11 55 ■ Open 4–
11:30pm daily ■ €€

Elegant Italian restaurant where you
can dine in the courtyard in summer.

See map on pp128–9

🔟 Prenzlauer Berg

Even when the city was divided, this former workers' district in East Berlin was favoured by artists and an alternative crowd. While it continues to exert a similar pull today, Prenzlauer Berg is being steadily transformed by young professionals and families. Cafés and restaurants have taken over tenement blocks around Kollwitzplatz and Husemannstraße, giving the streets an almost Parisian flair, while Kastanienallee, also known as "Casting Alley", is the catwalk of the hip young scene.

Gethsemane-kirche, detail

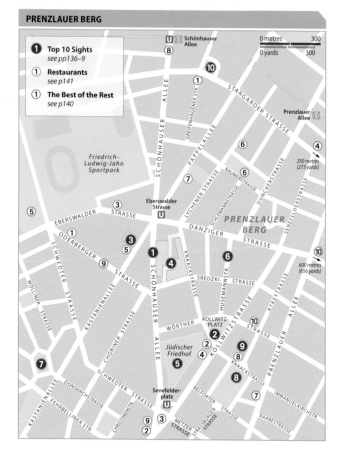

PRENZLAUER BERG

1	Top 10 Sights see pp136–9
1	Restaurants see p141
1	The Best of the Rest see p140

Schönhauser Allee U-Bahn station

1 Schönhauser Allee
MAP H1/2 ■ Prenzlauer Berg

Schönhauser Allee, 3 km (2 miles) long and lined with shops and pubs, is the main artery of the district. Down the centre of the road runs the high-level viaduct of U-Bahn line U2. A couple of buildings are still in their pre-1989 state and give a good impression of the old Prenzlauer Berg, especially between Senefelderplatz and Danziger Straße.

2 Kollwitzplatz
MAP H2 ■ Prenzlauer Berg

Once a quiet square, Kollwitzplatz is today the noisy heart of the district. All around the green square, locals congregate in the numerous cafés, pubs and restaurants. From the lavishly restored façades it is hard to tell that this was once one of the city's poorest areas. The district's 19th-century tenement blocks and impoverished past are today only recalled by the name of the square. The artist Käthe Kollwitz (see p59) once lived and worked at No. 25 (now destroyed), from where she highlighted the poverty of the local workers in her sculptures, drawings and sketches.

3 Prater
MAP H1 ■ Kastanienallee 7–9 ■ (030) 448 56 88 ■ Open 6–11pm Mon–Sat, noon–midnight Sun

The Prater is one of the few remaining entertainment complexes that were once common in big German cities. It was built in 1837 just outside the original city gates, and was first jokingly called "Prater" after its world-famous counterpart in Vienna. A concert hall was added in 1857 and by the turn of the century it had become so popular that the nickname stuck. Today, you can enjoy beer and food at the restaurant (see p141) of the same name.

4 Kulturbrauerei
MAP H1 ■ Schönhauser Allee 36–39 (entrance: Knaackstr. 97) ■ (030) 44 35 26 14 ■ kulturbrauerei. de/en

This giant complex of buildings originally housed the Schultheiss brewery, one of the breweries that once made Prenzlauer Berg famous. The complex, parts of which are over 150 years old, was designed by Franz Schwechten. It was completely restored in 1997–9 and has become a lively and popular spot. Cafés, restaurants, a cinema, shops and even a theatre have sprung up in the red and yellow brick buildings and the numerous interior courtyards.

The Kulturbrauerei complex

The peaceful Jewish Cemetery

5 Jewish Cemetery
MAP H2 ■ Schönhauser Allee 23–25 ■ Open 8am–4pm Mon–Thu, 7:30am–1pm Fri ■ www.jg-berlin.org

The small Jewish cemetery is among the city's most beautiful. The tombstones stand amid dense scrub and high trees. The cemetery was set up in 1827, when the former Jewish cemetery in Große Hamburger Straße was closed. Two of the famous personalities who have found their final resting places here are the painter and printmaker Max Liebermann (1847–1935) and the composer Giacomo Meyerbeer (1791–1864).

6 Husemannstraße
MAP H1 ■ Between Wörther and Danziger Str.

The East German regime undertook a perfect restoration of this idyllic street for Berlin's 750th anniversary celebrations. A stroll through the leafy roads lined with houses from the Gründerzeit (the years after the founding of the German Empire in 1871) is one of the loveliest ways to experience Prenzlauer Berg. Ancient-looking street lamps and signs,

cobbled streets, antiquated shop signs and a few atmospheric pubs take the visitor back to the late 19th century.

7 Zionskirche
MAP G2 ■ Zionskirchplatz ■ (030) 449 21 91 ■ Open 8–10pm Mon, 1–7pm Tue–Sat, noon–5pm Sun

Zionskirche, dating from 1866–73, and the square of the same name form a tranquil oasis in the middle of the lively district. The Protestant church has always been a political centre too. During the Third Reich, resistance groups against the Nazi regime congregated here and, during the East German period, the alternative "environment library" (an information and documentation centre) was established here. Church and other opposition groups who were active at Zionskirche played a decisive role in the political transformation of East Germany in 1989–90, which eventually led to the reunification of Germany.

8 Wasserturm
MAP H2 ■ Knaackstr.

The Wasserturm

The unofficial symbol of the district is this giant 30-m- (98-ft-) high water tower, built in 1877 as a water reservoir, but shut down in 1914. The engine house in the tower was used as an unofficial prison by the SA from 1933 to 1945, a period recalled by a memorial plaque. The water tower stands on Windmühlenberg (windmill hill), where some of the mills that had

---

PRENZLBERG OR PRENZLAUER BERG?

Many locals simply say Prenzlberg when talking about their quarter. But this name is used mainly by West Berliners and West Germans who have recently moved here – the real name is Prenzlauer Berg, just as it is written. The supposed nickname is just a new-fangled term for a neighbourhood that has become fashionable after the fall of the Berlin Wall.

made Prenzlauer Berg famous in the 19th century once stood. This round brick building has been converted into trendy apartments.

Interior of Synagoge Rykestraße

⑨ Synagoge Rykestraße
MAP H2 ▪ Rykestr. 53 ▪ (030) 88 02 83 16 ▪ Guided tours 2–6pm Thu ▪ www.jg-berlin.org/en.html

Built in 1904, this synagogue *(see p49)* is one of the few Jewish places of worship to have survived Kristallnacht on 9 November 1938, the violent attacks on Jewish property by the Nazis. The temple's historic interior was built from red bricks in the shape of a basilica. It is the largest synagogue in Berlin.

⑩ Gethsemanekirche
MAP H1 ▪ Stargarder Str. 77 ▪ (030) 445 77 45 ▪ Open May–Oct: 5–7pm Wed–Thu (otherwise by prior arrangement)

Outside this red-brick church, dating back to 1891–3, East German secret police beat up peaceful protesters. It was the starting point for the collapse of the East German regime.

Gethsemanekirche interior

A DAY IN PRENZLAUER BERG

▶ MORNING

Set off from the U-Bahn station in **Senefelderplatz** *(see p140)*, one of the lively spots in Prenzlauer Berg. From here, explore the old tenement blocks and backyards. Then continue west along Fehrbelliner Straße to Zionskirchplatz, and visit the eponymous **Zionskirche**. There are numerous cafés on the square, such as **Kapelle**, where you could stop for a coffee. Leave the square via Zionskirchstraße, then turn left into Kastanienallee. This is one of the most colourful streets in the neighbourhood. At the end of the street you could pop into **Prater** *(see p141)*. Then turn right into Oderberger Straße, one of the best preserved streets in the area. Continue east along Sredzkistraße until you reach **Husemannstraße**. Have a good look around the old Berlin streets, you may find something interesting to buy.

AFTERNOON

Stop for lunch at one of the numerous restaurants in **Kollwitzplatz** *(see p136)*: Gugelhof *(see p141)* and **Zander** are both recommended, the former for German and French cuisine, the latter for imaginative fish specialities. After lunch, walk along Knaackstraße to the **Synagoge Rykestraße**. From here it is a few paces back to the **Wasserturm**. Give your feet a rest at the small green space around the tower before continuing along Belforter Straße and Kollwitzstraße to Schönhauser Allee. Finish your walk at the tranquil **Jewish Cemetery**.

See map on p137 ⬅

The Best of the Rest

1 Greifenhagener Straße
MAP H1

Not the most beautiful, but one of the best-preserved red-brick residential streets of old Berlin.

2 Pfefferberg
MAP H2 ▪ Schönhauser Allee 176 ▪ (030) 44 38 30

This alternative cultural centre is set in a former brewery and hosts concerts, performance art events and festivals.

3 Senefelderplatz
MAP H2

The wedge-shaped square is named after Alois Senefelder, a pioneer of modern printing techniques. At its centre is a "Café Achteck", a historic octagonal public urinal.

4 Zeiss-Großplanetarium
Prenzlauer Allee 80 ▪ (030) 421 84 50 ▪ Open 9am–noon Tue–Thu, 6–9:30pm Fri, also pm Sat & Sun

Gaze at uncountable stars, planets and galaxies under the vast silvery dome of the planetarium.

5 Mauerpark
MAP G1 ▪ Am Falkplatz

The vast park near the former border, comprising Max Schmeling Hall and Jahn Sports Park, was built for the Berlin Olympic bid in 2000. Today, it hosts sports and music events, karaoke, and a Sunday flea market.

Buildings at Helmholtzplatz

6 Helmholtzplatz
MAP H1

Apart from the trendy cafés and bars, time seems to have stopped here in 1925, with buildings reminiscent of a social housing programme.

7 Museum Pankow
MAP H2 ▪ Prenzlauer Allee 227–228 ▪ (030) 902 953 917 ▪ Open 10am–6pm Tue–Sun

This museum charts the history of the district and its poor working-class inhabitants in the 19th century.

8 Konnopke's Imbiss
MAP H1 ▪ At the southern exit of U-Bahn Schönhauser Allee ▪ (030) 442 77 65 ▪ Open 10am–8pm Mon–Fri, noon–8pm Sat

This legendary *Currywurstimbiss* was opened in 1930 under the U-Bahn steel viaduct. The sausages served here are among the best in the city.

9 Oderberger Straße
MAP G1–H1

This leafy street is lined with cafés, boutiques and a few historic buildings. The old swimming baths of Prenzlauer Berg at No. 84 were renovated in 2015.

10 Thälmannpark
MAP H1 ▪ Prenzlauer Allee

One of few parks in the northeast of the city, dominated by Socialist prefabricated buildings. It has a monument to Ernst Thälmann, a communist murdered by the Nazis.

Toys at a stall, Mauerpark flea market

Restaurants

1 Oderquelle
MAP G1 ▪ Oderberger Str. 27 ▪ (030) 44 00 80 80 ▪ Open 6pm–1am daily ▪ €
Basic Berlin and German dishes are served up in an alternative, relaxed setting in this quaint little *Kiez* (neighbourhood) place.

2 Gugelhof
MAP H2 ▪ Knaackstr. 37 ▪ (030) 442 92 29 ▪ Open 5–11pm Mon & Wed–Fri, noon–11pm Sat & Sun ▪ €€
Bill Clinton was once a guest at this restaurant, which attracts clients from all over Berlin. The menu features an original combination of German and French cuisine.

Outdoor tables at Gugelhof

3 Cotto e Crudo
MAP G/H1 ▪ Eberswalder Str. 33 ▪ (030) 44 03 71 11 ▪ Open noon–midnight Tue–Sun ▪ €€
This homely restaurant offers an extensive pasta and pizza menu, plus classic Italian mains. It is located close to the southern end of Mauerpark.

4 Lucky Leek
MAP H2 ▪ Kollwitzstra. 54 ▪ (030) 66 40 87 10 ▪ Open 6–10pm Wed–Sun ▪ €€
Experience vegan dining here. There are no à la carte menus on Fridays and Saturdays, but you can choose from the three- or five-course meals.

PRICE CATEGORIES

For a three-course meal for one with half a bottle of wine (or equivalent meal), taxes and charges included.

€ under €30   €€ €30–60   €€€ over €60

5 Prater
MAP H1 ▪ Kastanienallee 7–9 ▪ (030) 448 56 88 ▪ Open 6pm–midnight Mon–Sat, noon–midnight Sun; beer garden: from noon Apr–Sep ▪ No credit cards ▪ €€
Surprises at the Prater include a beer garden, a rustic restaurant in the courtyard and free live concerts.

6 Sasaya
MAP H1 ▪ Lychener Str. 50 ▪ (030) 44 71 77 21 ▪ Open noon–3pm & 6–11:30pm Thu–Mon ▪ No credit cards ▪ €€
Head to Sasaya for some of Berlin's best sushi. Reservations needed.

7 Osmans Töchter
MAP H1 ▪ Pappelallee 15 ▪ (0172) 274 46 62 ▪ Open 5:30pm–1am daily ▪ €€€
This modern, family-run restaurant serves traditional Turkish cuisine.

8 Pasternak
MAP H2 ▪ Knaackstr. 22 ▪ (030) 441 33 99 ▪ Open 9am–1am daily ▪ €€
This Moscow-style venue has borscht, Russian music and vodka.

9 Schankhalle Pfefferberg
MAP H2 ▪ Schönhauser Allee 176 ▪ (030) 47 37 73 60 ▪ Open 4–11pm Tue–Sat ▪ €€
Enjoy home-brewed beer and snacks such as *Treberbrot* (bread made with malt left over from brewing beer).

10 MaoThai Stammhaus
MAP H2 ▪ Wörther Straße 30 ▪ (030) 441 92 61 ▪ Open noon–11:30pm daily ▪ €€
Berlin's first Thai restaurant, this friendly spot serves traditional and beautifully presented food.

See map on p137

🔟 Berlin's Southeast

Berlin's east and south are remarkably different in character. Friedrichshain, Lichtenberg and Hohenschönhausen in the east are densely built-up, with their old tenement blocks evoking stark memories of World War II and perhaps even more of life during the bleak days of the East German regime. Green Treptow and idyllic Köpenick in the far southeast, meanwhile, seem almost like independent villages and, together with Großer Müggelsee, are popular day trip destinations for visitors and Berliners alike.

Sculpture detail, Treptower Park

BERLIN'S SOUTHEAST

The charming small town of Köpenick across the Spree River

① Köpenicker Altstadt and Köpenicker Schloss

Schloss: Schlossinsel ▪ Open 11am–6pm Thu–Sun (winter: until 5pm) ▪ Adm ▪ www.smb.museum

The island community of Köpenick has a venerable history: as early as the 9th century, people had settled on Schlossinsel. The village stayed independent until 1920. Its coat of arms still features two fish, and the Altstadt (old town) on the Dahme River has 18th–19th-century fishers' huts. On 16 October 1906, Wilhelm Voigt, dressed as a captain, led soldiers into the Rathaus (town hall) on Alt-Köpenick, arrested the mayor and "confiscated" the municipal coffers. The "Hauptmann von Köpenick" (Captain of Köpenick) is commemorated by a statue (see p47) in front of the Rathaus. The 1904 structure is a good example of Gothic brick architecture from Brandenburg. The charming Baroque Köpenick palace, on Schlossinsel in the south of the district, was built in 1677–81 for the future King Frederick I by Dutch architect Rutger van Langervelt. It now houses collections from the Kunstgewerbemuseum (see p55).

② Mercedes-Benz Arena

Mühlenstr. 12–30/O2-Platz 1 ▪ Tickets: (030) 20 60 70 88 99 ▪ www.mercedes-benz-berlin.de

The city's largest entertainment arena, seating 17,000 people, hosts pop concerts and shows of all kinds, as well as being home to the Alba Berlin basketball team and the Eisbären Berlin ice-hockey club.

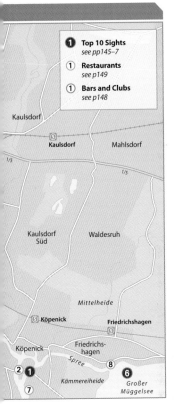

Kaulsdorf

Kaulsdorf   Mahlsdorf

Kaulsdorf Süd   Waldesruh

Mittelheide

Köpenick   Friedrichshagen

Köpenick   Friedrichs-hagen

Spree

Kämmereiheide   Großer Müggelsee

The Mercedes-Benz Arena

3 Stasi-Museum Berlin

Ruschestr. 103, Haus 1
■ Open 10am–6pm
Mon–Fri (from 11am
Sat & Sun) ■ Adm
■ www.stasimuseum.de

**Button spy camera,
Stasi-Museum**

The former headquarters
of the Stasi, East
Germany's secret police,
is now a memorial to the victims of
the East German regime and of Erich
Mielke, the minister in charge of the
secret police. Visitors can see his
offices, the canteen and spying equipment used by the Socialist regime.

4 Museum Berlin Karlshorst

Zwieseler Str. 4 ■ Open 10am–6pm
Tue–Sun ■ www.museum-karls
horst.de

World War II ended here on 8 May
1945, when Germany signed its
unconditional surrender. Documents, uniforms and photographs,
displayed in the former officers'
casino, relate the story of the war.

5 East Side Gallery

MAP H4 ■ Mühlenstraße
■ (030) 251 71 59 ■ Open 24 hours
■ www.eastsidegallery-berlin.de

A 1.3-km (0.8-mile) section of the
Berlin Wall was left standing next to
the Spree River. In 1990, 118 artists
from around the world painted onto
the concrete, making it a unique work
of art (see p78). Particularly famous
is a mural by Russian Dmitri Vrubel
showing Erich Honecker and Leonid

Brezhnev kissing. Most
murals were restored by
the original artists in 2009.

6 Großer Müggelsee

Treptow-Köpenick district
Nicknamed Berlin's "Large
Bathtub", the Großer
Müggelsee is the city's
biggest lake. Müggelsee is not as
popular as Großer Wannsee, mainly
because it is further from the centre.
It is known for the beer gardens on its
south side, which can be reached on
foot or by boat from Friedrichshagen.
You can swim in the lake, and around
it are great walking and cycling paths.

7 Treptower Park

Alt-Treptow
Established in the 19th century for
the city's working classes, Treptower
Park (see p61) is today best known
for its Sowjetisches Ehrenmal (Soviet
Memorial). In April 1945, 7,000 Red
Army soldiers who died during the
liberation of Berlin were buried here.
Beyond the mass graves is a 12-m
(39-ft) bronze statue of a Russian
soldier holding a child and a sword
with which he has destroyed the
Nazi Hakenkreuz (swastika) symbol.
The park's riverside location makes
it a popular picnic spot in summer.

8 Friedrichshain

MAP H2
This densely built-up area grew
rapidly during the industrialization
of the late 19th century. It became

Colourful murals at the East Side Gallery

an Allied target during the war and it was one of Berlin's most damaged districts. After the fall of the Wall, Friedrichshain attracted a young population, and it is now one of the city's most popular areas, home to trendy design and media companies, bars, clubs, and cafés, mostly set around Boxhagener Platz and Simon-Dach-Straße. Its Volkspark *(see p61)* houses Ludwig Hoffmann's Märchenbrunnen fountain, decorated with fairytale characters, and the wooded Großer and Kleiner Bunkerberg hillocks.

Märchenbrunnen, Volkspark

⑨ Tierpark Berlin
Am Tierpark 125 ▪ (030) 51 53 10 ▪ Hours vary, check website ▪ Adm ▪ www.tierpark-berlin.de/tierpark

Located in the Friedrichsfelde Palace park, Europe's largest zoological garden *(see p61)* hosts several rare species. The Siberian tigers in their rocky outdoor enclosures are worth a visit. The park is known for its successful elephant breeding programme. The 1695 palace sits in the middle of this estate.

⑩ Gedenkstätte Hohenschönhausen
Genslerstr. 66 ▪ English guided tours 11:45am, 2:15pm & 3:45pm daily ▪ Adm ▪ en.stiftung-hsh.de

This former secret police prison for political prisoners was in use until 1990. Before 1951, it served as a reception centre for the Red Army. You can visit the watchtowers and cells – particularly horrifying are the windowless "submarine cells" for solitary confinement and torture.

A DAY IN BERLIN'S SOUTHEAST

▶ MORNING

Begin your tour of Berlin's Southeast at Alexanderplatz. Sights on this tour are not always near each other, so using public transport is recommended.

Take the U-Bahn line U5 to Magdalenenstraße station, from where it is a short walk to the **Stasi-Museum Berlin**. Return to the station and continue on U5 to **Tierpark Berlin**, and spend some time exploring both the zoological garden and the beautifully restored Schloss Friedrichsfelde, built in early Neo-Classical style. Then catch bus No. 296 from the Tierpark U-Bahn station to the **Deutsch-Russisches Museum**.

AFTERNOON

From the museum, either walk (15 minutes) or take bus No. 296 southwest down Rheinsteinstraße to the S Karlshorst tram stop. No. 27 goes direct to Rathaus Köpenick. Stop for a typically German meal in the **Ratskeller** *(see p149)*, the town hall's cellar restaurant. Afterwards explore **Köpenick Old Town** *(see p145)*. The old fishing village is especially worth a visit. There are many cafés near **Köpenicker Schloss** *(see p145)* where you could stop for coffee and cake. Continue your journey by tram No. 60 to Friedrichshagen, the access point for the **Großer Müggelsee**. From here take one of the tourist boats for a trip around the lake before returning to Köpenick for the train back to the centre.

See map on pp144–5 ←

Bars and Clubs

 Berghain
Am Wriezener Bahnhof ▪ Open 10pm–6am Thu & Fri, 24hrs Sat

This club has a strict door policy. A good sound system and cool crowds make the wait worthwhile.

2 Arena
Eichenstr. 4 ▪ (030) 533 20 30

A post-industrial riverside complex, Arena is an unusual mix of concert halls, a club ship *(Hoppetosse)* and a moored swimming pool *(Badeschiff)*.

3 Cassiopeia
Revaler Str. 99 ▪ Open from 10pm Thu–Sat

Join hippies, punks and freestylers in this underground urban enclave for ungentrified clubbing and live gigs.

4 Sisyphos
Hauptstraße 15 ▪ www.sisyphos-berlin.net

Inside a former factory, this large techno club is famous for its parties.

5 Matrix
Warschauer Platz 18 ▪ Open 10pm–5am daily

Inside vaults under the Warschauer Straße train station, Matrix is one of the largest clubs in the city. It attracts a young crowd and Berlin's best DJs.

Matrix, set under railway arches

6 Festsaal Kreuzberg
Am Flutgraben 2 ▪ (030) 403 65 56 30 ▪ Open 5–11pm Thu & Sun (until 1am Fri & Sat)

One of Berlin's best live music halls, this venue hosts rock, alternative and indie bands. It has a lovely beer garden.

7 Monster Ronson's Ichiban Karaoke Bar
Warschauer Str. 34 ▪ (030) 89 75 13 27 ▪ Open from 7pm daily

At this lively bar, karaoke fans either practise their art in soundproof booths that can fit up to 16 people, or sing on a stage. Try the brunch on Sundays.

8 Salon zur Wilden Renate
Alt Stralau 70 ▪ (030) 25 04 14 26 ▪ Open 6pm–2am Wed–Thu (until 8am Fri, until 6am Sat & Sun) ▪ No credit cards

Styled like a living room, this club plays house and techno music. It gets crowded shortly after opening.

9 Zenner
Alt Treptow 15 ▪ (030) 533 73 70 ▪ Open noon–9pm Mon–Thu, 11am–10pm Fri–Sun ▪ www.zenner.berlin

One of the largest and oldest beer gardens of Berlin, Zenner is a leafy space situated in Treptower Park on the Spree River. There is also a hall where live music events take place on weekends.

10 Revier Südost
Schnellerstr. 137 ▪ Open 4–11pm Mon–Thu (until 1am Fri–Sun) ▪ www.reviersuedost.de

Set in the premises of the former Bärenquell brewery in the up-and-coming neighbourhood Schöneweide, Revier Südost hosts club nights, concerts, and theatre and art events.

Restaurants

PRICE CATEGORIES

For a three-course meal for one with half a bottle of wine (or equivalent meal), taxes and charges included.

€ under €30   €€ €30–60   €€€ over €60

1 Il Ritrovo
Gabriel-Max-Str. 2
■ (030) 29 36 41 30 ■ Open noon–midnight daily ■ €

Enjoy delicious, reasonably priced wood-fired pizza in a friendly and cosy atmosphere. There is also a wine bar here.

Vast vaults of Ratskeller Köpenick

2 Ratskeller Köpenick
Alt-Köpenick 21 ■ (030) 655 51 78 ■ Open 11am–11pm Tue–Sat (until 10pm Sun) ■ €€

Traditional fare is served in the vaulted cellars where Wilhelm Voigt famously conned *(see p145)* local civil servants.

3 Klipper Schiffsrestaurant
Bulgarische Str. ■ (030) 53 21 64 90 ■ Open 10am–1am daily ■ No credit cards ■ €

This two-masted 1890 boat has been turned into a restaurant; the menu features fish and game dishes.

4 Freischwimmer
Vor dem Schlesischen Tor 2 ■ (030) 61 07 43 09 ■ Open from noon Mon–Fri (from 10am Sat & Sun) ■ €€

Head to Freischwimmer, a restaurant and bar floating on a wooden terrace over the Flutgraben Canal, for brunch.

5 Burgeramt
Krossener Str. 21–22 ■ (030) 66 76 34 53 ■ Open noon–midnight daily ■ €

A wide variety of burgers are available at this burger joint, from beef patties to many vegetarian options.

6 Khao Taan
Gryphiusstr. 10 ■ (030) 58 61 74 00 ■ Open 6–10pm Tue–Sat ■ €€

Impeccable Thai dishes served as a set menu. Diners need to book weeks in advance to be able to get a table here.

7 Krokodil
Gartenstr. 46–48 ■ (030) 65 88 00 94 ■ Open 4–11pm Mon–Fri, 3–11pm Sat (from noon Sun) ■ €

Situated in Köpenick's Old Town, near the river baths in Gartenstraße, this is one of the nicest garden venues, especially in summer.

8 Bräustübl
Müggelseedamm 164 ■ (030) 37 44 67 69 ■ Open noon–10pm Mon–Sat (from 11am Sun) ■ €

This typical beer garden, belonging to the neighbouring Berliner Bürger-Brau brewery, serves excellent game dishes.

9 Hafenküche
Zur alten Flußbadeanstalt 5 ■ (030) 42 21 99 26 ■ Open 6–11pm Wed–Fri, noon–11pm Sat & Sun ■ €€

Tucked away in the waterfront east of the Spree River, this port restaurant serves casual meals. The picnic baskets on offer are perfect for a weekend ride in a boat hired from the neighbouring shop.

10 Jäger & Lustig
Grünberger Str. 1 ■ (030) 29 00 99 12 ■ Open noon–midnight daily ■ €

A rustic restaurant and beer garden, Jäger & Lustig specializes in typical German cuisine; options include game and some vegetarian dishes.

See map on pp144–5

📐 Grunewald and Dahlem

Berlin's green southwest, which includes the districts of Grunewald and Dahlem, is dotted with lakes, rivers, residential villas, private estates and small castles. Grunewald and Dahlem have a charming suburban character that has always drawn affluent and famous Berliners. Visitors can enjoy extensive walks in the Grunewald forest, take a ferry ride across picturesque Wannsee to the romantic ruins at Pfaueninsel or relax at Europe's largest inland beach. Dahlem's Museum of Europäischer Kulturen has a terrific collection, while the Haus der Wannsee Konferenz and Alliiertenmuseum recall a darker period in Berlin's history.

Schloss Glienicke, detail

GRUNEWALD AND DAHLEM

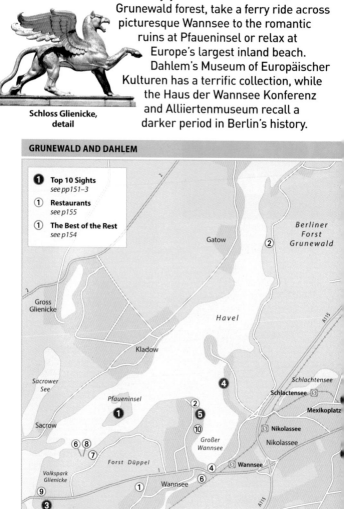

- **1** Top 10 Sights
  see pp151–3
- **1** Restaurants
  see p155
- **1** The Best of the Rest
  see p154

Gatow

Berliner Forst Grunewald

Gross Glienicke

Havel

Kladow

Sacrower See

Schlachtensee
Schlachtensee Ⓢ

Mexikoplatz

Pfaueninsel

Nikolassee Ⓢ
Nikolassee

Sacrow

Großer Wannsee

Forst Düppel

Wannsee Ⓢ

Volkspark Glienicke

Wannsee

Friedrich Wilhelm II's charming ruined castle folly on Pfaueninsel

1 Pfaueninsel
Pfaueninselchaussee ■ (030) 80 58 68 30 ■ Castle: closed for renovation until 2024 ■ www.spsg.de

Visitors to Pfaueninsel *(see p60)* are immediately enchanted by the romantic palace ruins and the eponymous peacocks that run around here. The Wannsee island, which can only be reached by ferry, is one of the most charming spots for a walk in Berlin.

2 Museum Europäischer Kulturen
Arnimallee 25 ■ Open 10am–5pm Tue–Fri, 11am–6pm Sat & Sun ■ Adm ■ www.smb.museum

Out of the three museums in Dahlem, only the Museum of European Cultures will remain once the Museum of Asian Art and the Museum of Ethnology (both currently closed) move to the Humboldt Forum *(see p85)*. The museum's vast array of objects, including graphic art and jewellery, represent life in Germany and other European countries from the 18th century to the present day.

3 Schloss Glienicke
Königstr. 36 ■ (0331) 969 42 00 ■ Open Apr–Oct: 10am–6pm Tue–Sun (Nov, Dec & Mar: until 5pm Sat & Sun) ■ Adm ■ www.spsg.de

One of Berlin's most beautiful Hohenzollern palaces, the Schloss Glienicke is a romantic castle built by Schinkel in 1824–60. It served as a summer residence for Prince Carl of Prussia. The landscaped garden was designed by Lenné and includes pavilions called "Große" and "Kleine Neugierde" (large and small curiosity), a restaurant and the Orangerie.

White-sand artificial beach at the beautiful Wannsee lake

4 Strandbad Wannsee

Wannseebadeweg 25
■ (030) 803 54 50 ■ Hours vary,
call to check ■ Adm

Europe's largest inland beach,
which is almost 2 km (1 mile) long
and 80 m (262 ft) wide *(see p61)*, is a
picturesque spot on the edge of the
city. The renovated swimming baths
were built in 1929–30 as a recreation
area for workers.

5 Haus der Wannsee-Konferenz

Am Großen Wannsee 56–58 ■ (030)
805 00 10 ■ Open 10am–6pm daily
■ www.ghwk.de

It is hard to believe that something
as abhorrent as the Holocaust could
have been planned at this elegant
villa. Built by Paul Baumgarten in
1914–15 in Neo-Baroque style for
businessman Ernst Marlier, it hosted
the Nazi elite, among them the infamous Adolf Eichmann, on 20 January
1942. They met to discuss the details
of the mass extermination of Jews.
An exhibition documents the conference and its consequences, as
well as the history of the villa.

6 Alliiertenmuseum

Clayallee 135 ■ (030) 818 19
90 ■ Open 10am–6pm Sun–Tue
■ www.alliiertenmuseum.de/en

This museum recalls the 50 or so
years of partnership between West
Berliners and the Western Allies.
Based in a former US barracks, it uses
uniforms, documents, weapons and
military equipment to tell the story of
Berlin's post-war history, though not
only from the military point of view.

7 Grunewald Villas

Some of Berlin's most
attractive 19th-century villas are
found in the streets around the
Grunewald S-Bahn station. Especially
worth seeing are Nos. 15 and 11 in
Winklerstraße, the latter of which was
built by Hermann Muthesius in the
style of an English country house. Villa
Maren at No. 12 is a beautiful example
of the Neo-Renaissance style. The
villas on Furtwänglerstraße and Toni-
Lessler-Straße are also worth visiting.

PRUSSIA AND ANTIQUITY

From 1821, Lenné and Schinkel tried to
turn the Potsdam countryside into an
"island paradise". Their idea was based
on Classical ideas of the
harmonious ensemble of
architecture and landscape,
in line with the idealized
views of antiquity
prevalent in the Neo-
Classical period. The
architectural style of
Prussian palaces such
as Sanssouci **(left)**
thus harks back to
Greek and Roman
models and the
Italian Renaissance.

8 Jagdschloss Grunewald

Hüttenweg 100, Grunewaldsee
■ (0331) 969 42 00 ■ Open Apr–Oct:
10am–6pm Tue–Sun; Nov, Dec & Mar:
tours only, 10am–4pm Sat & Sun
■ Adm ■ www.spsg.de

This small white 1542 palace is
the oldest of its kind in the city area.
It was once a hunting lodge for the
Electors. Built in the Renaissance
and Baroque styles, it holds paintings by Cranach the Elder and
16th–19th-century portraits of
Hohenzollern rulers.

9 Museumsdorf Düppel

Clauertstr. 11 ■ (030) 802 66
71 ■ Open late Mar–Oct: 10am–6pm
Sat & Sun ■ Adm ■ www.dueppel.de

This lively open-air museum serves
as a reminder that Berlin was once
a series of villages dating back to
the 13th century. Costumed actors
enact the daily life of the Middle
Ages, with bread-baking, pottery
and basket-weaving demonstrations. The gardens are fascinating.

Villas of Mexikoplatz

10 Mexikoplatz

Idyllic Mexikoplatz in the
southern district of Zehlendorf is
one of the most atmospheric and
architecturally fascinating squares
in Berlin. It is flanked by elegant
semicircular Jugendstil apartment
blocks, and in front of these stands
Berlin's last remaining Art-Deco-
style S-Bahn station. In summer,
the buildings' balconies are decked
with greenery and flowers. Some of
Berlin's most magnificent mansion
houses line Argentinische and
Lindenthaler Allees, the streets
leading into the magnificent square.

A DAY IN THE SOUTHWEST

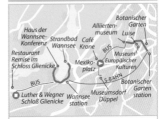

▶ MORNING

Start your morning walk through
Berlin's southwestern districts
by taking the S-Bahn (line S1) to
Mexikoplatz. Admire the beautiful
villas and the lovely green square
before dropping in at **Café Krone**
(No. 2 Argentinische Allee) for a
late breakfast. Then take bus No.
118 southwards to the open-air
museum **Museumsdorf Düppel**.
From there, take bus No. 115
north to the **Alliiertenmuseum**.
Afterwards, a 20-minute walk
through the park opposite leads
right up to the beer garden **Luise**
(see p155) near Freie Universität,
where you can have lunch.

AFTERNOON

Resume your explorations with a
stop at the **Museum Europäischer
Kulturen** (see p151), a 2-minute
walk south of the café, or discover
tropical flora in the giant greenhouses of the **Botanischer Garten**
(pp60–61), a 20-minute walk east.
The seasonal displays are spectacular at any time of year. Then
find your way to the Botanischer
Garten S-Bahn station to take the
train to the Wannsee station, gate-
way to the sights of southwestern
Berlin. When the weather is right,
head to the beaches of **Strandbad
Wannsee**. Alternatively, pay a
visit to the **Haus der Wannsee-
Konferenz** and then admire
the park and **Luther & Wegner
Schloß Glienicke** (see p155). After
your day out, recharge
with coffee and cake or supper
at **Restaurant Remise im Schloss
Glienicke** (see p155). Your best
option for the return journey is
the S-Bahn from Wannsee.

See map on pp150–51

The Best of the Rest

 Open Air Museum Domäne Dahlem

Königin-Luise-Str. 49 ■ Museum: open 10am–5pm Sat & Sun; grounds: open 7am–10pm daily ■ Adm ■ www.domaene-dahlem.de

Learn about modern organic farming techniques at this historic working farm.

 Grunewaldturm
Havelchaussee

■ Open 10am–10pm daily

This Neo-Gothic brick tower was built in 1897 as a memorial to Kaiser Wilhelm I. There is also a viewing platform on top.

Grunewaldturm

 Onkel Toms Hütte
Argentinische Allee

The "Uncle Tom's Hut" settlement, developed in 1926–32 according to designs by Bruno Taut and others, was intended to create a modern housing estate for workers.

④ **Freie Universität**
Habelschwerdter Allee 45
■ Library: open 9am–10pm Mon–Fri (until 5pm Sat & Sun)

Berlin's largest university, founded in 1948 as a rival to the Humboldt University in East Berlin. It is worth looking at the 1950s Henry-Ford-Bau here, and the Philological Library, designed by Lord Norman Foster.

Norman Foster's Philological Library

⑤ **Teufelsberg**
Open 11am–sunset Wed–Sun
■ Adm

Situated on top of a hill, this Cold War era listening tower is a landmark viewpoint. The surrounding forests are popular for biking and the Teufelsee lake for swimming and sunbathing (nude if you wish).

⑥ **Heinrich von Kleist's Grave**
Bismarckstr. 3, Am Kleinen Wannsee

German playwright Kleist and his companion Henriette Vogel committed suicide by shooting themselves in 1811; they are buried here together (near the S-Bahn overpass).

⑦ **St-Peter-und-Paul-Kirche**
Nikolskoer Weg 17 ■ (030) 805 21 00
■ Open 11am–4pm daily

This stone church on the Havel was built in 1834–7 by Stüler and resembles Russian-Orthodox churches.

⑧ **Blockhaus Nikolskoe**
Nikolskoer Weg 15 ■ (030) 805 29 14 ■ Open noon–6pm daily

This wooden, Russian-style *dacha*, built in 1819, was a gift from King Friedrich Wilhelm III to his daughter Charlotte and his son-in-law, the future Tsar Nicholas I.

⑨ **St-Annen-Kirche**
Königin-Luise-Str./Pacelliallee

This 14th-century Gothic church has attractive murals depicting scenes from the life of St Anna, as well as late Gothic figures of saints and a Baroque pulpit.

⑩ **Liebermann-Villa**
Colomierstr. 3 ■ Open summer: 10am–6pm Wed–Mon; winter: 11am–5pm Wed–Mon

The home of Berlin painter Max Liebermann, on the Wannsee shore, is now a museum of his art.

Restaurants

PRICE CATEGORIES

For a three-course meal for one with half a bottle of wine (or equivalent meal), taxes and charges included.

€ under €30 €€ €30–60 €€€ over €60

The Blockhaus Nikolskoe restaurant

1 Mutter Fourage
Chausseestrasse 15a ▪ (030) 805 23 11 ▪ Open summer: 9am–7pm; winter: 10am–6pm daily ▪ €
Hidden in the yard of a market garden and an atelier, this charming café has a delicious selection of homemade cakes and snacks.

2 Haus Sanssouci
Am Großen Wannsee 60 ▪ (030) 805 30 34 ▪ Open 11:30am–11pm Tue–Sun ▪ €€
Offering great views of Wannsee, this idyllic cottage-style restaurant serves up mostly German food, but it has lobster nights and other specials too.

3 Floh
Am Bahnhof Grunewald 4 ▪ (030) 892 93 56 ▪ Open noon–11pm daily ▪ €
A rustic pub, Floh (Flea) is known for its homemade dishes. Its beer garden is right next to the Grundewald S-Bahn station.

4 Loretta am Wannsee
Kronprinzessinnenweg 260 ▪ (030) 80 10 53 33 ▪ Open noon–10pm Wed–Sun ▪ €€
Overlooking the lake, Loretta am Wannsee serves hearty German dishes and has a large beer garden.

5 Alter Krug Dahlem
Königin-Luise-Str. 52 ▪ Open 10am–midnight daily ▪ (030) 832 70 00 ▪ No credit cards ▪ €
Relax in the porch swings of this large beer garden. A barbecue provides the food at mealtimes.

6 Blockhaus Nikolskoe
Nikolskoer Weg 15 ▪ (030) 805 29 14 ▪ Open noon–6pm daily ▪ No credit cards ▪ €€
Traditional German fare is on offer at this historic cabin with a water view.

7 Luise
Königin-Luise-Str. 40 ▪ (030) 84 18 88 0 ▪ Open 11am–11pm Mon–Thu (until midnight Fri), 10am–midnight Sat (until 11pm Sun) ▪ €
One of Berlin's nicest beer gardens on the Freie Universität campus, Luise's always has a good atmosphere. Try the delicious salads and sandwiches.

8 Englers
Englerallee 42 ▪ (030) 36 42 36 ▪ Open noon–10pm Tue–Thu & Sun (until 11pm Fri & Sat) ▪ €€
This refined restaurant serves pan-European food, such as veal liver and Weinberg snails, paired with German and Austrian wines.

9 Luther & Wegner Schloß Glienicke
Königstr. 36 ▪ (030) 805 40 00 ▪ Open noon–9pm Wed–Sun ▪ €€
Sophisticated surroundings and cuisine. Fish dishes and salads in summer, game and roasts in winter.

10 Chalet Suisse
Clayallee 99 ▪ (030) 832 63 62 ▪ Open noon–midnight daily ▪ €€
Enjoy local and Swiss cooking in a cosy atmosphere at Chalet Suisse.

See map on pp150–51

![TOP 10] Potsdam and Sanssouci

Marmorpalais

Potsdam is an important part of European cultural history – a splendid centre of the Enlightenment, which reached its climax in the 18th century in the architectural and artistic design of Frederick the Great's palace of Sanssouci. The palace complex, with its beautiful, extensive park, is both magnificent and playful. It has been designated a World Heritage Centre of Culture by UNESCO and enchants millions of visitors every year.

The town of Potsdam, with more than 150,000 inhabitants, is the capital of the federal province of Brandenburg. This former garrison town has much to delight visitors, including small palaces and old churches, idyllic parks and historic immigrant settlements.

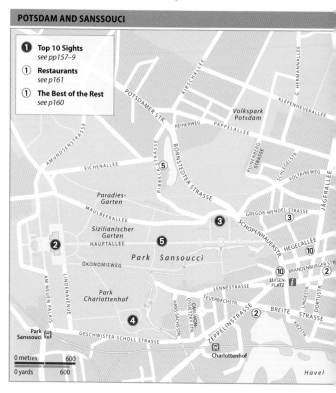

POTSDAM AND SANSSOUCI

- **1** Top 10 Sights
  see pp157–9
- **1** Restaurants
  see p161
- **1** The Best of the Rest
  see p160

1 Museum Barberini
Alter Markt, Humboldtstr. 5-6
■ **(0331) 23 60 14 499** ■ **Open 11am–7pm Tue–Sun** ■ **Adm** ■ **www.museum-barberini.com**

This private art museum, once Palace Barberini, was built in 1771–72 by Frederick the Great. Destroyed during the war, it was reconstructed by Hasso Plattner, and opened to the public in 2017. The rooms house 250 paintings and sculptures from Mr. Plattner's collection and others on loan.

2 Neues Palais
Am Neuen Palais ■ **(0331) 969 42 00** ■ **Open 10am–6pm Wed–Mon (Nov–Mar: until 5pm)** ■ **Visitor centre is at the south gate; audio guide available** ■ **Adm** ■ **www.spsg.de**

One of Germany's most beautiful palaces, the Baroque Neues Palais

The beautiful Baroque Neues Palais

was built in 1763–9 for Frederick the Great by Johann Gottfried Büring, Jean Laurent Le Geay and Carl von Gontard. The vast structure has 200 rooms, including the Marmorsaal (marble hall), a lavish ballroom, and the Schlosstheater, where plays are once more performed today. Frederick's private chambers are equally splendid, especially his Rococo study, the upper gallery with valuable parquet flooring and the Oberes Vestibül, a room clad in marble.

3 Schloss Sanssouci
Maulbeerallee ■ **(0331) 969 42 00** ■ **Open Apr–Oct: 10am–6pm Tue–Sun; Nov–Mar: 10am–5pm Tue–Sun; guided tour obligatory** ■ **Adm** ■ **www.spsg.de**

Frederick the Great wished to live "sans souci" ("without worries") in a palace outside the city. In 1745, he commissioned architect Georg Wenzeslaus von Knobelsdorff to construct this Rococo palace using his own designs. The structure rises above the former terraced vineyards, leading up to the domed building and its marble hall at the centre of the complex. The hall pays homage to Rome's Pantheon. To its left and right are rooms designed by Johann August Nahl and von Knobelsdorff; these include the concert room and the king's library. Here, the monarch liked to play the flute or to philosophize with Voltaire. Works by Antoine Watteau adorn the palace walls.

4 Schloss Charlottenhof
Geschwister-Scholl-Str. 34a
■ (0331) 969 42 28 ■ Open May–Oct:
10am–6pm Tue–Sun ■ www.spsg.de

A small Neo-Classical palace
in Park Sanssouci, the Schloss
Charlottenhof was built in 1829
by Schinkel for the heir to the
throne, Friedrich Wilhelm IV.
Particularly worth seeing here
is the tent-like Humboldtsaal.

5 Schlosspark Sanssouci
Chinesisches Haus: Am
Grünen Gitter; (0331) 969 42 25;
open May–Oct: 10am–6pm Tue–
Sun ■ Römische Bäder: Lennéstr.;
(0331) 969 42 25; open May–Oct:
10am–6pm Tue–Sun ■ Orangerie:
An der Orangerie 3–5; (0331) 969
42 22; open Apr: 10am–6pm Sat
& Sun (May–Oct: until 6pm Tue–
Sun) ■ www.spsg.de

It is easy to spend a day in a park
as large as this one. Among the
many charming buildings hidden
in the landscaped garden is the
Rococo-style Chinesisches Haus,
built in 1754–6 by Johann Gottfried
Büring. It originally served as a
teahouse and dining room, and
now houses an exhibition of East
Asian porcelain. The Römische
Bäder (Roman Baths) are lakeside
pavilions modelled on an Italian
Renaissance villa. They were built
as bath- and guesthouses between
1829 and 1840 by Schinkel. The
Orangerie, built in 1851–60 by Stüler,
was also originally intended for the
king's guests. Today it houses a
small gallery of paintings.

6 Schloss Cecilienhof
Im Neuen Garten ■ (0331)
969 42 00 ■ Open Apr–Oct: 10am–
6pm Tue–Sun (Nov–Mar: until 5pm)
■ www.spsg.de

The 1945 Potsdam Conference was
held in this palace, built in 1914–17 in
the style of an English country house.
Now a UNESCO World Heritage Site, it
houses a hotel and a small exhibition.

House in the Holländisches Viertel

7 Holländisches Viertel
Friedrich-Ebert-, Kurfürsten-,
Hebbel-, Gutenbergstr.

A pleasant way to explore Potsdam
is a walk through the historic Old
Town. Built between 1733 and
1742, the area originally served
as a settlement for Dutch workers
after whom it is now named.

THE POTSDAM CONFERENCE
In July and August 1945, the heads of the
governments of the United States (Harry
Truman), the USSR (Joseph Stalin) and Great
Britain (Winston Churchill) met in Schloss
Cecilienhof in order to seal the future of
Germany through a treaty. Vitally important
points such as the level of reparations to be
paid by Germany, the demilitarization of the
country, its new borders, the punishment
of war criminals, and the resettlement of
Germans from Poland were decided here.

8 Marmorpalais
Heiliger See (Neuer Garten)
■ (0331) 969 45 50 ■ Open May–
Oct: 10am–6pm Tue–Sun (Nov–Apr:
until 4pm Sat & Sun) ■ www.spsg.de

This small, early Neo-Classical
palace by the Heiliger See was
built in 1791–7 by architect Carl
Gotthard Langhans and others.
It features an elegant concert
hall as well as contemporary
furniture and porcelain.

9 Marstall (Filmmuseum)
Breite Str. 1a ■ (0331) 271
81 12 ■ Open 10am–6pm Tue–Sun
■ www.filmmuseum-potsdam.de

Set in the Baroque former stable
buildings of the king's town residence,
this small museum uses old cameras,
props and projectors to document
the history of German film.

10 Nikolaikirche
Am Alten Markt ■ (0331)
270 86 02 ■ Open 9am–6pm
Mon–Sat, 11:30am–5pm Sun

Potsdam's most attractive church,
Nikolaikirche was designed by
Schinkel in 1830 in a Neo-Classical
style. Its giant dome is particularly
striking, and you can ascend it for
a view over the Stadtschloss, which
is now home to the parliament
of Brandenburg.

The Neo-Classical Nikolaikirche

A DAY IN POTSDAM

◉ MORNING

Begin your exploration in the
Schlosspark Sanssouci as early
as possible in order to get ahead
of the daily influx of visitors. Start
with **Schloss Sanssouci** (see p157)
and **Neues Palais** then visit the
Chinesisches Haus, Römische
Bäder and Orangerie. From the
orangery's viewing terrace you
will have magnificent views over
the entire palace complex. If you
are up for it, you could also climb
up to Schloss Belvedere on top of
the hill. From Schlosspark walk
along Voltaireweg to Neuer Garten
in the northeast of Potsdam,
where you can recover over a
tasty lunch at **Brauerei Meierei**
(Im Neuen Garten 10).

AFTERNOON

Start the afternoon at **Schloss
Cecilienhof** (see p158) and stroll
through Neuer Garten. Stop for a
break at Heiliger See, then head
to the centre of Potsdam, starting
with the **Holländisches Viertel**
(Dutch quarter) where you could
pop into one of the numerous
cafés. Stroll past the St Peter-
und-Paul Kirche (see p160), the
Französische Kirche (see p160),
the **Nikolaikirche** and the **Altes
Rathaus** (see p160) to the **Marstall**
film museum and Museum
Barberini. If you have time, extend
your tour by driving to nearby
Babelsberg. You could either visit
the Filmpark (see p160), admire
Schloss Babelsberg or walk up
Telegrafenberg. Round off your
day with a delicious evening meal
at **Pino** (see p161) in Potsdam.

See map on pp156–7 ←

The Best of the Rest

① Alexandrowka
Russische Kolonie/Puschkinallee

The Russian colony feels like a village in Tsarist Russia. Decorated log cabins with gardens were built here in 1826 for a Russian military choir. Don't miss the museum and the Alexander Newski church.

② Dampfmaschinen-haus
Breite Str. 28 ▪ (0331) 969 42 25 ▪ Open May–Oct: 10am–6pm Sat & Sun ▪ www.spsg.de

This building, resembling a mosque with minarets, is the water pumping station for Sanssouci. The 1842 pump can be seen inside.

③ Telegrafenberg
Albert-Einstein-Str. ▪ Einsteinturm tours Oct–Mar: (0331) 29 17 41 ▪ Adm

The Einstein tower on top of Telegraph Hill was designed by Erich Mendelssohn in 1920.

④ Schloss Babelsberg
Park Babelsberg ▪ Closed for renovation until 2024 ▪ www.spsg.de

Built by Schinkel, this Neo-Gothic building sits in an idyllic park on the banks of the Havel River. The building is closed for renovation but the park is open to visitors. Check the website for details of temporary exhibitions.

Altes Rathaus

⑤ Potsdamer Stadtschloss
Neuer Markt

The Hohenzollern palace, once the residence of Frederick the Great, was badly bombed in World War II and had to be demolished in 1960. It is the cultural centre and the seat of the Potsdam legislative assembly.

⑥ Altes Rathaus
Am Alten Markt

The old town hall, built in 1753, is decorated with sculptures and Potsdam's coat of arms – two gilded Atlas figures, each carrying a globe on its back. Today, it is home to the city's museum.

⑦ Filmpark Babelsberg
Großbeerenstr. 200, Potsdam ▪ Open late Mar–early Nov: 10am–6pm daily; check website for park closing days ▪ Adm ▪ www.filmpark-babelsberg.de

The Filmpark *(see p65)* offers visitors a tour of the legendary UFA-Studios, complete with U-boat trips and stunt performances.

⑧ Französische Kirche
Am Bassinplatz ▪ (0331) 29 12 19 ▪ Open late Mar–mid-Oct: 1:30–5pm Tue–Sun

In 1752, Johann Boumann built this elliptical Huguenot church with its columned portico; Schinkel designed the beautiful interior in the 1830s.

⑨ St-Peter-und-Paul-Kirche
Am Bassinplatz ▪ (0331) 230 79 90 ▪ Open 10am–6pm daily (winter: until 5pm)

Based on Haghia Sophia in Istanbul, the Catholic church of St Peter and St Paul was built in 1867–70 by Stüler.

⑩ Brandenburger Tor
Luisenplatz

The most attractive of five former town gates was built by Gontard and Unger in 1770 to celebrate Prussian victory in the Seven Years' War.

The Neo-Gothic Schloss Babelsberg

Restaurants

PRICE CATEGORIES
For a three-course meal for one with half a bottle of wine (or equivalent meal), taxes and charges included.

€ under €30   €€ €30–60   €€€ over €60

1 Zum Starstecher
Leiblstr. 12 ▪ (0331) 28 79 05 05 ▪ Open 5–10pm Wed–Fri (from noon Sat & Sun) ▪ €€

This restaurant serves Brandenburg dishes such as *Königsberger Klopse* (Königsberg meat balls).

2 Zanotto
Dortustr. 53 ▪ (0331) 23 54 74 06 ▪ Open 6–10pm Wed–Sun ▪ €€

This Italian restaurant uses fresh seasonal ingredients and home-made pasta.

3 Pino
Weinbergstr. 7 ▪ (0331) 270 30 30 ▪ Open 6pm–midnight Mon–Sat ▪ €€

Close to Park Sanssouci, Pino serves a daily changing menu of exquisite Sicilian fare. The wine list reads like a Who's Who of Italian vintages.

4 Restaurant Juliette
Jägerstr. 39 ▪ (0331) 270 17 91 ▪ Open 5–10pm Wed–Sun (also noon–2:30pm Sat & Sun) ▪ Closed Jul ▪ €€

A former manor house is the setting for this French restaurant, one of the most charming in Potsdam. It serves top-quality French classics.

5 Krongut Bornstedt
Ribbeckstr. 6–7 ▪ (0331) 55 06 50 ▪ Open from noon Wed–Sun ▪ €€

Set in the brewery of a historic country manor, Krongut Bornstedt serves hearty meals with local fish, game, sausages and home-brewed beers.

6 Maison Charlotte
Mittelstr. 20 ▪ (0331) 280 54 50 ▪ Open noon–10pm daily ▪ €€

An old-world wine bar in a red-brick Dutch house with outdoor seating in a pleasant courtyard, Maison Charlotte serves French country fare and fine wines.

7 Villa Kellermann
Mangerstr. 34 ▪ (0331) 20 04 65 40 ▪ Open 6–11pm Wed–Fri, noon–4:30pm & 6–11pm Sat ▪ €€€

This elegant Michelin-starred restaurant by Heiliger See features uniquely designed rooms. Locals come here to enjoy traditional German cuisine with a modern twist.

8 Waage
Am Neuen Markt 12 ▪ (0331) 817 06 74 ▪ Open 4–11pm Tue–Sat, noon–10pm Sun ▪ €€

The regional meat and fish dishes at this attractive historic restaurant in central Potsdam are particularly worth trying.

Café Heider's vintage car shuttle

9 Café Heider
Friedrich-Ebert-Str. 29 ▪ (0331) 270 55 96 ▪ Open 9am–10pm daily ▪ €

This lovely café in the middle of Potsdam's Old Town offers a fantastic breakfast, which you can enjoy outside on the terrace in summer. A vintage Ford can be hired.

10 La Madeleine
Lindenstr. 9 ▪ (0331) 270 54 00 ▪ Open noon–10pm daily ▪ No credit cards ▪ €

A little bistro serving all sorts of crêpes, such as sweet with jam or savoury with ham – the ideal spot for a quick snack.

See map on pp156–7

Streetsmart

Interior of Berlin Hauptbahnhof

Getting Around

Arriving by Air

After nine years of delays, Berlin's two international airports, Tegel (TXL) and Schönefeld (SXF) are to be replaced in late 2020 by a new regional hub, the long-awaited **Berlin-Brandenburg (BER).** Situated some 18 km (11 miles) southeast of the city on the former sight of Schönefeld airport, Berlin-Brandenburg is extremely well connected and will receive regular flights from Europe, North America and Asia. Schönefeld will operate as Brandenburg's fifth terminal. The old Tegel airport that served the city for 46 years went out of operation in early 2020.

The fastest way to and from Berlin-Brandenburg is the S-Bahn commuter train RE7 or RB14, which stops at various stations in and around the city centre, or the FEX Airport Express, which whisks you directly to Berlin Hauptbahnhof, Berlin's central station, in around 30 minutes. Regular city buses conveniently link the airport to Berlin's vast U-Bahn network.

International Train Travel

International high-speed trains connect **Berlin Hauptbahnhof** to other cities across Europe. Reservations for these services are essential.

Tickets and passes for multiple international journeys and rail services are an excellent option for those planning to visit more than one European destination. Tickets and passes are available from **Eurail** or **Interrail**. As well as the price of the pass, travellers should note that, depending on the service, an additional reservation fee may apply. Always check that your pass is valid on the service on which you intend to travel before boarding the train; travelling without reservations can incur a hefty fine.

Eurostar runs a regular service from London, via the Channel Tunnel, to Brussels, where you can change for Berlin. This can be a very economical way to travel if booked in advance.

Deutsche Bahn (DB), Germany's national rail network, also runs a regular high-speed service to and from other European destinations.

Students and those under the age of 26 can benefit from discounted rail travel both to and in Germany. For more information on discounted tickets and passes, visit the Eurail or Interrail websites.

Long-Distance Bus Travel

Eurolines offers a variety of coach routes to Berlin from other European cities. Fares start from £19, with additional discounts for students, children and seniors. Other services include **FlixBus**, **Student Agency Bus** and **Ecolines**.

The **Zentraler Omnibus Bahnhof (ZOB)** is the city's largest long-distance bus station with connections to towns all over Germany and the rest of Europe. Check its website for timetables and tickets.

Public Transport

Berliner Verkehrsbetriebe (BVG) is Berlin's main public transport authority and service provider. Timetables, ticket information and transport maps can be found online.

Tickets

Berlin has a convenient universal ticketing system. This means that tickets for regional rail services are also valid on the S-Bahn and U-Bahn, as well as on other public transport services such as trams, buses and ferries. Tickets can be bought from automatic machines on station platforms or from ticket offices. Special offers include a five-person ticket valid for one day.

The city is divided into three travel zones for the purposes of ticket pricing: A, B and C. Zone A covers the city centre, Zone B the outskirts of town, and Zone C includes Berlin's suburban areas, Potsdam and its environs, as well as Berlin-Brandeburg airport. Tickets for any combination of zones are available to buy.

A single ticket is valid for up to two hours, and allows as many changes as required. Travel is only valid in one direction, so a second ticket is required for the return journey.

Short-trip (kurzstrecke) tickets are cheaper, but can only be used for three stops on trains and six stops on buses and trams.

Daily (tageskarte) and seven-day tickets (24-stunden-karte), costing €8.80 and €36 respectively for zones A–B, work out at much better value if you plan on making multiple journeys during your stay in Berlin. Seven-day tickets also allow you to travel with one extra adult or up to three children for free after 8pm on weekdays, anytime at weekends, public holidays and on 24 and 31 December.

Discounted tickets are available with tourist cards that offer combined public transport and museum entry (see p171).

All tickets must be validated in the red or yellow time-stamping machine near the ticket machine at platform entrances or on board buses. If caught without a valid ticket you may face a €60 fine.

Regional and Local Trains

Germany's railways are operated by Deutsche Bahn (DB). Regional Bahn and Regional Express (RB and RE) trains service the wider Berlin-Brandenburg region and beyond. Use this service for day trips to Potsdam (see p156) and other towns near Berlin.

U-Bahn and S-Bahn

Don't let the name confuse you; Berlin's "underground" trains also run on elevated tracks above ground. There are ten U-Bahn lines in total, each connecting with the S-Bahn and other U-Bahn lines at various points across the city.

The service usually closes between 12:30am and 4am. However, on weekends all lines are open 24 hours except the U4 and U55.

U-Bahn stations are easily identifiable – each station is marked by a rectangular blue sign with a large, white letter U.

The S-Bahn is faster than the U-Bahn, and its stations are further apart from one another. Berlin has 16 S-Bahn lines in total, running well beyond the confines of the city. Trains run every 10 or 20 minutes or so, or more frequently during peak travel times.

S-Bahn stations are marked by a round, green sign, featuring a large, white letter S.

Buses

Several bus services operate in Berlin, and conveniently they all use the same ticket tariffs. Berlin's city buses are marked by three-digit route codes and operate every 20 minutes between 5am and midnight. Major routes are serviced by Metro buses (marked by a letter "M" before the route number), operating 24 hours a day, and running every 10 to 20 minutes, while express buses (marked by a letter "X") run every 5 to 20 minutes.

The night bus service operates every half an hour from midnight until 4am when the U-Bahn service resumes. Regular tickets are not valid on this service. Night bus tickets can be bought directly from the driver (cash only).

All bus routes have a detailed timetable on display at each stop, and inner-city bus stops are equipped with digital screens indicating waiting times. Consult the BVG website for specific route information.

DIRECTORY

ARRIVING BY AIR
Berlin-Brandenburg (BER)
w berlin-airport.de

INTERNATIONAL TRAIN TRAVEL
Berlin Hauptbahnhof
MAP F3 ■ Europaplatz 1
w bahnhof.de/
bahnhof-de/Berlin_
Hauptbahnhof.html

Deutsche Bahn
w bahn.com

Eurail
w eurail.com

Eurostar
w eurostar.com

Interrail
w interrail.eu

LONG-DISTANCE BUS TRAVEL
Ecolines
w ecolines.net

Eurolines
w eurolines.com

FlixBus
w flixbus.de

Student Agency Bus
w studentagencybus.
com

Zentraler Omnibus Bahnhof (ZOB)
MAP A4 ■ Messedamm 2-4
w zob-berlin.de

PUBLIC TRANSPORT
BVG
w bvg.de

Trams

Despite only servicing the eastern parts of the city, trams (strassenbahn) are a popular way to get around for locals and tourists alike, particularly if you are travelling from Mitte to any part of Prenzlauer Berg.

Important routes are serviced by Metro trams running every 10 or 20 minutes, 24 hours a day. Some run a reduced service on weekends. Other tram services run every 20 minutes between 5 or 6am and midnight.

Visitors should note that Berlin's integrated transport system allows the use of tram tickets on buses, S-Bahn and U-Bahn train services, and vice versa. Tickets can be purchased at the usual vending points, or by using machines (coin only) on board

Taxis

Official Berlin taxis are cream, have a "Taxi" sign on the roof and have a meter on the driver's dashboard. Taxi apps such as Uber and Lyft also operate in Berlin.

Taxis can be hailed on the street, picked up at official taxi ranks (würfelfunk), which are usually conveniently situated in popular locations, or booked in advance online or over the phone from firms such as **Taxi Funk Berlin** or **Würfelfunk**. If you are travelling 2 km (1 mile) or less, ask for a short trip (kurzstrecke) for €5 – this can only be requested in taxis that you have hailed from the street.

Driving

Berlin is easily reached by car from most European cities via E-roads, which form the International European Road Network.

Germany's regional roads (landesstrassen) when marked with yellow road signs, while motorways (autobahnen) are marked with blue road signs. Although some stretches of motorway have variable speed limits depending on weather and road conditions, others have no enforced speed limit at all. German drivers therefore tend to zoom along at high speeds reaching up to 200 km/h (125 miles/h).

Berlin is surrounded by a circular motorway called the Berliner Ring, which has numerous signposted exits that lead straight to the city centre.

Drivers must carry their passport and insurance documentation if driving a foreign-registered vehicle.

Driving licences issued by any of the European Union member states are valid throughout the EU. If visiting from outside the EU, you may need to apply for an International Driving Permit. Check with your local automobile association if this applies to you ahead of travelling.

You must be 21 or over and have held a valid driver's licence for at least one year to rent a car in Germany. By law, drivers aged 21–22 must buy a Collision Damage Waiver (CDW). Drivers under the age of 25 may incur a young-driver surcharge.

In the event of a break-down or accident, or if you require assistance on the road, contact **ADAC Auto Assistance**.

Berlin itself is relatively straightforward to navigate by car; road layouts are clear and streets are well signposted. Parking is not hard to find and is relatively cheap when compared to other major European cities.

If you are planning on driving during your stay, familiarize yourself with the rules of the road prior to getting behind the wheel of a vehicle. Always drive on the right. Unless otherwise signposted, vehicles coming from the right always have priority. Beware of cyclists and trams in the city. Trams take precedence; take care when turning; and allow cyclists right of way.

The wearing of seatbelts is compulsory in a hired car, lights must be used in tunnels and underground. The use of a mobile phone while driving is prohibited, with the exception of a hands-free system. The drink-drive (see p168) limit is strictly enforced.

All drivers must have third-party insurance (hapflichtversicherung) – it is the minimum insurance requirement in Germany. Also compulsory is an environmental badge for vehicles driving within **Environmental Green Zones** (umweltzonen). Most of downtown Berlin is an Umweltzone. Certification can be purchased online for a small fee. If you are flying to Berlin and staying within the Metro area the most efficient way to travel is by public transport. There are park-and-ride facilities on the outskirts of the city, which are cheaper than inner-city parking.

Cycling in Berlin

Berlin is generally a very bike-friendly city; it has many designated cycle lanes and there are traffic lights at intersections.

Should you get tired of pedalling, bicycles can be taken on the U-Bahn, S-Bahn and trams, but they are prohibited on buses, except night buses, which can carry up to two at the driver's discretion. For all public transport an additional bicycle *(fahrrad)* ticket is required.

Deutsche Bahn (DB) operates an excellent public bicycle system called **LIDL Bike**. Bikes can be picked up from train stations and major intersections, and they can be dropped off at any of the LIDL Bike stations conveniently dotted throughout the city. To rent a LIDL Bike, you must register by providing your credit card details. A one-off registration fee of €3 applies. The first 30 minutes cost €1.50, and you will be charged €1 for every additional half hour. You can also hire bikes at many cycling shops for similar or cheaper rates; one of the most reliable is **Fahrradstation**. There are a number of bike sharing apps, like Nextbike or Call a Bike. Be aware that drink-drive limits also apply to cyclists.

Cyclists should ride on the right. If you are unsure or unsteady, it is a good idea to practise in one of the inner-city parks before taking to the city roads. If in doubt, dismount: many cyclists cross junctions on foot; if you do so, switch to the pedestrian section of the crossing. Beware of tram tracks; try to cross them at an angle to avoid getting the wheels stuck.

For your own safety, do not walk with your bike in a bike lane or cycle on pavements, on the left side of the road, in designated pedestrian zones or in the dark without lights. The locals usually don't bother, but wearing a helmet is highly recommended.

Berlin by Boat

Visitors to Berlin may be surprised to discover that the city has miles of tranquil waterways. In fact, an extensive system of canals and lakes links Berlin's city centre with neighbour-ing Potsdam, Spandau, Charlottenburg and the area of Müggelsee, mak-ing boating in the city not only a fun way to see the sights, but also a viable way to get around.

Six ferry lines operate in Berlin as part of the city's integrated public transport system. Marked by a letter F, they provide cross-river connections in locations to the east of the centre where there are fewer bridges. The regular F10 ferry service provides a particularly charming trip from Wannsee (near Potsdam) to the beautiful lakeside village of Alt-Kladow.

Those who wish to see the sights from the the water should embark on a river tour along the Spree or Landwehrkanal.

Tour operators such as **Reederei Bruno Winkler**, **Reederei Riedel** and **Stern und Kreisschiffahrt** offer tours in both English and German.

Potsdam and its lakes and rivers make for an excellent day out on the water, and the town is teeming with boat rental companies offering a large number of rental opportunities. Book in advance online or you can make enquiries at the **Potsdam Tourist Information Centre** on the day.

DIRECTORY

TAXIS

Taxi Funk Berlin
ⓦ funk-taxi-berlin.de

Würfelfunk
ⓦ wuerfelfunk.de

DRIVING

ADAC Auto Assistance
ⓦ adac.de

Environmental Green Zones
ⓦ umwelt-plakette.de

CYCLING IN BERLIN

Fahrradstation
ⓦ fahrradstation.com

LIDL Bike
ⓦ lidl-bike.de

BERLIN BY BOAT

Potsdam Tourist Information Centre
ⓦ potsdam-tourism.com

Reederei Bruno Winkler
ⓦ reedereiwinkler.de

Reederei Riedel
ⓦ reederei-riedel.de

Stern und Kreisschiffahrt
ⓦ sternundkreis.de

Practical Information

Passports and Visas

For entry requirements specific to your home country, including visas, consult your nearest German embassy or consult the **German Federal Foreign Office** website. Citizens of the UK, US, Canada, Australia and New Zealand do not need a visa for stays of up to three months but, from late 2023, must apply in advance for the European Travel Information and Authorization System (**ETIAS**). Visitors from other countries may also require an ETIAS, so check before travelling. EU nationals do not need a visa or an ETIAS.

Travel Safety Advice

Now more than ever, it is important to consult both your and the German government's advice before travelling. The **UK Foreign, Commonwealth & Development Office (FCDO)**, the **US Department of State**, the **Australian Department of Foreign Affairs and Trade** and the German Federal Foreign Office offer the latest information on security, health and local regulations for travellers.

Customs Information

You can find information on the laws relating to goods and currency taken in or out of Germany on the German Federal Foreign Office website.

For EU citizens there are no limits on most goods. Non-EU citizens can claim back VAT on purchases over €25 at the airport when leaving.

Insurance

We recommend that you take out a comprehensive insurance policy covering theft, loss of belongings, medical care, cancellations and delays, and read the small print carefully.

UK citizens are eligible for free emergency medical care in Germany provided they have a valid European Health Insurance Card (EHIC) or UK Global Health Insurance Card (**GHIC**). Visitors from outside these areas must arrange their own private medical insurance. Prescriptions have to be paid for upfront. Non-EU visitors should check if their home country has a reciprocal arrangement.

Health

Emergency medical care in Germany is free for all EU and Australian citizens. If you have an EHIC or GHIC, present this immediately. You may have to pay after your treatment and claim the money later. For other visitors, the payment of medical expenses is the patient's responsibility. Hence it is important to arrange comprehensive medical insurance.

Ambulances arrive swiftly when called. Those able to reach a hospital themselves should use the entrance marked *Notaufnahme* (Accident and Emergency). **Charité Krankenhaus**, Berlin's main central hospital, has a 24-hour emergency room.

Chemists or pharmacies (*apotheken*) are signalled by a red "A" sign. After 8pm, the address of the nearest all-night pharmacy is posted on the door of each outlet; alternatively, you can call the **Ärztlicher Bereitschaftsdienst der KV Berlin**. Those with private health insurance can contact **Doctors on Call**.

Visitors who suspect they have caught a sexually transmitted disease (STD) can be tested at **Berliner AIDS-Hilfe**. Emergency contraception is available from pharmacies.

No innoculations are required for Germany. Unless otherwise stated, tap water is safe to drink.

Smoking, Alcohol and Drugs

Germany has a smoking ban in all public places, including bars, cafés, restaurants and hotels.

Possession of narcotics is strictly prohibited and could result in prosecution and a prison sentence.

Unless stated otherwise, it is permitted to drink alcohol on the streets and in public parks. A strict drink-drive limit of 0.05 per cent BAC (blood alcohol content) is enforced.

ID

Visitors are not required to carry ID, but in the event of a routine check you may be asked to show your passport. If you don't have it with you, the police may escort you to wherever your passport is being kept so that you can show it to them.

Personal Security

Berlin is a relatively safe city, but as in most cities, use common sense. Pickpocketing is common, particularly on crowded buses and at tourist sites.

For emergency **police** dial 110, for **ambulance** or **fire brigade** services dial 112. There are also hotlines for **emergency dentists**, and **narcotics** and **poison** emergencies.

Contact your embassy if your passport has been stolen, or in the event of a serious crime or accident.

Germans, and Berliners in particular, are generally accepting of all people, regardless of their race, gender or sexuality. Although long celebrated as a liberal and tolerant country, homosexuality was only legalized in Germany in 1994. Despite all the freedoms that the LGBTQ+ community enjoy in Berlin, acceptance is not always a given. If you do at any point feel unsafe, the **Safe Space Alliance** pinpoints your nearest place of refuge.

The **Maneo** emergency hotline run by **Mann-O-Meter** supports victims of homophobic behaviour. **Lesbenberatung** is a lesbian safe space.

Travellers with Specific Requirements

Berlin is well-equipped for visitors with mobility needs. Pavements are sloped at junctions and most public buildings, malls and cinemas are fitted with lifts, ramps and extra-wide doors. The **German Red Cross (DRK)** rents out wheelchairs.

S- and U-Bahn trains are wheelchair accessible, but not all stations have lifts. If you are in the U-Bahn, wait at the head of the platform, and the driver will put up a ramp. In the S-Bahn, speak to the station manager to have a ramp set up. BVG maps show all of the accessible stations. Buses with a wheelchair symbol have one door with a ramp that can be lowered down.

Berlin's charitable association for the blind and sight-impaired, the **Allgemeiner Blinden-und Sehbehindertenverein**, offers useful information.

DIRECTORY

PASSPORTS AND VISAS

ETIAS
w etiasvisa.com

German Federal Foreign Office
w auswaertiges-amt.de

TRAVEL SAFETY ADVICE

Australian Department of Foreign Affairs and Trade
w smartraveller.gov.au

UK Foreign, Commonwealth & Development Office (FCDO)
w gov.uk/foreign-travel-advice

US Department of State
w travel.state.gov

INSURANCE

GHIC
w ghic.org.uk

HEALTH

Ärztlicher Bereitschafts-dienst der KV Berlin
c 11 61 17
w kvberlin.de

Berliner AIDS-Hilfe
MAP A5 ◼ Kurfürstenstr. 130
w berlin-aidshilfe.de

Charité Krankenhaus
MAP J3 ◼ Charitéplatz 1
c (030) 450 50

Doctors on Call
c (030) 89 00 91 00

PERSONAL SECURITY

Ambulance and Fire Brigade
c 112

Emergency Dentists
c (030) 89 00 43 33

Lesbenberatung
w lesbenberatung-berlin.de

Maneo
c (030) 216 33 36
w maneo.de

Mann-O-Meter
w mann-o-meter.de

Narcotics
c (030) 192 37

Police
c 110

Poison
c (030) 192 37

Safe Space Alliance
w safespacealliance.com

TRAVELLERS WITH SPECIFIC REQUIREMENTS

Allgemeiner Blinden-und Sehbehindertenverein
Auerbacherstr. 7
c (030) 89 58 80
w absv.de

German Red Cross (DRK)
Bundesallee 73
c (030) 60 03 00
w drk-berlin.de/reservierung.html

Time Zone

Germany is on Central European Time (CET), one hour ahead of Greenwich Mean Time (GMT), 6 hours ahead of US Eastern Standard Time (EST) and 11 hours behind Australian Eastern Standard Time (AEST). The clock moves forward 1 hour during daylight saving time from the last Sunday in March until the last Sunday in October.

Money

Germany is one of the 19 European countries using the euro (€). Major credit, debit and prepaid currency cards are widely accepted. Contactless payments are becoming the norm since the COVID-19 pandemic. It is always worth carrying some cash on you. Cash machines are located at various points throughout the city centre.

It is common to leave a tip of 5–10 per cent if service is good.

Electrical Appliances

The electric current is 220 volts. Many electrical appliances such as hair dryers have 110/220V transformers built in, so converters may be less of a concern, especially if you're coming from North America. Bring an adaptor with two round pins.

Mobile Phones and Wi-fi

Visitors travelling to Berlin with EU tariffs will be able to use their devices abroad without being affected by data roaming charges; instead they will be charged the same rates for data, SMS and voice calls as they would pay at home. Visitors with non-EU tariffs will need to be equipped for GSM network frequencies 900 and 1800 MHz. It is advisable to sign up for an international usage plan to keep costs down. Europe-based companies such as Ortel also offer prepaid plans at competitive rates. Upon arrival consider buying a local SIM card or cheap mobile phone with a German number so you can take advantage of local rates. If needed, ask your home carrier for the unlock code to use a different SIM card/service.

While connection speeds can lag behind in some other European countries, Germany is extremely well connected. Berlin has over 400 wireless internet hotspots, many of which are free, in bars, cafés, department stores, hotels and public places. Deutsche Bahn gives you up to 30 minutes of free surf time per day at over 100 stations across the country. Vodafone Kabel Deutschland does the same thing at 75 outdoor WiFi hotspots in town.

Postal Services

German mail is efficient, reliable and fast. Offices of **Deutsche Post**, the national mail service, usually open 8am–6pm (until noon on Saturday). Offices in train stations and airports also open on Sunday. Buy stamps from the post office counter or vending machines.

Public postboxes in Berlin generally have two slots: *Postleitzahlen* (postal codes) 10000–169999 for addresses in Brandenburg and Berlin, and *Andere Postleitzahlen* (other postal codes) for destinations elsewhere in Germany and abroad.

Weather

The weather in Berlin is better than its reputation. The continental climate guarantees mild and dry weather from May to September. Spring and autumn can be cold and wet, and from November to February it is often cloudy, with a biting cold, easterly wind whistling through the city.

Opening Hours

On weekdays, small retailers generally open at 9am or 10am and shut by 7pm, while department stores close at 10pm. Large supermarkets open 8am–10pm. Most shutters go down at 4pm on Saturdays. Shops in large train stations and service stations and convenience stores *(spätkauf)* stay open until at least midnight, and are also open on Sundays.

Banks in the city centre work 9am–4pm Monday to Wednesday, till 6pm on Thursday, and till 2pm on Friday. Larger post offices work 8am–6pm Monday to Friday, and untill at least noon on Saturday. Pharmacies open 9am–7pm Monday to Friday, and until 4pm on Saturday.

Public museums are generally open 10am–6pm; many close on Monday.

The COVID-19 pandemic proved that situations can change suddenly. Always check before visiting attractions and hospitality venues for up-to-date hours and booking requirements.

Visitor Information

The municipal **Berlin Tourist Info** service has seven offices in the city. Here you can book tickets for events and sightseeing tours, buy the **Museum Pass** or **WelcomeCard** (which gives unlimited access to the transport network and discounts on many attractions), and make reservations at hotels and hostels (for a €3 fee). The city-run website **Berlin.de**, available in English, also provides useful information.

There is a wide variety of apps available. Good ones in English include **BVG Fahrinfo Plus**, which provides real-time public transport connections, and 360° Berlin which offers guided walks, gives a good historical overview of the city and pinpoints scenic panoramas. Both are available on Android and iPhone. WhatWasHere_ Berlin is an interactive city guide for iPhone.

Taxes and Refunds

VAT is 19 per cent in Germany. Non-EU residents are entitled to a tax refund subject to conditions. In order to do this, you must request a tax receipt and export papers (ausfuhrbescheinigung)

when you purchase your goods. When leaving the country, present these papers, along with the receipt and your ID, at Customs to receive your refund.

Local Customs

Germany has very strict laws on hate speech and symbols linked to Hitler and Nazism. Disrespectful behaviour in public places can warrant a f ine, or even prosecution. Be respectful when visiting Berlin's historical sights and monuments. Pay attention to signage indicating when photos aren't allowed and think carefully about how you compose your shots.Visitors have come under serious criticism for posting inappropriate photos taken in front of sites such as the Holocaust Denkmal (see p87) on social media.

Dress respectfully when visiting churches, synagogues and other religious buildings.

Language

German is the offcial language, but Berlin is an international city. The use of English is almost as prevalent as German, particularly in business and tourism. The majority of Berliners speak English, and you can easily get by in shops and restuarants without knowing a word of German, but it's always appreciated if you can handle a few niceties before continuing the conversation in English.

Accommodation

Whatever your budget, finding a good, affordable place to stay generally isn't a problem, especially in eastern Berlin. There is a range of options from luxury and boutique hotels to B&Bs and quirky stays in camping trailers and former East German prison cells. Youth hostels are well-equipped and attract guests of all ages. Kreuzberg has several pensionen (guesthouses) and small hotels. Most business hotels are in west Berlin. Places outside the city centre can offer good value in green areas, and are often close to S- and U-Bahn lines.

Rates are fairly reasonable by European standards. Premium/middle/cheap double rooms in great locations are available for around €200/120/80. The average hotel room price is around €100.

Places to Stay

PRICE CATEGORIES
For a standard double room per night (with breakfast if included), taxes and extra charges.

€ under €120   €€ €120–€250   €€€ over €250

Luxury Hotels

Hotel Intercontinental Berlin
MAP N6 ■ Budapester Str. 2 ■ (030) 260 20 ■ www.berlin.intercontinental.com ■ €€
A luxury hotel in the Tiergarten, nicely situated with great views over the central park, this establishment is popular with business travellers. The building itself is not particularly attractive, but the rooms are furnished in a timelessly elegant style. Its two restaurants offer first-class food – the elegant, fine-dining Hugos (see p74) has a Michelin star – and the Marlene Bar, the Cigar and Rum Lounge, and the pool and fitness area are also excellent.

Radisson Collection Hotel
MAP K5 ■ Karl-Liebknecht-Str. 3 ■ (030) 23 82 80 ■ www.radissonhotels.com ■ €€
Conveniently located on the banks of the Spree between Alexanderplatz and the Museumsinsel, this modern hotel is ideal for exploring city centre sights. It has one of the best rooftop bars in town, with spectacular views of Berlin's downtown skyline. Some of the hotel's bright rooms offer views of the Berliner Dom. Its chic restaurant HEat (see p109) serves Asian fusion cuisine. In the warmer months, you can enjoy alfresco dining on the elegant terrace, watching the boats go by.

Hotel Bristol Berlin
MAP P4 ■ Kurfürstendamm 27 ■ (030) 88 43 40 ■ www.bristolberlin.com ■ €€€
One of Berlin's most famous hotels, the Bristol has it all – a magnificent, cosmopolitan blend of elegance and modern amenities. Among them is a luxury spa and three on-site restaurants, including the classy Reinhard's at Kurfürstendamm. Its international reputation has attracted a host of famous guests, from Fidel Castro to Tina Turner.

Hotel de Rome
MAP K4 ■ Behrenstr. 37 ■ (030) 460 60 90 ■ www.roccofortehotels.com ■ €€€
Located off Bebelplatz near the State Opera, just steps away from Unter den Linden, Hotel de Rome is sited within the historic 19th-century Dresdner Bank building. After World War II, the GDR State Bank used the structure. The interior is now a vision of postmodern ideas, while the Italian restaurant, the Opera Court café (see p93) and the spa area live up to the expectations of a hotel geared towards the international jet-set crowd.

The Mandala Hotel Potsdamer Platz
MAP L2 ■ Potsdamer Str. 3 ■ (030) 590 050 000 ■ www.themandala.de/en ■ €€€
This apartment hotel is set in a great spot at Potsdamer Platz. It has suites of varying sizes between 35–200 sq m (375–2,153 sq ft), each equipped with a kitchenette, fitness area, sauna, stereo, daily newspapers and anything else you could possibly wish for. The Michelin-starred, light-filled restaurant Facil (see p75) is a peaceful haven away from the hubbub of Potsdamer Platz.

Orania
MAP H5 ■ Oranienstraße 40 ■ (030) 695 396 80 ■ www.orania.berlin ■ €€€
A refined boutique hotel, Orania is set in a former commercial building. It is located in the edgy and vibrant eastern part of the Kreuzberg district. There are 25 rooms and 16 suites available, all of which are beautifully furnished with wooden fittings. Downstairs guests will find a bar, a restaurant and a cosy lounge with an open fireplace. Every Thursday and Tuesday jazz and classical concerts are also held on the premises.

Sheraton Grand Hotel Esplanade

MAP N6 ■ Lützowufer 15 ■ (030) 25 47 80 ■ www. esplanade.de ■ €€€

Glitzy and modern, with furnishings somewhere between Bauhaus style and functional sobriety. Service at this Sheraton group hotel is excellent and its first-class facilities include a state-of-the-art spa and fitness centre, with a pool, massage area, gym, solarium and three saunas. The hotel's Unique Bar serves up cocktails with unexpected ingredients such as rosemary, pepper and paprika.

Soho House

MAP H2 ■ Torstr. 1 ■ (030) 405 04 40 ■ www.soho houseberlin.com ■ €€€

This six-storey Bauhaus monument started life as a Jewish-owned department store before eventually housing the archives of the ruling party in East Germany (SED). The heated rooftop pool, fancy art and a private cinema seem at home alongside exposed cement walls. This is an excellent spot for celebrity sightings.

Waldorf Astoria

MAP N4 ■ Hardenberg straße 28 ■ (030) 814 00 00 ■ www.waldorfastoria berlin.de ■ €€€

The first and only Waldorf Astoria in Germany, this hotel takes up 32 floors of the "Zoofenster" sky-scraper. The sleek, visually stunning building has a glass exterior which offers a view of the neighbouring zoo. The hotel with its 232 rooms and suites has an elegant Art-Deco style. The service is excellent. Over 900 original works

of art are featured in the hotel and the views from the library lounge on the 15th floor are stunning.

Westin Grand Hotel

MAP K4 ■ Friedrichstr. 158–164 ■ (030) 202 70 ■ www.westin-berlin. com ■ €€€

This Westin hotel offers luxury accommodation in a historic spot at the corner of Friedrichstraße and Unter den Linden, with large, elegant rooms and good service. The lobby and the grand stairs are breathtaking. There's also a café and a bar.

Designer Hotels

art'otel berlin-mitte

MAP L6 ■ Wallstr. 70–73 ■ (030) 24 06 20 ■ www. artotelberlinmitte.com ■ €€

This designer hotel emphasises every detail and has styled everything, from the furniture to the soap in the bathroom. Blending architectural style with art-inspired interiors, each art'otel focuses on a contemporary artist. The historic building is decorated with paintings by the Neo-Expressionist postmodern artist Georg Baselitz. The hotel is centrally located, close to Nikolaiviertel.

Casa Camper

MAP J5 ■ Weinmeisterstr. 1 ■ (030) 20 00 34 10 ■ www.casacamper.com ■ €€

This modern hotel near Hackescher Markt in the hip part of Mitte is beautifully appointed. It offers excellent service and free Wi-Fi and iPod docking stations in every

room. The small spa and snacks and breakfast in the 24/7 rooftop bar are included in the price. Rooms on the upper floors have great views over the city.

Stilwerk Hotel Kantgaragen

MAP N2 ■ Kantstraße 126 ■ (030) 31 51 55 01 ■ €€

Opened in 2022, this hotel is affiliated to the art and design centre Stilwerk. It is housed in a protected building, which was built in 1930 and was formerly a multi-storey car park. The 61 modern studios on offer here feature furniture and accessories by famous designers. Some studios have kitchenettes. The private parking facilities have e-charging stations.

Hotel Q!

MAP P3 ■ Knesebeckstr. 67 ■ (030) 810 06 60 ■ www.hotel-q.com ■ €€

Stylish and discreet, this is a favourite among Hollywood stars. The rooms here are designed as "living landscapes" with furniture integrated into the walls.

Ku'Damm 101

MAP G1 ■ Kurfürsten-damm 101 ■ (030) 520 05 50 ■ www.kudamm 101.com ■ €€

This minimalist hotel, one of the few based on the Bauhaus design principles of Le Corbusier, caters to an art-oriented clientele, who appreciate the simple, comfortable rooms and large bathrooms, the stylish, modern interiors and the great views from the breakfast room. Prices are highly competitive.

Maritim proArte Hotel Berlin
MAP K4 ■ Friedrichstr. 151 ■ (030) 203 35 ■ www.maritim.de ■ €€
Predominantly styled in tones of green and blue, this modern business hotel has almost 300 modern paintings decorating its rooms.

nhow Hotel
Stralauer Allee 3 ■ (030) 290 29 90 ■ www.nhow-hotels.com ■ €€
Formerly a warehouse on the Spree River, nhow is a "music and lifestyle" hotel, complete with a recording studio. Cutting-edge facilities in rooms include a flat-screen TV that doubles as a mirror.

Park Plaza Wallstreet Berlin Mitte
MAP L6 ■ Wallstr. 23–24 ■ (030) 847 11 70 ■ www.radissonhotels.com ■ €€
With dollar-bill carpets and murals of stockbrokers' and industry maxims all around the building, the New York Stock Exchange is the theme here. This is a pleasant hotel in a central location.

Sir Savigny
MAP C4 ■ Kantstraße 144 ■ (030) 21 78 26 38 ■ www.sirhotels.com/de/savigny ■ €€
Set inside a 19th-century tenement building, this hotel has 45 rooms and suites. The on-site restaurant doubles as a bar.

Lux Eleven
MAP J6 ■ Rosa-Luxemburg-Str. 9–13 ■ (030) 936 28 00 ■ www.lux-eleven.com ■ €€€
This stylish, modern apartment hotel is a designer's dream come true. Old townhouses have been converted into mostly white, sleek rooms with all the gadgets of a business hotel. The Prince restaurant and bar, with its understated elegance, adds to the upmarket flair of the hotel.

Quirky Hotels and Guesthouses

Eastern Comfort
Mühlenstr. 73–77 ■ (030) 66 76 38 06 ■ www.eastern-comfort.com ■ €
Moored on the Spree near the Oberbaumbrücke, this popular boat-hotel draws visitors to the hard-partying districts of Kreuzberg and Friedrichshain. Some 24 snug berths are spread over two decks. The East Side Gallery is nearby.

Easy Lodges Berlin
Columbiadamm 160 ■ (030) 68 05 03 41 ■ www.easy-lodges.atberlinhotels.com ■ €
These smartly-furnished wooden units in cool Scandinavian design have all the amenities including free Wi-Fi. Located on the grounds of a swimming pool near Tempelhofer Feld, each cabin can take up to four guests, year-round. An affordable hybrid of hotel and campsite.

Ostel
Wriezener Karree 5 ■ (030) 25 76 86 60 ■ www.ostel.eu ■ €
Located in Berlin's trendy Mitte district, Ostel is designed to look like an Eastern Bloc-era hotel. The choice of rooms includes doubles with shared or private bathrooms, rooms with double- or triple-decker bunk beds as well as apartments that can sleep up to six people.

25hours Hotel Bikini Berlin
MAP N5 ■ Budapester Str. 40 ■ (030) 26 36 95 94 ■ www.25hours-hotels.com ■ €€
Part of the Bikini Berlin shopping mall, this smart 10-storey hotel offers guests the Monkey Bar, a rooftop restaurant with a 360° panorama and a ringside view of the primate enclosure and elephant house at the city's Zoologischer Garten. The "jungle sauna" has windows overlooking the green expanse of the Tiergarten.

Almodóvar Hotel
Boxhagener Str. 83 ■ (030) 692 097 080 ■ www.almodovarhotel.de ■ €€
Berlin's first biohotel flaunts its pedigree with flourish. The in-house Bardot bistro serves organic vegetarian dishes, as well as lactose- and gluten-free and vegan. Every room comes with its own yoga mat. Guests can also relax in the top-level spa and admire the Berlin panorama.

Arte Luise Kunsthotel
MAP J3 ■ Luisenstr. 19 ■ (030) 28 44 80 ■ www.luise-berlin.com ■ €€
This charming hotel has 50 rooms all individually and imaginatively decorated by local artists, with themes that range from loud pop art to classic Modernism. Near Unter den Linden and the Hauptbahnhof.

Hollywood Media Hotel

MAP P3 ▪ Kurfürsten-damm 202 ▪ (030) 88 91 00 ▪ www.filmhotel.de ▪ €€

Located right on glitzy Kurfürstendamm, this hotel has loads of cine-matic knick-knacks including props, movie posters and photos of stars. Each of the 182 rooms is dedicated to a film legend. The owner is Artur Brauner, an esteemed Polish-born film producer.

Hotel Neuer Fritz Berlin

MAP J4 ▪ Friedrichstr. 105 ▪ (030) 28 49 00 ▪ www. neuerfritz.com ▪ €€

Housed in a former GDR car dealership, this small hotel combines Baroque features, a spa and an excellent location on the Spree. The interior decor and the excellent service make it a popular choice.

Michelberger Hotel

Warschauer Str. 39 ▪ (030) 29 77 85 90 ▪ www.michelberger-hotel.com ▪ €€

Set right in the heart of the Friedrichshain enter-tainment district, the Michelberger Hotel offers guests quirky urban sophistication and a young, fun dynamic. Amenities include free Wi-Fi and a cool lounge area strewn with books and magazines.

Propeller Island City Lodge

MAP B5 ▪ Albrecht-Achilles Str. 58 ▪ (030) 891 90 16 ▪ www. propeller-island.de ▪ €€

If you're staying at this unusual lodge, you will share it with the German audio-visual artist Lars Stroschen, who designed all the rooms himself, each in a wildly unique style.

Cosy Hotels

Midi Inn City West Kurfürstendamm

MAP P2 ▪ Wielandstr. 26 ▪ (030) 881 64 85 ▪ kudamm.midi-inn.de ▪ €

A small guesthouse close to Ku'damm – a handful of atmospheric rooms, retrofitted in a non-fussy, mock 1920s style. Free Wi-Fi and flatscreen TVs.

Nürnberger Eck

MAP P5 ▪ Nürnberger Str. 24A ▪ (030) 235 17 80 ▪ www.nuernberger-eck. de ▪ €

A 5-minute stroll from Ku'damm, this handsome edifice has been a guest-house since the 1920s. The eight rooms are a time capsule of furnish-ings. A highlight is the early 20th-century bridal suite, with pink rose wall-paper, carved wooden bedstead and bird motifs.

Pension Peters

MAP N3 ▪ Kantstr. 146 ▪ (030) 312 22 78 ▪ www.pension-peters-berlin.de ▪ €

Located just off the café-filled Savignyplatz, this friendly little pension run by a German Swedish crew is thought-fully furnished, with Belle Epoque details even in the marble fittings and frescoes. Rooms are large and bright – make sure you ask for one over-looking the peaceful rear courtyard.

Gorki Apartments

MAP G2 ▪ Weinbergsweg 25 ▪ (030) 48 49 64 80 ▪ www.gorkiapartments. com ▪ €€

Stylish, self-contained serviced apartments in a renovated former East Berlin apartment complex. The house is located in the Mitte district so it can be a little noisy on the street-side of the apartments.

Hotel Johann

MAP G5 ▪ Johanniterstr. 8 ▪ (030) 225 07 40 ▪ www. hotel-johann-berlin.de ▪ €€

This small hotel with friendly staff offers mod-erately priced comfort. It is located in a quiet street a 10-minute walk from Jüdisches Museum Berlin, near Sommerbad Kreuzberg, an open-air swimming pool complex.

Hotel-Pension Funk

MAP P4 ▪ Fasanenstr. 69 ▪ (030) 882 71 93 ▪ www. hotel-pensionfunk.de ▪ €€

Based in the apartment of the silent-film star Asta Nielsen, this guesthouse is close to Ku'damm. The rates are unbeatable, while furnishings and service are personal and friendly. There are only 15 rooms, so book in advance.

Living Hotel Henriette

MAP L6 ▪ Neue Roßstr. 13 ▪ (030) 24 60 09 00 ▪ www. living-hotels.com ▪ €€

A stylish hotel with classic decoration – warm oak-panelled walls and thick carpets and curtains adorn the rooms, which are arranged around an inner courtyard. Few hotels in town are better than this, and the service is very friendly.

For a key to hotel price categories see p172

Myer's Hotel

MAP H2 ▪ Metzer Str. 26 ▪ (030) 44 01 40 ▪ www.myershotel.de ▪ €€

A family-run hotel in the centre of Prenzlauer Berg, Myer's is ideal for families or couples. Located in an historic part of town, the service is attentive and the atmosphere relaxed.

Sarotti Höfe

MAP F6 ▪ Mehringdamm 52–57 ▪ (030) 600 31 68 0 ▪ www.hotel-sarottihoefe.de ▪ €€

Located in a converted chocolate factory, this unique hotel has rooms with high ceilings and vintage furniture. A series of courtyards and stairs lead to the rooms; there are no lifts.

Ackselhaus, Blue Home and Club del Mar

MAP H2 ▪ Belforter Str. 21 ▪ (030) 44 33 76 33 ▪ www.ackselhaus.de ▪ €€€

This small boutique with a Mediterranean garden has stylish, themed rooms. It is located near Kollwitzplatz, a popular area with bustling bars and cafés.

Hotels in Green Surroundings

Hotel Bayrisches Haus

Im Wildpark/Elisenweg 2, Potsdam ▪ (0331) 550 50 ▪ www.bayrisches-haus.de ▪ €€

Nestled in a former game reserve outside Potsdam, this deluxe take on Bavarian country living has marbled bathrooms, gorgeous linens, the Michelin-starred Friedrich Wilhelm restaurant (see p161) and an indoor pool.

Hotel Müggelsee Berlin

Müggelheimer Damm 145 ▪ (030) 65 88 20 ▪ www.hotel-mueggelsee-berlin.de ▪ €€

A comfortable hotel combining near-unspoilt nature and closeness to the city. There are tennis courts, boat and bicycle hire and plenty of leisure activities.

Hotel Spree-idyll am Yachthafen

Müggelseedamm 70 ▪ (030) 641 94 00 ▪ hotel-spree-idyll.berlin ▪ €€

A small family-run house on the Müggelspree, not far from a bathing beach and a boat-hire booth – the ideal place to relax and forget all about the hustle and bustle of the big city, which is, however, only a short distance to the northwest. Come here to relax and take part in the various kinds of watersports.

Landhaus Schlachtensee

Bogotastr. 9 ▪ (030) 809 94 70 ▪ www.hotel-landhaus-schlachtensee.de ▪ €€

A 20-minute walk from the Schlachtensee (see p61) and Krumme Lanke, this villa oozes the charm of old rural Berlin. The furnishings in its rooms are a little old-fashioned, but the service is personable. The lovely beach at Strandbad Wannsee is just 4 km (2.5 miles away).

Locanda 12 Apostoli

Hüttenweg 90 ▪ (030) 818 19 10 ▪ www.12-apostoli.de ▪ €€

Sited in the southwestern Grunewald forest, this hotel is housed in an 1871 hunting lodge used by Kaiser Wilhelm II. There is a restaurant and lakeside terrace, a large dog-walking area, as well as a private riding club nearby.

Pentahotel Berlin-Köpenick

Grünauer Str. 1 ▪ (030) 65 47 90 ▪ www.pentahotels.com ▪ €€

The slightly sterile and impersonal atmosphere of this hotel is more than made up for by its location. It is in the centre of the southeastern district of Köpenick, right on the banks of the Dahme River, and Müggelsee is not far away. The hotel is just a short walk from the S-Bahn station.

Ringhotel Seehof Berlin

MAP A4 ▪ Lietzenseeufer 11 ▪ (030) 32 00 20 ▪ www.hotel-seehof-berlin.de ▪ €€

Centrally located in Charlottenburg, not far from the Messegelände, in a picturesque spot on the Lietzensee. The well-run hotel has a beautiful indoor pool as well as a delightful sun terrace.

Schlosshotel by Patrick Hellman

MAP A6 ▪ Brahmsstr. 10 ▪ (030) 895 84 30 ▪ www.schlosshotelberlin.com ▪ €€

This historic villa has been transformed into an exquisite boutique hotel with luxury furnishings, and a lovely garden, pool and sauna.

Schlosspark-Hotel
MAP A/B3 ■ Heubnerweg 2A ■ (030) 326 90 30 ■ www.schlossparkhotel. de ■ €€€
The only hotel near Schloss Charlottenburg, next to the Schlosspark, this is just a few minutes from the west of the city centre. The facilities are good and service is impeccable.There are only 40 rooms.

Das Stue
Drakestr. 1 ■ (030) 311 72 20 ■ www.so-berlin-das-stue.com ■ €€€
Housed in the former royal Danish embassy, this impressive five-star hotel is conveniently located next to the Tiergarten. There's luxury at every turn at this tranquil hide-away, including an acclaimed Michelin-starred restaurant.

Medium-Priced Hotels

Henri Hotel Kurfürstendamm
MAP P4 ■ Meinekestr. 9 ■ (030) 88 44 30 ■ www. hotel-residenz.com ■ €€
Based in one of the most beautiful old Berlin townhouses near Ku'damm, this hotel offers guests an intimate, characterful atmosphere. The late-19th-century rooms are tastefully furnished, and the restaurant has outdoor seating in summer.

Honigmond Garden Hotel
MAP F2 ■ Invalidenstr. 122 ■ (030) 28 44 55 77 ■ www. honigmond.de ■ €€
Exuding nostalgia with a hint of luxury, this hotel

is set within a listed 1845 building and has original antiques, stucco ceilings and a pretty courtyard with a Japanese fishpond.

Hotel AMANO
MAP G2 ■ Augustr. 43 ■ (030) 809 41 50 ■ www. amanogroup.com ■ €€
In a narrow street lined with galleries, this chic hotel is an excellent base from which to explore the Hackescher Markt area, Scheunenviertel and the Museumsinsel. Rooms and fully serviced apartments are available. Open bathrooms make this a better choice for couples. The view from the roof terrace is spec-tacular, and extras such as bike hire, pedestrian navigation systems and iPod walking tours help guests make the most of their stay.

Hotel Kastanienhof
MAP G2 ■ Kastanienallee 65 ■ (030) 44 30 50 ■ www.kastanienhof. berlin ■ €€
A charming hotel set in a turn-of-the-20th-century building. The rooms are basic but well equipped. An ideal base for explor-ing Prenzlauer Berg.

Hotel MANI
MAP G2 ■ Torstr. 136 ■ (030) 53 02 80 80 ■ www. amanogroup.de ■ €€
Just a heartbeat from lively Rosenthaler Platz, this stylish hotel is a favourite with fashion-istas and weekend partygoers. Its rooms are compact but beautifully appointed, with parquet floors and ultramodern, open-plan bathrooms. Rent bicycles from the reception and explore

nearby modern art galleries, well-known landmarks and lovely cafés.

Hotel Riehmers Hofgarten
MAP F6 ■ Yorckstr. 83 ■ (030) 78 09 88 00 ■ www.riehmers-hofgarten-berlin.de ■ €€
Here you can live the life of a Prussian officer. This remarkable hotel is part of a large complex of 19th-century Neo-Gothic buildings – old Kreuzberg apartments, with sombre rooms and elegant bathrooms, are the perfect setting for trying out the 19th-century lifestyle. The hotel has free Wi-Fi and docking stations in every room. The restaurant has con-temporary variations of traditional dishes.

Living Hotel Großer Kurfürst
MAP L6 ■ Neue Roßtr. 11–12 ■ (030) 24 60 00 ■ www.living-hotels.de ■ €€
Close to the Spree south of the Museumsinsel, the hotel offers guests rooms and fully furnished apartments. It also has useful extras, such as a gym, sauna and bike hire.

Ellington Hotel Berlin
MAP P5 ■ Nürnberger Str. 50–55 ■ (030) 68 31 50 ■ www.ellington-hotel.de ■ €€€
This distinctive hotel is a beacon of modern design set within listed 1920s Bauhaus archi-tecture. It is conveniently located close to KaDeWe, Ku'damm and the zoo, offering a stylish alter-native to a young and international clientele.

For a key to hotel price categories see p172

Hotel Bleibtreu

MAP P3 ■ Bleibtreustr. 31 ■ (030) 88 47 40 ■ www. bleibtreu.com ■ €€€

The hotel's stylish inner courtyard – reminiscent of Tuscany – and bright, tasteful rooms are an oasis of tranquillity. The international clientele is equally stylish. The hotel has its own restaurant, pool and sauna.

Hotel Hackescher Markt

MAP J5 ■ Große Präsidentenstr. 8 ■ (030) 28 00 30 ■ www.hotel-hackescher-markt.com ■ €€€

A charming hotel in an unbeatable location right opposite Hackesche Höfe. Its large, bright, elegantly furnished rooms, friendly service, excellent restaurant and attractive patio guarantee a pleasant stay.

Hotels for Business Travellers

Hotel Catalonia Berlin Mitte

Köpenicker Str. 80–82 ■ (030) 24 08 47 70 ■ www.cataloniahotels. com ■ €

This centrally located boutique hotel has 131 rooms, a cocktail bar and the Kunstwerk restaurant. There are two meeting rooms available, one seating up to 60 people, and a business centre. The hotel is a short walk from Heinrich-Heine-Straße U-Bahn.

Meliá Berlin

Friedrichs. 103 ■ (030) 22 38 57 62 ■ www.melia. com ■ €

Meliá is located in the heart of the city, near Friedrichstraße train station and the Spree River. The hotel has six different-sized conference rooms, a meeting area and a space for events, plus a tapas bar, fitness area, sauna and terrace.

ARCOTEL John F

MAP K5 ■ Werdescher Markt 11 ■ (030) 405 04 60 ■ www.arcotelhotels. com/JohnF ■ €€

Very conveniently located within walking distance of Unter den Linden and the stores of Friedrichstraße, and midway between the Museumsinsel and Gendarmenmarkt, this is a smart, modern hotel with various business and conference facilities. The breakfast includes sparkling wine and vegan food options.

Grand Hyatt Berlin

Marlene-Dietrich-Platz 2 ■ (030) 25 53 12 34 ■ www.hyatt.com ■ €€

The Grand Hyatt at Potsdamer Platz has comfortable rooms, a spa, fitness centre and pool, plus the excellent Vox restaurant (see p74). For business travellers, it has six meeting spaces and a boardroom, with catering available.

Leonardo Hotel Berlin Mitte

MAP J4 ■ Bertolt-Brecht-Platz 4 ■ (030) 374 40 50 00 ■ www.leonardo-hotels.de ■ €€

This four-star hotel has modern, air-conditioned rooms equipped with tea and coffee facilities. The hotel also offers 24-hour room service, a luxurious business lounge, a sauna and a fitness centre. It is located within walking distance of the Friedrichstrasse train station, the Reichstag building and many government institutions.

The Mandala Suites

MAP L4 ■ Friedrichstr. 185–190 ■ (030) 20 29 20 ■ www.themandalasuites. de ■ €€

Sister establishment of the Mandala Hotel in Potsdamer Platz, this is also a central apartment hotel with suites elegantly equipped as offices. Cleaning service is available and newspapers are delivered each morning.

Estrel Residence Congress Hotel

Sonnenallee 225 ■ (030) 683 12 25 22 ■ www. estrel.com ■ €€€

With more than 1,000 rooms, this hotel is one of Europe's largest, offering three- to four-star service. Its numerous conference rooms and latest technology make it perfect for international business meetings and the individual business traveller.

Hilton Berlin

MAP L4 ■ Anton-Wilhelm-Amo-Straße 30 ■ (030) 20 23 00 ■ www.hilton.de ■ €€€

Executives favour this hotel because of its central location and the views across the Gendarmenmarkt and Französischer and Berliner Doms, and specially designed executive rooms.

Pullman Berlin Schweizerhof

MAP N5 ■ Budapester Str. 25 ■ (030) 269 60 ■ www. pullmanhotels.com ■ €€€

One of Berlin's top luxury hotels, the Schweizerhof is set right in the centre of western Berlin and features clean lines, elegant furnishings and a large, well-designed fitness area.

Sofitel Berlin Kurfürstendamm

MAP P4 ▪ Augsburger Str. 41 ▪ (030) 800 99 90 ▪ www.sofitel-berlin-kurfuerstendamm.com ▪ €€€

Designed by star architect Jan Kleiheus, this hotel offers the largest rooms in Berlin and spectacular views over Ku'damm. Other perks include free Wi-Fi, efficient service and a helpful concierge desk.

Budget Hotels and Hostels

Baxpax Hotel Kreuzberg

MAP H5 ▪ Schlesische Str. 18 ▪ (030) 69 51 83 22 ▪ www.baxpax.de ▪ €

Much better than a youth hostel yet much cheaper than a guesthouse, this refurbished factory is unusual – you may be sleeping in a decommissioned VW Beetle. Plus you'll meet friendly people from around the world.

Bed and Breakfast Ring

www.bandb-ring.de ▪ €

This hotel offers shared accommodation in private homes all over town. You'll normally have your own room with one or two beds or an apartment to yourself. The rooms are mostly priced moderately, from €25 per person.

The Circus Hotel

MAP G2 ▪ Weinbergsweg 1A ▪ (030) 20 00 39 39 ▪ www.circus-berlin.de ▪ €

Near Alexanderplatz, this hostel offers great value

accommodation close to many sights. Dorm beds and single, double and triple rooms are available as well as a rooftop apartment with good views. There is a restaurant, a garden courtyard, and bike and scooter rental.

EastSeven Berlin Hostel

MAP H2 ▪ Schwedter Str. 7 ▪ (030) 93 62 22 40 ▪ www.eastseven.de ▪ €

In the lively Prenzlauer Berg neighbourhood brimming with bars and cafés, this friendly hostel with a garden is also just a 20-minute walk from Alexanderplatz and the Museumsinsel.

Grand Hostel Berlin

MAP F5 ▪ Tempelhofer Ufer 14 ▪ (030) 20 09 54 50 ▪ www.grandhostel-berlin.de ▪ €

Housed in a building dating from 1874, this hostel with a friendly and helpful staff is in a central location in trendy Kreuzberg. It offers safe, clean, spacious dorms and private rooms, some with their own bathrooms. There is also a lounge with computers, free Wi-Fi, bike rental and a large buffet for breakfast.

Hotel Transit

MAP F6 ▪ Hagelberger Straße 53–4 ▪ (030) 789 04 70 ▪ www.hotel-transit.de ▪ €

Housed on two floors of a former factory, this international youth hostel is located in a lively area close to the town centre. It has 50 large loft-style rooms, includ-ing singles, doubles and dorms.

Hüttenpalast

MAP H6 ▪ Hobrechtstr. 66 ▪ (030) 37 30 58 06 ▪ www.huettenpalast.de ▪ €

Tucked away in an old Neukölln vacuum-cleaner factory, this unique boutique hotel lets you slumber in designer caravans and Alpine huts placed inside the factory. Relax in the peaceful green courtyard, or sample organic treats in the streetside café.

Meininger Berlin East Side Gallery

MAP D5 ▪ Am Postbahnhof 4 ▪ (030) 31 87 97 67 ▪ www.meininger-hotels.com/en ▪ €

Close to the Mercedes Benz Arena, this budget hotel has 245 rooms ranging from two- to six-seater occupancy. Cook your own meal, or opt to dine at the on-site restaurant. It also features a bar with a great atmosphere where you can relax.

St Christopher's Inn Berlin Mitte

Ziegelstr. 28 ▪ (030) 27 87 48 80 ▪ www.st-christophers.co.uk ▪ €

Pod beds, free breakfast, a rooftop bar and a fun atmosphere make this centrally located hostel a reliable choice.

Three Little Pigs Hostel

Stresemannstr. 66 ▪ (030) 26 39 58 80 ▪ www.three-little-pigs.com ▪ €

Located in a historical convent in the Mitte district, this hostel offers light-filled rooms overlooking a central courtyard. It is conveniently located for visiting key sights, and also isn't far from Kreuzberg for some after-dark adventures.

For a key to hotel price categories see p172

General Index

Acknowledgments

This edition updated by

Contributor Petra Falkenberg
Senior Editors Dipika Dasgupta, Alison McGill
Senior Designer Vinita Venugopal
Project Art Editor Bharti Karakoti
Assistant Art Editor Divyanshi Shreyaskar
Project Editor Tijana Todorinovic
Assistant Editor Anjasi N.N.
Picture Research Administrator Vagisha Pushp
Picture Research Manager Taiyaba Khatoon
Publishing Assistant Halima Mohammed
Jacket Designer Jordan Lambley
Cartographer Ashif
Cartography Manager Suresh Kumar
Senior DTP Designer Tanveer Zaidi
Senior Production Editor Jason Little
Senior Production Controller Samantha Cross
Managing Editors Shikha Kulkarni, Beverly Smart, Hollie Teague
Managing Art Editor Sarah Snelling
Senior Managing Art Editor Priyanka Thakur
Art Director Maxine Pedliham
Publishing Director Georgina Dee

DK would like to thank the following for their contribution to the previous editions: Hilary Bird, Petra Falkenberg, Anna Streiffert.

The publisher would like to thank the following for their kind permission to reproduce their photographs:

Key: a-above; b-below/bottom; c-centre; f-far; l-left; r-right; t-top

123RF.com: Heike Jestram 150cla.
4Corners: SIME/Giovanni Simeone 2tr, 44–5.
Alamy Images: AA World Travel Library 13br; A. Astes 62bl; Agencja Fotograficzna Caro 2tl, 8–9, 16cl, 20crb, 69cr, 140tr, 153cl, / Sorge 21bl; B.O'Kane 26tl; Pat Behnke 130cra; Bildagentur-online / Schoening 93tl; Bildagentur-online/ Schickert 136tl, 139bl; Chromorange 56cr; David Davies 32cb; Stephan Dost 27b; dpa picture alliance 88br, 115crb, 133tl; dpics 11ca; Adam Eastland Art + Architecture 57tl; Reiner Elsen 30–1c; epa european pressphoto agency b.v. 63cr; Sina Ettmer 152t; Hemis 53cr, 125br, 138tl; Peter Horree 32br, 49tr;image-BROKER 34bl, 36crb, 47cl, 89bc, 139tl; imageBROKER / Ingo Schulz 120t; Image Professionals GmbH / Karl Johaentges 154bl; INTERFOTO 37tl, 37b; ITAR-TASS News Agency / TASS 59br; Keystone Pictures USA 158bl; Art Kowalsky 91cl; LOOK Die Bildagentur der Fotografen GmbH 14br; Lothar Steiner 155tr; MARKA 48; Iain Masterton 25tr, 39tl, 146tc; mauritius images GmbH 16–7c; Michel Meijer 81tr; Novarc Images 137br; Roussel Photography 121bl; Riccardo Sala 35crb; Schoening 125cla; John Stark 99cla; travelstock44 107tl, / Juergen Held 132cl; Werner Otto 33cl; Julie G Woodhouse 23cl, 123clb; World History Archive 46br.
Ankerklause: olfgang Borrs 134tl.
Bandol Sur Mer: 101tr.

Becketts Kopf: 72cr.
Berlinale: Andreas Teich 80b.
Berliner Kaffeerösterei: 126tl.
Borchardt: 75cl.
Bröhan-Museum: 57b.
Corbis: Eye Ubiquitous/Stephen Rafferty 88tl; Hemis / Borgese Maurizio 116cra; Hulton-Deutsch Collection 59ca; Ocean/John Harper 110–1; Reuters / Fabrizio Bensch 27tl; Schoening 16bl, 119tr; VCG Wilson 40cb, 56tl.
DDR Museum: 90tl.
Deutches Technikmuseum/ © SDTB: C. Kirchner 64tl.
Deutsche Kinemathek: Hans Scherhaufer 22tl, Marian Stefanowski 20clb, 22crb.
Deutsche Oper: Marcus Lieberenz 66tr.
Deutsches Historisches Museum, Berlin: 18bl.
Dreamstime.com: Rostislav Ageev 11cr; Andreykr 128tl; Atosan 15cr; David Beaulieu 4cra; Michal Bednarek 86bl; Goran Bogicevic 96tr; Gunold Brunbauer 107cb; Buschmen 33br, 118tl, 122bl; Carolannefreeling 115tl, 144tl; Ccat82 103t, 113t; Claudiodivizia 7tl, 10bl; 11clb, 24br, 39bc, 41tl; Andrea La Corte 60bl; Mikael Damkier 10clb; Digitalsignal 95tr; Matthew Dixon 10br, 32–3c; Dennis Dolkens 129cr; Diego Gorzalczany 11br; Christian Draghici 4crb, 46t, 51t, 79bl, 102tl, 151t, 159bl; Elenaburn 86t, 104bl; Elxeneize 158cra; Alexandre Fagundes De Fagundes 16crb, 17l; Joerg Franzen 51bc; Kevin George 61c, 84tl, 147cla; Simone Gobbo 11tl; Gudmund1 14cl; Jorg Hackemann 4clb; Hanohiki 145br; Hel080808 12bl, 87cl; Hugoht 146b; Juliane Jacobs 130bl; Javarman 105clb; Josefkubes 137tl; Dragan Jovanovic 13clb; Junede 122–3t; Tom K 48tl; Karinhamich 89cla; Katatonia82 98tl; Sergey Kelin 4b, 11crb, 17cb, 35c; Jan Kranendonk 6cla; Ivan Kravtsov 85tr; Axel Lauer 74tl; Miroslav Liska 34–5cla; Locha79 7cr; Markwaters 15bl, 52br, 114bl; Vasilii Maslak 4cla; Mateuszsloszу 41b; Matteocozzi 114tr; Lucian Milasan 12cl; Mishkacz 96bl; Luciano Mortula 55t, 129tr, 145t; Kalin Nedkov 3tr, 162–3; Noppasinw 79tr; Olena Buyskykh 25clb; Andrey Omelyanchuk 61tr; Vladimir Ovchinnikov 160bl; Sean Pavone 24–5c, 157tr; Petarneychev 78tl; Andrey Popov 12–3c; Peter Probst 60cr; Romangorielov 10cra; Rudi1976 3tl,4t, 82–3; Mario Savoia 30cl; Spongecake 145t; Petr Švec 124t; Sylvaindeutsch 52cl; Tmscherzer 120bl; Totalpics 142–3; Anibal Trejo 49b, 8cb,112tl; Ferenc Ungor 138c; Voevale 7tr, 24cl, 26bc, 76tl; Jannis Werner 152br; Jeff Whyte 50cla; Alex Zarubin 116bc.
Facil Restaurant: Lukas Roth 75tr.
©Filmpark Babelsberg: 65bl.
Friedrichstadt-Palast: Götz Schleser 67tr.
Brauhaus Georgbrau: 108bl.
Getty Images: 58crb; DeAgostini 51bc; John Freeman 31cra; Sean Gallup 68clb; Heritage Images 19bc, /The Merchant Georg Gisze, 1532 by Hans Holbein, the Younger (1497-1543) collection of the Staatliche Museen, Berlin 40cla; Lonely Planet 36tl; Travelstock44 - Juergen Held 20–1c; ullstein bild 132br.
Grand Hyatt Berlin: 117tr
Gugelhof: 141cl.
Restaurant & Café Heider: 161crb.
House of Weekend: 70b.

iStockphoto.com: DigitalVision Vectors / Grafissimo 47br.

Jewish Museum Berlin: Gift of Dieter und Si Rosenkranz /Jens Ziehe 43tl, Burkhard Katz 43cra, Spertus Institute Chicago /Roman März 43clb, Yves Sucksdorff 42bl, 42–43ca.

Klunkerkranich: Julian Nelken 134br.

Kulturforum Berlin: © Philipp Eder 4cl 38cl, 38crb.

Kunst-Werke: 99br.

Labyrinth Kindermuseum: 64bl.

La Lavanderia Vecchia: 135tr.

James MacDonald: 73br.

Matrix: 148bl.

Mein Haus am See: 71cr.

Mr Susan: 100b.

Museum für Naturkunde: A. Dittmann 64cr.

Overkill GmbH: 133crb

Ratskeller Kopenick: 149cl.

Restaurant Lubitsch Berlin: 127cra.

Robert Harding Picture Library: Hubertus Blume 31tl; Siegfried Grassegger 20bc; Thomas Robbin 13tl, 30clb; Ingo Schulz 28–9, 33tl; Lothar Steiner 23b.

Schwules Museum: Tobias Wille 69b.

Shutterstock.com: f11photo 1.

Sra Bua Bar: 92bl.

Staatliche Museen Zu Berlin: 38bl, David von Becker 38-39c.

SuperStock: Javier Larrea / age fotostock 18ca.

Tim Raue Restaurant, Berlin: 74t

Victoria Bar: 73t.

Zillestube: 109tr.

Cover
Front and spine: **Shutterstock.com:** f11photo.

Back: **AWL Images:** Sabine Lubenow cla; **Dreamstime.com:** Erix2005 tl; **iStockphoto. com:** jotily tr, Nikada crb; **Shutterstock.com:** f11photo b.

Pull out map cover
Shutterstock.com: f11photo.

All other images are: © Dorling Kindersley. For further information see www.dkimages.com.

Commissioned Photography Dorota Jarymowicz and Mariusz Jarymowicz, Britta Jaschinski, Rough Guides/Tim Draper, Rough Guides/Diana Jarvis, Rough Guides/Roger d'Olivere Mapp, Rough Guides/Roger Norum

Illustrator www.chrisorr.com

First edition created by DK Verlag, Munich

Penguin Random House

First edition 2002

Published in Great Britain by Dorling Kindersley Limited DK, One Embassy Gardens, 8 Viaduct Gardens, London SW11 7BW, UK

The authorised representative in the EEA is Dorling Kindersley Verlag GmbH. Arnulfstr.124, 80636 Munich, Germany

Published in the United States by DK Publishing, 1745 Broadway, 20th Floor, New York, NY 10019, USA

Copyright ©2002, 2023 Dorling Kindersley Limited
A Penguin Random House Company

23 24 25 26 10 9 8 7 6 5 4 3 2 1

The publishers cannot accept responsibility for any consequences arising from the use of this book, nor for any material on third party websites, and cannot guarantee that any website address in this book will be a suitable source of travel information.

A CIP catalogue record is available from the British Library.

A catalogue record for this book is available from the Library of Congress.

ISSN 1479-344X
ISBN 978-0-2416-2104-2

Printed and bound in Malaysia

www.dk.com

As a guide to abbreviations in visitor information blocks: **Adm** = admission charge; **D** = dinner; **L** = lunch.

MIX
Paper | Supporting responsible forestry
FSC™ C018179

This book was made with Forest Stewardship Council™ certified paper – one small step in DK's commitment to a sustainable future.
For more information go to www.dk.com/our-green-pledge

Phrase Book

In an Emergency

Where is the telephone?	Wo ist das Telefon?	voh ist duss tel-e-fone?
Help!	Hilfe!	hilf-uh
Please call a doctor	Bitte rufen Sie einen Arzt	bitt-uh roof'n zee ine-en artst
Please call the police	Bitte rufen Sie die Polizei	bitt-uh roof'n zee dee poli-tsy
Please call the fire brigade	Bitte rufen Sie die Feuerwehr	bitt-uh roof'n zee dee foyer-vayr
Stop!	Halt!	hult

Communication Essentials

Yes	Ja	yah
No	Nein	nine
Please	Bitte	bitt-uh
Thank you	Danke	dunk-uh
Excuse me	Verzeihung	fair-tsy-hoong
Hello	Guten Tag	goot-en tahk
Goodbye	Auf Wiedersehen	owf-veed-er-zay-ern
Good evening	Guten Abend	goot'n-ahb'nt
Good night	Gute Nacht	goot-uh nukht
Until tomorrow	Bis morgen	biss morg'n
See you	Tschüss	chooss
What is that?	Was ist das?	voss ist duss
Why?	Warum?	var-room
Where?	Wo?	voh
When?	Wann?	vunn
today	heute	hoyt-uh
tomorrow	morgen	morg'n
month	Monat	mohn-aht
night	Nacht	nukht
afternoon	Nachmittag	nahkh-mit-tahk
morning	Morgen	morg'n
year	Jahr	yar
there	dort	dort
here	hier	hear
week	Woche	vokh-uh
yesterday	gestern	gest'n
evening	Abend	ahb'nt

Useful Phrases

How are you? (informal)	Wie geht's?	vee gayts
Fine, thanks	Danke, es geht mir gut	dunk-uh, es gayt meer goot
Where is/are?	Wo ist/sind…?	voh ist/sind
How far is it to…?	Wie weit ist es…?	vee vite ist ess
Do you speak English?	Sprechen Sie Englisch?	shpresh'n zee eng-glish
I don't understand.	Ich verstehe nicht	ish fair-shtay-uh nisht
Could you speak more slowly?	Könnten Sie langsamer sprechen?	kurnt-en zee langsamer shpresh'n

Useful Words

large	gross	grohss
small	klein	kline
hot	heiss	hyce
cold	kalt	kult
good	gut	goot
bad	böse/schlech	burss-uh/shlesht
open	geöffnet	g'urff-nett
closed	geschlossen	g'shloss'n
left	links	links
right	rechts	reshts
straight ahead	geradeaus	g'rah-der-owss

Making a Telephone Call

I would like to make a phone call	Ich möchte telefonieren	ish mer-shtuh tel-e-fon-eer'n
I'll try again later	Ich versuche noch ein mal später	ish fair-zookh-uh nokh ine-mull shpay-ter
Can I leave a message?	Kann ich eine Nachricht hinterlassen?	kan ish ine-uh nakh-risht hint-er-lahss-en
answer phone	Anrufbeant-worter	an-roof-be-ahnt-vort-er
telephone card	Telefonkarte	tel-e-fohn-kart-uh
receiver	Hörer	hur-er
mobile	Handy	han-dee
engaged (busy)	besetzt	b'zetst
wrong number	Falsche Verbindung	falsh-uh fair-bin-doong

Sightseeing

library	Bibliothek	bib-leo-tek
entrance ticket	Eintrittskarte	ine-tritz-kart-uh
cemetery	Friedhof	freed-hofe
train station	Bahnhof	barn-hofe
gallery	Galerie	gall-er-ree
information	Auskunft	owss-koonft
church	Kirche	keersh-uh
garden	Garten	gart'n
palace/castle	Palast/Schloss	pallast/shloss
place (square)	Platz	plats
bus stop	Haltestelle	hal-te-shtel-uh
national holiday	Nationalfeier-tag	nats-yon-ahl-fire-tahk
theatre	Theater	tay-aht-er
free admission	Eintritt frei	ine-tritt fry

Shopping

Do you have/ Is there…?	Gibt es…?	geept ess
How much does it cost?	Was kostet das?	voss kost't duss?
When do you open/ close	Wann öffnen Sie? schliessen Sie?	vunn off'n zee shlees'n zee
this	das	duss
expensive	teuer	toy-er
cheap	preiswert	price-vurt
size	Grösse	gruhs-uh
number	Nummer	noom-er
colour	Farbe	farb-uh
brown	braun	brown
black	schwarz	shvarts
red	rot	roht
blue	blau	blau
green	grün	groon
yellow	gelb	gelp

Types of Shop

antique shop	Antiquariat	antik-var-yat

chemist (pharmacy)	**Apotheke**	*appo-**tay**-kuh*
bank	**Bank**	*bunk*
market	**Markt**	*markt*
travel agency	**Reisebüro**	*rye-zer-boo-roe*
department store	**Warenhaus**	*vahr'n-hows*
chemist's drugstore	**Drogerie**	*droog-er-ree*
hairdresser	**Friseur**	*freezz-**er***
newspaper kiosk	**Zeitungskiosk**	*tsytoongs-kee-osk*
bookshop	**Buchhandlung**	*bookh-hant-loong*
bakery	**Bäckerei**	*beck-er-**eye***
post office	**Post**	*posst*
shop/store	**Geschäft/Laden**	*gush-**eft/lard'n***
film processing shop	**Photogeschäft**	*fo-to-gush-**eft***
self-service shop	**Selbstbedie-nungsladen**	*selpst-bed-ee-nungs-lard'n*
shoe shop	**Schuhladen**	*shoo-lard'n*
clothes shop	**Kleiderladen**	*klyder-lard'n*
clothes store	**Boutique**	*boo-**teek**-uh*
food shop	**Lebensmittel-geschäft**	*lay-bens-mittel-gush-eft*
glass, porcelain	**Glas, Porzellan**	*glars, Port-sellahn*

Staying in a Hotel

Do you have any vacancies?	**Haben Sie noch Zimmer frei?**	*harb'n zee nokh tsimm-er-fry*
with twin beds?	**mit zwei Betten?**	*mitt tsvy bett'n*
with a double bed?	**mit einem Doppelbett?**	*mitt ine'm dopp'lbet*
with a bath?	**mit Bad?**	*mitt bart*
with a shower?	**mit Dusche?**	*mitt doosh-uh*
I have a reservation	**Ich habe eine Reservierung**	*ish harb-uh ine-uh rez-er-veer-oong*
key	**Schlüssel**	*shlooss'l*
porter	**Pförtner**	*pfert-ner*

Eating Out

Do you have a table for …?	**Haben Sie einen Tisch für…?**	*harb'n zee ine-uhn Tisch für…?*
I would like to reserve a table	**Ich möchte eine Reservierung machen**	*ish mer-shtuh ine-uh rezer-veer-oong makh'n*
I'm a vegetarian	**Ich bin Vegetarier**	*ish bin vegg-er-tah-ree-er*
Waiter!	**Herr Ober!**	*hair oh-bare!*
The bill (check), please	**Die Rechnung, bitte**	*dee resh-noong bitt-uh*
breakfast	**Frühstück**	*froo-shtock*
lunch	**Mittagessen**	*mit-targ-ess'n*
dinner	**Abendessen**	*arb'nt-ess'n*
bottle	**Flasche**	*flush-uh*
dish of the day	**Tagesgericht**	*tahg-es-gur-isht*
main dish	**Hauptgericht**	*howpt-gur-isht*
dessert	**Nachtisch**	*nahkh-tish*
cup	**Tasse**	*tass-uh*
wine list	**Weinkarte**	*vine-kart-uh*
tankard	**Krug**	*khroog*
glass	**Glas**	*glars*

spoon	**Löffel**	*lerff'l*
teaspoon	**Teelöffel**	*tay-lerff'l*
tip	**Trinkgeld**	*trink-gelt*
knife	**Messer**	*mess-er*
starter (appetizer)	**Vorspeise**	*for-shpize-uh*
the bill	**Rechnung**	*resh-noong*
plate	**Teller**	*tell-er*
fork	**Gabel**	*gahb'l*

Menu Decoder

Aal	*arl*	eel
Apfel	*upf'l*	apple
Apfelschorle	*upf'l-shoorl-uh*	apple juice with sparkling mineral water
Apfelsine	*upf'l-seen-uh*	orange
Aprikose	*upri-**kawz**-uh*	apricot
Artischocke	*arti-**shokh**-uh*	artichoke
Aubergine	*or-ber-jeen-uh*	aubergine (eggplant)
Banane	*bar-**narn**-uh*	banana
Beefsteack	*beef-stayk*	steak
Bier	*beer*	beer
Bockwurst	*bokh-voorst*	a type of sausage
Bohnensuppe	*burn-en-zoop-uh*	bean soup
Branntwein	*brant-vine*	spirits
Bratkartoffeln	*brat-kar-toff'ln*	fried potatoes
Bratwurst	*brat-voorst*	fried sausage
Brötchen	*bret-tchen*	bread roll
Brot	*brot*	bread
Brühe	*bruh-uh*	broth
Butter	*boot-ter*	butter
Champignon	*shum-pin-yong*	mushroom
Currywurst	*kha-ree-voorst*	sausage with curry sauce
Dill	*dill*	dill
Ei	*eye*	egg
Eis	*ice*	ice/ ice cream
Ente	*ent-uh*	duck
Erdbeeren	*ayrt-beer'n*	strawberries
Fisch	*fish*	fish
Forelle	*for-**ell**-uh*	trout
Frikadelle	*Frika-dayl-uh*	rissole/ hamburger
Gans	*ganss*	goose
Garnele	*gar-nayl-uh*	prawn/shrimp
gebraten	*g'**braat**'n*	fried
gegrillt	*g'grilt*	grilled
gekocht	*g'kokht*	boiled
geräuchert	*g'rowk-ert*	smoked
Geflügel	*g'floog'l*	poultry
Gemüse	*g'mooz-uh*	vegetables
Grütze	*grurt-ser*	groats, gruel
Gulasch	*goo-lush*	goulash
Gurke	*goork-uh*	gherkin
Hammelbraten	*hamm'l-**braat**'n*	roast mutton
Hähnchen	*haynsh'n*	chicken
Hering	*hair-ing*	herring
Himbeeren	*him-beer'n*	raspberries
Honig	*hoe-nikh*	honey
Kaffee	*kaf-fay*	coffee
Kalbfleisch	*kalp-flysh*	veal
Kaninchen	*ka-**neensh**'n*	rabbit
Karpfen	*karpf'n*	carp
Kartoffelpüree	*kar-toff'l-poor-ay*	mashed potatoes

German	Pronunciation	English
Käse	*kayz-uh*	cheese
Kaviar	*kar-vee-ar*	caviar
Knoblauch	*k'nob-lowkh*	garlic
Knödel	*k'nerd'l*	noodle
Kohl	*koal*	cabbage
Kopfsalat	*kopf-zal-aat*	lettuce
Krebs	*krayps*	crab
Kuchen	*kookh'n*	cake
Lachs	*lahkhs*	salmon
Leber	*lay-ber*	liver
mariniert	*mari-neert*	marinated
Marmelade	*marmer-lard-uh*	marmalade, jam
Meerrettich	*may-re-tish*	horseradish
Milch	*milsh*	milk
Mineral-wasser	*minn-er-arl-vuss-er*	mineral water
Möhre	*mer-uh*	carrot
Nuss	*nooss*	nut
Öl	*erl*	oil
Olive	*o-leev-uh*	olive
Petersilie	*payt-er-zee-li-uh*	parsley
Pfeffer	*pfeff-er*	pepper
Pfirsich	*pfir-zish*	peach
Pflaumen	*pflow-men*	plum
Pommes frites	*pomm-fritt*	chips/ French fries
Quark	*kvark*	soft cheese
Radieschen	*ra-deesh'n*	radish
Rinderbraten	*rind-er-brat'n*	joint of beef
Rinderroulade	*rind-er-roo-lard-uh*	beef olive
Rindfleisch	*rint-flysh*	beef
Rippchen	*rip-sh'n*	cured pork rib
Rotkohl	*roht-koal*	red cabbage
Rüben	*rhoob'n*	turnip
Rührei	*rhoo-er-eye*	scrambled eggs
Saft	*zuft*	juice
Salat	*zal-aat*	salad
Salz	*zults*	salt
Salzkartoffeln	*zults-kar-toff'l*	boiled potatoes
Sauerkirschen	*zow-er-keersh'n*	cherries
Sauerkraut	*zow-er-krowt*	sauerkraut
Sekt	*zekt*	sparkling wine
Senf	*zenf*	mustard
scharf	*sharf*	spicy
Schaschlik	*shash-lik*	kebab
Schlagsahne	*shlahgg-zarn-uh*	whipped cream
Schnittlauch	*shnit-lowkh*	chives
Schnitzel	*shnitz'l*	veal or pork cutlet
Schweinefleisch	*shvine-flysh*	pork
Spargel	*shparg'l*	asparagus
Spiegelei	*shpeeg'l-eye*	fried egg
Spinat	*shpin-art*	spinach
Tee	*tay*	tea
Tomate	*tom-art-uh*	tomato
Wassermelone	*vuss-er-me-lohn-uh*	watermelon
Wein	*vine*	wine
Weintrauben	*vine-trowb'n*	grapes
Wiener Würstchen	*veen-er voorst-sh'n*	frankfurter
Zander	*tsan-der*	pike-perch
Zitrone	*tsi-trohn-uh*	lemon
Zucker	*tsook-er*	sugar
Zwieback	*tsvee-ba*	rusk
Zwiebel	*tsveeb'l*	onion

Numbers

0	null	*nool*
1	eins	*eye'ns*
2	zwei	*tsvy*
3	drei	*dry*
4	vier	*feer*
5	fünf	*foonf*
6	sechs	*zex*
7	sieben	*zeeb'n*
8	acht	*uhkht*
9	neun	*noyn*
10	zehn	*tsayn*
11	elf	*elf*
12	zwölf	*tserlf*
13	dreizehn	*dry-tsayn*
14	vierzehn	*feer-tsayn*
15	fünfzehn	*foonf-tsayn*
16	sechzehn	*zex-tsayn*
17	siebzehn	*zeep-tsayn*
18	achtzehn	*uhkht-tsayn*
19	neunzehn	*noyn-tsayn*
20	zwanzig	*tsvunn-tsig*
21	einundzwanzig	*ine-oont-tsvunn-tsig*
30	dreissig	*dry-sig*
40	vierzig	*feer-sig*
50	fünfzig	*foonf-tsig*
60	sechzig	*zex-tsig*
70	siebzig	*zeep-tsig*
80	achtzig	*uhkht-tsig*
90	neunzig	*noyn-tsig*
100	hundert	*hoond't*
1000	tausend	*towz'nt*
1,000,000	eine Million	*ine-uh mill-yon*

Time

one minute	eine Minute	*ine-uh min-oot-uh*
one hour	eine Stunde	*ine-uh shtoond-uh*
half an hour	eine halbe Stunde	*ine-uh hullb-uh shtoond-uh*
Monday	Montag	*mohn-targ*
Tuesday	Dienstag	*deens-targ*
Wednesday	Mittwoch	*mitt-vokh*
Thursday	Donnerstag	*donn-ers-targ*
Friday	Freitag	*fry-targ*
Saturday	Samstag/ Sonnabend	*zums-targ zonn-ah-bent*
Sunday	Sonntag	*zon-targ*
January	Januar	*yan-ooar*
February	Februar	*fay-brooar*
March	März	*mairts*
April	April	*april*
May	Mai	*my*
June	Juni	*yoo-ni*
July	Juli	*yoo-lee*
August	August	*ow-goost*
September	September	*zep-tem-ber*
October	Oktober	*ok-toh-ber*
November	November	*no-vem-ber*
December	Dezember	*day-tsem-ber*
spring	Frühling	*froo-ling*
summer	Sommer	*zomm-er*
autumn (fall)	Herbst	*hairpst*
winter	Winter	*vint-er*